TOWNS *of* TWO HALVES

A TOURIST'S GUIDE TO FOOTBALL TOWNS

David Guest

www.townsof2halves.co.uk
Rosewood Publishing Ltd

TOWNS OF TWO HALVES
www.townsof2halves.co.uk

First published by Rosewood Publishing Ltd 2018

ISBN 978-0-9956787-2-9

Printed and bound by CPI Group (UK) Ltd,
Croydon CR0 4YY

Rosewood Publishing Ltd
www.townsof2halves.co.uk

By the same author
A PRESSURE OF THE HAND

For Joe Royle, with thanks

Contents

Football Towns

Carlisle

Newcastle
Sunderland

Middlesbrough

Morecambe
Fleetwood
Blackpool
Preston
Blackburn
Accrington
Burnley
Bradford
Leeds
Hull
Bolton
Huddersfield
Scunthorpe
Liverpool
Rochdale
Barnsley
Grimsby
Wigan
Bury
Oldham
Doncaster
Tranmere
Manchester
Rotherham
Sheffield
Lincoln
Macclesfield
Crewe
Burslem
Mansfield
Stoke
Derby
Nottingham
Shrewsbury
Burton
Wolverhampton
Leicester
Peterborough
Norwich
Walsall
West Bromwich
Birmingham
Coventry
Cambridge
Northampton
Ipswich
Milton Keynes
Stevenage
Cheltenham
Colchester
Nailsworth
Oxford
Wycombe
Luton
Swansea
Newport
Reading
Watford
Southend
Cardiff
Swindon
LONDON
Bristol
Gillingham
Crawley
Yeovil
Southampton
Brighton
Portsmouth
Exeter
Bournemouth
Plymouth

Distance no object?
Plan your awaydays
and weekend breaks
for the season

Introduction

This is a book about football only in the sense that time spent watching football can easily feel like time wasted. Less long-winded than Marcel Proust but riddled with the same anxiety, the book tries to calm those nerves.

There are two ways to tackle the problem. The more obvious is to ignore football altogether. That's a rare example of cutting off your nose to spite your face and throwing it out with the bathwater.

Alternatively you could take literally the idea of following your team. In casual conversation, 'following' a particular team demands no more of you than looking out for their results. But football, bless it, takes place all over the country in diverse cities, towns and suburbs, many of them unregarded. And when you look closely, each of the 92 places with a football league club turns out to have much more to offer.

This, then, is a book about an accidental, self-service form of tourism. If it were a piece of academic reasearch it would grope hesitantly towards the conclusion that anywhere in the country might be a tourist destination.

On that basis, your awaydays or city breaks will be to places like Accrington or Bradford rather than Amsterdam or Bruges, but the principle is much the same.

Finding unexpectedly interesting things to do or to look at in ordinary places, you will notice that the tourism begins to take precedence over the football. The two hours that you would devote to a football match... Can you really spare that much time? I'd imagine it will take longer to reach that point if your team plays attractive, winning football. On the other hand, if you follow one of the big clubs you won't always be able to get a ticket. In that event, the unique attractions of an unfamiliar town or city will be all the more important.

At the very least, you may never visit the place again. Do you really want to come away from a town having seen no more of it than its football ground, its Wetherspoon's and its shopping mall?

Not a football book, then, but as a travel book it has serious shortcomings. It is by no means systematic. An authentic travel writer would have done a much more thorough job, the resultant work would run to a dozen volumes and it would be out of date within days of being printed.

On which subject... The composition of the Football League changes every year. At the end of each season two teams drop out of League 2 and two from the National League (or whatever it happens to be called that year) take their places. To that extent, this book will be 2.17% out of date by May 2019. If any readers feel short-changed, I refer them to the book's website:

• www.townsof2halves.co.uk

There they will find updates where necessary and additional material. The website will also include links to places listed in the book.

Another risk of printing almost any kind of information, with the best will in the world, is that things change. Where I've mentioned a particular price or an opening time, it has usually been for the sake of illustration or emphasis; please don't rely on it still applying. And in most of the book I'm referring to the towns as I found them on the day of my visit. That was usually the date of the football match at the foot of each chapter. I'd make that clear in the text each time, but to do it here saves having to say "on the day I was there" on every other page.

There are, inevitably, some elements of a memoir. The matches I've attended go back to the early 1960s. The book is a record of what I have done with at least 92 days of my life – $1/250$th, I estimate. I can't decide whether this was time well spent. It's a startling statistic, though, and one to consider carefully before going to a football match again.

Accrington Stanley

"I wouldn't trust anybody in Accrington with that," the young man said. "Keep it with you."

'That' was a rucksack. I'd arrived at Accy on the Lancashire altiplano with an overnight bag. I was looking for a way to avoid lugging it around all day. The youth with the low opinion of his fellow citizens was as close as Accrington had that afternoon to an Information Centre. Outside the Town Hall the universal 'i' sign was on display, but anyone lured in by it was intercepted by this youth and turned away: the hall was closed for a private party.

He had the weary indifference of the local council factotum, and his outfit – neither a suit nor a uniform – matched the building itself: smart enough, but with a top half apparently designed by someone unable to see the bottom half.

As he ushered me from the premises I asked whether he could suggest anywhere in town to leave a rucksack for half a day: a hotel, perhaps, or the police station. Left luggage is a serious problem in our Orwellian age of perpetual conflict. His mistrust was misplaced, as Accrington promptly demonstrated.

The bag contained nothing of any value: some clothes ready for washing, basic toiletries and a couple of second-hand books. Entrusting it to anyone, anywhere, would not have entailed much of a risk. Just a few minutes later, at another Accrington service desk, I asked if they could help.

The young man there didn't have to think about it for long. "What you could do," he suggested, "is leave it lying around, as it were, and we'd have to put it over there [he indicated a corner of a table] as Lost Property. Then you'd come back later on and reclaim it. If there was a supervisor here, you might lay it on a bit. 'What am I like?' you might say, that sort of thing." He smiled broadly.

"What time do you close?" I asked.

"Six o'clock," he replied. "I finish at three, but I'll let the guy who takes over know what's going on and it'll be there when you come for it."

And so it was, with no sign that anybody had given it a second look.

The rucksack had already accompanied me on the first of the day's excursions. The stop before Accrington on the railway line into the Pennines from Preston is for Church & Oswaldtwistle. Vaguely aware of Oswaldtwistle Mills and happy to explore aspects of my Lancastrian heritage, I left the train there. As promised, Oswaldtwistle Mills was only three minutes' walk from the station. It was not, however, a heritage site; it was a shopping village.

People visiting an area for the first and possibly only time may be as interested in shopping opportunities as in galleries, museums, cathedrals etc. Or more so. I entered Oswaldtwistle Mills in a glass-half-full spirit. Besides, I'd had no breakfast.

As it turned out there were heritage displays in the Mills. On the threshold of a soft furnishings section, a sign proclaiming 'Textile Museum' pointed to a slim doorway protected by a grubby PVC strip curtain. Within, the Textile Museum lived up to this unpromising start. In places the warp and weft of the cobwebs provided a fitting 21st century commentary on the fate of the Lancashire textile industry.

It wasn't a bad museum, just small, neglected and confined to dark, ill-favoured spaces (thus replicating the atmosphere of the original mills, perhaps, though without the noise, dust and general threats to health). The transition from cottage industry to Industrial Revolution was explained clearly enough, and there were machines standing motionless and silent, like a line of dinosaur skeletons, in one workshop.

The main distinction of the Oswaldtwistle area is that James Hargreaves, inventor of the Spinning Jenny, was from these parts. Local reaction to his invention was so un-neighbourly that the family removed to Nottingham for its own safety. There was a glorious hand-written correction to one of the commentary panels on this subject. Describing the irruption of a furious mob into the Hargreaves' cottage, the text dropped an aitch in its excitement and a capital 'H' had been grafted by hand on to the front of 'argreaves'.

Back in the retail experience, signs leading to Toilets and Victorian Arcade delivered another heritage bonus. Off the Arcade, a room offered a more extensive chronological treatment of the Oswaldtwistle story, from archaeological beginnings to close to the present. This introduced Oswald, King of Northumbria in the seventh century. A 'twistle', it claimed, was the meeting place of two streams, but you may prefer to think of the sainted Oswald (as he became in the Middle Ages) as some sort of Dark Ages Roger Whittaker, putting his lips together and blowing to keep his spirits up.

This room also held particularly fine scale models of beam engines, and a less detailed but equally evocative model of the mills of Clayton-le-Moors in about 1920. The career of Robert Peel was celebrated – not the famous Prime Minister and founder of the Metropolitan Police, but his grandfather, a man whose innovative use of vegetable motifs in calico printing led to him becoming known as 'Parsley Peel'. Did he ever experiment with anything that actually had to be peeled? We weren't told.

Finally, this display introduced what became a theme of the day: the Accrington Pals, the 11th (Service) Battalion (Accrington) East Lancashire Regiment. This was one of the battalions raised in the early days of World War I in response to Kitchener's call for volunteers. On 8 September 1914 the Accrington newspaper reported the proposal to form a local unit; by 24 September the Accrington battalion had almost reached full strength (1,100 men). Training occupied most of 1915.

The battalion's first major action was an attack on the fortified village of Serre, on the opening day of the Battle of the Somme in July 1916. The first troops went over the top at 7.20am and by 8am, according to the Pals website, the battle was effectively over. Of about 720 Accrington Pals who took part in the attack, 584 were killed, wounded or missing. Brigadier-General HC Rees said: "Not a man wavered, broke the ranks or attempted to go back. I have never seen, indeed could never have imagined such a magnificent display of gallantry, discipline and determination."

You'll encounter the Pals again in the Hyndburn Heritage

Museum, in Accrington's Arndale Centre. That local initiative is mainly about artefacts and the daily lives of the different kinds of people who used them. There are also reminders of other Accrington distinctions:

- The Ewbanks carpet-sweeper
- The invention of Terylene
- And the Accrington NORI brick, supposedly the hardest in the building world, used in the foundations of Blackpool Tower and the Empire State Building. After Oswaldtwistle, NORI is the second of the day's etymological teasers. The brick is said to be iron-hard, and the word IRON, carelessly not reversed in the moulds, left the legend NORI on the bricks that came out of them. Or so they say.

Accrington's brightest, most surprising cultural jewel is the Haworth Gallery, perhaps 10 minutes out of the town centre by bus towards Bury or Rochdale. Sit on the left-hand side so that as the bus leaves the town you can admire the remarkable and wholly unexpected avenues ascending the slopes to the east, seeming to disappear eventually in distant coniferous woodland. The Pennines redeem many a view in East Lancs.

The Gallery is in Haworth Park, where you will also find a rose garden. Here a cherry blossom commemorates the Queen's diamond jubilee in 2013 – she visited Accrington that year – and two oaks are dedicated to the Accrington Pals. In the woodland, students from the nearby college have built a memorial to the Pals identical to one in Serre.

The house, in the Arts & Crafts style, was bequeathed to the people of Accrington in 1920; which is only appropriate, since the sweat of the local textile workers would have paid for it in the first place. Most of the exhibition space is on the first floor. Pride of place goes to Europe's largest public collection of Tiffany glass.

"Have you been here before?" the lady on the front desk asked me.

"No, it's my first time in Accrington," I said.

"Did you come specially for the Tiffany?"

"No," I said. Sensing that I might as well have been visiting

Venice and disclaiming any interest in canals I added apologetically, "For a football match. Oldham Athletic are playing a pre-season friendly at Accrington Stanley this afternoon."

She was not at all put out, as we used to say in the north – Ken Barlow would have said 'discountenanced'. "Oh, yes," she said cheerily, "we've got another couple from Oldham inside," gesturing towards the gallery.

It was not such a large place that I would miss my fellow fans. They were in the Tiffany & Interior Design room. He was a piratical-looking fellow, with a Captain Jack headscarf, a single gold earring and a replica shirt. She was more quietly dressed and was moving among the exhibits, while he appeared to be listening through earphones to a commentary. I toyed with the idea of trying to sell them a book but it seemed kinder just to leave them to it.

The unlikely presence of so much Tiffany glass here arises from the career of Accrington design apprentice Joseph Briggs, who left the town to seek his fortune in the USA in the late 19th century. He worked for the Tiffany company for 40 years, eventually becoming its managing director. The Haworth holds what Briggs sent back in the 1930s.

It's possible that most people associate Tiffany with a particular style of lampshade, or perhaps with stained glass. The pieces in Accrington, numbering over 140, are mainly but not exclusively vases and tiles. The Sulphur-Crested Cockatoos mosaic alone is said to be make a visit worthwhile, but along with several other pieces this was on loan to the Corning Museum of Glass in New York when I was in Accrington.

The collection is arranged thematically in four rooms: Tiffany and Interior Design; and the Past; and Nature; and The Tiffany Phenomenon. Marvel at the beauty of the vases in particular and at the technical skills involved. Learn more about glass-making techniques (Cypriote, intaglio, millefiore etc) than you ever expected to. And stay for lunch in the Gallery Kitchen, where the wine is served in what may be the heaviest glass you'll ever have drunk from.

Elsewhere in the building there are paintings and, on the

day of my visit, the Accrington Camera Club's annual exhibition. Haunting the corridors were three heavily made-up young women in period dress who may have been volunteers, visitors or ghosts, it was hard to tell.

A few minutes back into town on the bus and another 15 walking up the hill towards Clitheroe and you're at the Wham Stadium, so-called because Accrington Stanley's sponsors are What More UK. And the final conundrum of the day: why are they called Stanley? Nobody is quite sure.

The generally accepted explanation is that regulars at the Stanley Arms, on Stanley Street in Accrington, formed a club called Stanley Villa. Accrington FC, one of the founders of the Football League, had to resign from the league in 1893 and Stanley Villa absorbed the name. As Accrington Stanley they joined the Third Division North in 1921. In 1962 they dropped out of the league again. In 2006, as Conference champions, they rose a third time to the Football League. Not for nothing are they known as The Club that Wouldn't Die.

And that is largely why I decided on a simple alphabetical arrangement for this book. It places Accrington Stanley first. I hope no football fan would argue with the sentiment.

Accrington Stanley 2 Oldham 2
The Wham Stadium, 22 July 2017

Arsenal

This is the most exalted of my 'home' teams. I lived about half a mile from top-class football at Highbury Stadium for seven years in the late 1980s and early 90s.

Football wasn't a factor when we bought the house; we could have been much closer had we wanted to be. When we were house-hunting we made an appointment to see a place that proved to be next door to the visiting supporters' entrance. We didn't even get out of the car to look at that one. I still feel faintly guilty thinking about the estate agent fuming inside.

The main difference proximity to Highbury Stadium made to my life was that I avoided using the car on match days – traffic came to a standstill and parking was impossible. I attended just a handful of matches. Two were on corporate hospitality tickets: for a European tie against, I think, Brondby, and a cup-tie against Aston Villa. I can't remember who my hosts were on either occasion: so much for the marketing power of corporate hospitality...

More memorably, Oldham played there four times – three times in the league and once in the League Cup – while I was a taxpayer in the People's Republic of Islington. I went to all of them. To be able to walk to an Oldham game was a rare treat but, looking back, it makes me wonder whether I would have bought a season ticket had I lived in Oldham. The answer is almost certainly No; to express it in Arsenal terms, I may have lived near the ground but I never inhabited the obsessive territory of *Fever Pitch*.

Oldham played two Saturday afternoons and two evening matches at Highbury. To one of the evening games I took a young friend of the family. I can't remember the friend's name but she was an Australian of Mediterranean extraction who was returning home after a spell in London and wanted to see a football match before she went.

The atmosphere of a night match has always been special. For us that night it began some way from the stadium, with the smells of hand-rolled cigarettes and fried onions, and growing numbers of excited people. At the gates a degree of claustrophobia set in. Turnstiles were and remain ridiculous, awkward contraptions (not improved by the modern requirement to swipe a barcode or QR code). When we got through it wasn't immediately apparent which way to go, and the crowd's movement swept us up. We found ourselves climbing through the digestive tract of the stand, in semi-darkness, surrounded by dark, bulky shapes of people. And then the darkness parted abruptly as we reached the portal that brought us back into the night air, and the field lay unfurled beneath us, flooded by light and radiating a startlingly vibrant shade of emerald green. And at that point I heard her gasp: for a moment the sight literally took her breath away.

I'm not sure how much she enjoyed the following two hours. Oldham struggled gamely against superior opponents, but that would hardly have taken the gloss off her enjoyment of the evening.

With an hour to spare in London recently I caught the Victoria Line to Finsbury Park and walked down Blackstock Road to Highbury Fields. The Finsbury Park end of Blackstock Road is pretty much as I remember it – very much Arsenal territory, with the huge club shop at the tube/railway station. From the junction of Gillespie Road onwards, it became less recognisable.

For that reason I'd be reluctant to suggest places to go except in the most general terms. Islington is great for restaurants and pubs, but if you head north instead, to and beyond Finsbury Park, the cuisine becomes more exotic and the independent sector more predominant – Ethiopian deli, Vietnamese takeaway, Jamaican specialities etc.

For a walk to work up an appetite you might take a diversion through Highbury Fields. Opposite the house in which Walter Sickert lived, and beyond the Art Nouveau Boer War memorial, there's a woodland area where nature looks to be regaining the upper hand. That leads past a good children's play area into Highbury Fields – an open space at first, then tennis courts and all-weather football pitches and a large open-air café further up. At the top of Highbury Fields you'll find a clocktower put up to mark the 60th anniversary of Queen Victoria, and then you're on Blackstock Road.

Between here and the Emirates is the Gillespie Park wildlife and nature reserve, which looks a perfect place to take the kids for an hour or two; but it's not open on match days. You could look instead at Freightliners Farm, occupying a flank of Paradise Park on the other side of Holloway Road; that's set up as somewhere an urban community can see farm animals, and watch or take part in pastoral activities, or just sample the freshest food imaginable in the Strawbale Café.

At the Emirates Stadium you can take stadium tours and visit a museum. At the old Highbury Stadium, for a casual visitor, there is just the magnificent Art Deco frontage of the East Stand to admire. Just... It still looks sensational, hovering above the end of Conewood Street as if the 20th century's most enormous and stylish wave was about to sweep down the road towards you. If anything it's in better shape than ever, the paint fresh and bright – though no longer cream – and the old 'A-Football-C' crest resplendent in its hexagonal frame at intervals along the facade. The marble halls remain as a reception area, and Epstein's bust of Herbert Chapman monitors the comings and goings.

A plan to put a public footpath through the redeveloped site didn't happen. The gardens that occupy what was the playing surface are therefore private, as in many other London squares (a 2015 report by estate agent Knight Frank said that access to a private garden square added 25% to a property's value). Perhaps, in future, the gardens of Highbury Stadium Square will be included in the London Parks & Gardens Trust's open weekends.

Arsenal 2 Oldham 1
Highbury, 10 March 1992

Aston Villa

Aston Villa was one of a handful of football matches I cycled to. My journey that May morning started near Holyhead, on Anglesey, and was a kind of La-Z-Boy triathlon. Large stretches of it were accomplished by car and train. The cycling probably accounted for no more than 18 miles.

Still, it was a satisfying link with past generations. My father, as a boy in north Manchester, often cycled to football matches (perhaps wearing clogs). In later life we were approaching Bury in my car one Boxing Day and, still a couple of miles from the football ground, he became increasingly agitated about finding somewhere to park. I asked if he had ever previously gone to Gigg Lane in a car. No, he replied, only ever on a bike or by bus. Parking near Bury FC, then, was not something he had any experience of, even in the glory days of record crowds (35,000 for a cup-tie with Bolton Wanderers in 1960). We eventually found somewhere that left us with a walk of no more than 200 yards. As someone else said later: "You could have parked in the centre circle and it wouldn't have inconvenienced anybody."

The Aston Villa game on the first Sunday in May 1993 attracted more than 37,000. It was freighted with context. In the league, newly rebranded the Premiership, Villa were pressing for the title. At the paupers' end of the table Oldham occupied a relegation place and the annual game of musical chairs was close to its conclusion. They were eight points adrift with three games to play. The previous day – the Saturday – Crystal Palace, the only team Oldham could conceivably catch, had done a lap of honour at the end of their last home game.

The personal context was that my marriage was in disarray. I was on Anglesey to reflect on matters free of distractions. I'm not sure whose brainwave that was – I was happy in my own company, and the brief holiday would have put into my head the idea that more time to myself, not less, was what I needed.

I drove my mother's car back from Holyhead to my parents'

home in the Footballers' Wives belt of Cheshire. There I had the usual difficulty coaxing the bike's front wheel back into its quick-release forks – so much for transition – and cycled to Crewe railway station. From Crewe I took a train to Birmingham New Street and rode north along one of the city's many fine dual carriageways to Villa Park. I found a park, though no villa, and shackled the bicycle to some railings to join the throng heading for the football ground.

Among Oldham's travelling support there was a festive atmosphere. After a season of deepening anguish they had reconciled themselves to relegation and were determined to enjoy what remained of the club's day in the Premiership sun. Their good humour extended even to that usually reliable hate-figure, the former favourite in the opposition's strip: they cheered Earl Barrett, now a Villain.

Around the rest of the ground the mood was equally festive. Villa were assumed to be heading for the top of the league, barely breaking stride to give the doomed Oldham Athletic a salutary thumping. Their team included stars from all over the world: Mark Bosnich of Australia, Dwight Yorke of Trinidad & Tobago, Dean Saunders of Wales, Irishmen Ray Houghton, Paul McGrath and others. Demand for tickets among Villa fans was so great that a number of sheepish individuals at the visiting supporters' end could only have been displaced persons unable to find seats in more congenial company.

Oldham won 1-0. Tony Henry scored the winning goal after about half an hour. Plenty of time, everyone thought, for Villa to put the visitors in their place... But it never looked like happening and Oldham were more comfortable as the match wore on.

Their supporters, by contrast, began to look pale and drawn. At the final whistle there were celebrations, of course, and more applause – perhaps slightly patronising now – for Earl Barrett. But as they filed back to their cars, coaches and bicycle in the bright sunshine of a warm May afternoon many of their faces had a greenish tinge. Hope was reborn and with it, dread.

The anxiety lasted only a few more days. On the following Wednesday Oldham beat Liverpool 3-2 at Boundary Park while

Crystal Palace gained a 0-0 draw at Manchester City. On Saturday 8 May, the last day of the season, Palace lost 3-0 at Arsenal and Oldham beat Southampton 4-3. An eight-point deficit was overturned in six days against teams that finished in 2nd, 6th and 18th positions. Oldham stayed in the Premiership by dint of having scored a couple more goals over the 42-game season than Crystal Palace.

It was a temporary reprieve. Oldham went down the following season with barely a whimper. My marriage lasted only a little longer. Neither turn of events was the end of the world.

Aston Villa 0 Oldham 1
Villa Park, 2 May 1993

Barnsley

Yorkshire is God's Own Country, as all Yorkshiremen acknowledge. It also turns out to be Pharoah's Own Country.

Yes, Yorkshire has:

- More pyramids than any other county in Britain[1]
- More monuments inspired by Egyptian architecture than you could shake a stick at
- Many pioneering archaeologists, explorers and artists – Egyptologists, in other words.

In Barnsley in December 2017 you could hardly move for sarcophagi and scarabs. Well, in Barnsley's museums and galleries, anyway. In the market and the Alhambra Centre you wouldn't have been able to move for Christmas shoppers. (What is it with Yorkshire and Alhambras? Is it to do with the moors?) And at Premier Foods in the north-west of the town you wouldn't have been able to move for mince pies, 2.3m being turned out every day at that time of year.

I had my first encounter with Middle Kingdom Barnsley at Cannon Hall, a few miles west of the town. By coincidence the organiser of the Ancient Egypt in Yorkshire festival, Professor Joann Fletcher, was giving a talk there. Such was the enthusiasm for the topic, the talk was sold out and the crush made it difficult to get into the place. Once in, though, and away from the auditorium, I had the Hall largely to myself.

Downstairs, the displays are presented as furnished rooms, as if the Spencers (succeeded by the Spencer-Stanhopes) might arrive to dine, draw or read at any moment. An unusually candid note in one room recalls the slave-ship the *Cannon Hall*, owned by an opportunist son, but the family wealth came primarily from iron, coal and exploitation of the local working classes. In fact the Spencer-Stanhope in charge at Cannon Hall at the turn of the 19th century was an anti-slavery campaigner and a friend of William Wilberforce, who visited the hall often.

---

1 *Up to a Point – in search of pyramids in Britain and Ireland*, by David Winpenny.

Upstairs are the collections. The pictures they're most proud of are by Constable and Canaletto; among the pottery, they claim the Moorcroft collection is second only to the company's own in Burslem; crossing over between painting and ceramics is the De Morgan collection, with the Arts & Crafts pottery of William and the Pre-Raphaelite paintings of Evelyn; there's glass from the first to the 20th centuries, including some Lalique; and some gorgeous metalwork, especially in the Art Nouveau style.

Finding a door closing softly and spontaneously behind me, I asked one of the volunteers on duty in the gallery rooms whether the Hall was haunted. She replied that she had seen a ghost there herself and had been inclined to doubt it until three firemen, not unduly impressionable, had seen it during a call-out that proved to be a false alarm; and someone ascending the circular stairs by the butler's pantry had been startled to see a pair of white stocking-clad legs ascending into the darkness ahead of him.

The museum and gallery work hard to appeal to children – dressing-up opportunities, video etc – but the more obvious family attraction is Cannon Hall Farm next door to the Hall. It has farm animals and more exotic creatures (reptiles, ferret-racing and so forth) with play areas indoors and out.

Back in town, signs direct you to Experience Barnsley. It's an exuberant jumble of an exhibition, celebrating Barnsley at work (coal, iron, linen, glass) and play (heroes of Oakwell) down the ages. It's free, and many of the exhibits have been contributed by local people; it's as authentic and lively a local museum as you could wish to find, and it's not afraid to make fun of itself.

In a separate room there's more from the Nile Valley. Almost immediately, a sign warns you that "exhibits beyond this point include human remains". What could be more enticing to a young visitor? Curators can be as inventive as they like with interactivity, time-lines, dressing-up and so on, but human remains thousands of years old... Step this way, kids.

One truly peculiar feature of Experience Barnsley: the Gents across the corridor from the Egyptian annex includes a full-height floor urinal of very unusual design. Two units form an isosceles triangle with the wall, jutting back at a jaunty Pythagorean angle towards the wash-basins.

The Cooper Gallery was a case of saving the best until last where Egyptian relics were concerned. Barnsley-born artist Ernest Harold Jones, 1877-1911, travelled to Egypt for the sake of his health and produced some exquisite paintings and drawings of tomb decorations. As the notes alongside his work explain, an artist was a better bet for a good image than the cameras of the day. Harold Jones' vibrant, painstakingly accurate illustrations and his work as an explorer and archaeologist provide a glimpse of the way people worked in those far distant, Indiana Jones days. Unfortunately, the work and the conditions did nothing for his health. Some of the pictures are incomplete, the artist having died at the age of 34.

The Cooper Gallery is an interesting old building, once a school, now completely renovated. The paintings on display would normally have included a Turner but that was out on loan. I had to make do with Vanessa Bell, Edward Lear, John Ruskin and others.

In the café one of the first items on the menu was Barnsley Pie. Might this, I asked (having been paying attention at Experience Barnsley), be a famous Barnsley Goose Pie? The serving lady smiled and said no, she didn't have a recipe. This seemed a lame excuse – how can a goose pie be more complicated than a chicken pie? But what do I know about making pies? I opted for Barnsley Lasagne, which was as exotic as it sounds.

Over the road is St Mary's Church. In a small memorial garden adjacent there's a plaque on the wall honouring the contribution of the people of Barnsley to the cause of democracy in the Spanish Civil War. You don't see that often, do you? And just around the corner is an imposing sculpture commemorating a mining disaster. It is, still, Yorkshire.

Barnsley 0 Derby County 3
Oakwell, 9 December 2017

Birmingham City

Welcome to this week's edition of *The Lobotomist's Chair*, in which we tease out the inner secrets of a much-loved or, at least, famous celebrity. Following complaints that too many replies in our Q&A format were beginning "Obviously...", indicating that the questions were mindless, we're taking a break from sports stars. This week's national treasure is none other than the city of Birmingham.

The Lobotomist's Chair Does Birmingham have a persecution complex?

Birmingham Why would you ask that? We don't get the respect we should, but that's a different matter.

TLC You mean you deserve respect as the country's second city?

B Exactly. That should count for something, surely?

TLC Perhaps. But it was an inconsequential market town through most of British history...

B You make the point for me. It can't have been inconsequential, can it, if the consequence is the country's second city? And yet you casually throw in the disparaging adjective, to add to the impression of Birmingham as somewhere that doesn't need to be taken too seriously.

TLC OK, I withdraw 'inconsequential'. How about 'modest'?

B And if I quibble with that, am I immodest? How about 'thriving'?

TLC Let's move on. Isn't it the case that most people in this country don't actually realise Birmingham is the second city? A poll conducted by BMG at the beginning of 2017 found 38% of the people it spoke to identified Manchester as the UK's number two, against 36% for Birmingham. A YouGov poll two years earlier made the same finding.

B That's gobby Mancs for you. Birmingham exceeds Manchester in population and in contribution to GDP. And what has Manchester really got apart from derelict mills all over the place and the world's least popular motorway? Birmingham, by contrast, is the city of a thousand trades.

TLC Or, depending on who you talk to, "the largest village in Europe"; perhaps Birmingham's character is a touch sprawling or diffuse. Does its cultural and social diversity mitigate against a strong sense of identity?

B Rubbish. The city was the crucible of the Industrial Revolution, and three times as many patents originate in Birmingham as in Manchester; I doubt you'll find as many Michelin-starred restaurants anywhere else; and then there's the fantastic collection of Pre-Raphaelite art, the Jewellery Quarter, the canals and some magnificent Georgian and Victorian architecture. This is a vibrant modern city with a wonderful heritage.

TLC I thought you might want to keep the discussion away from architecture. Wasn't Sir Herbert Manzoni, the man chiefly responsible for the post-war reconstruction of Birmingham, uncompromisingly modern: "I have never been very certain as to the value of tangible links with the past. They are often more sentimental than valuable... As to Birmingham's buildings, there is little of real worth in our architecture. Its replacement should be an improvement."

B But we have the best of both worlds: fine classical buildings and sensational modern ones. Have you been to see the Library of Birmingham, on Centenary Square?

TLC Is that the one Prince Charles said looked like somewhere books would be burnt?

B If that's what an incinerator looks like, there isn't a Green Belt, Woodland Trust or Site of Special Scientific Interest in the country that wouldn't want one. It's stunning, inside and out. Inside, especially on the upper floors, the arrangement of circular balconies around a hive-shaped ascent through the building is gorgeous. Where archive copies of periodicals and books are brought together with spines of consistent colour, the aesthetic impact is startling. Walkways and escalators criss-cross the space in such a way as to persuade you that you're approaching the science-fiction section. In fact most of the contemporary fiction is on the ground or sub-ground floors, but it's worth going upstairs just for the sensational interiors and the viewing platforms.

TLC Did anything escape Manzoni's modernising zeal?

B Yes, and let's not forget the Luftwaffe – Birmingham was the most bombed city in the country after London and Liverpool.

TLC So what should we look for?

B Victorian neo-classical, Gothic Revival, Arts & Crafts... there's plenty to admire. Largely from the Edwardian period the Birmingham Museum & Art Gallery, which charges no admission price, is a building worthy of a second city. Take your time here, but don't miss:

- The Staffordshire Hoard gallery, with gorgeous gold, silver, garnet and glass pieces from Anglo-Saxon connoisseurs
- Claimed to be the most important collection of Pre-Raphaelite art in the world, including the picture (*Proserpine* by Dante Gabriel Rosetti) of which Northcote Parkinson (of Parkinson's Law fame) said: "It is now widely agreed that the glum expression of the model, Mrs William Morris, reflects not her anxieties about Victorian plumbing but the growing suspicion that she would have been happier had she married Dante Gabriel Rosetti"
- Epstein's *Lucifer*. This is one of the first things you'll see and it may be the piece that stays with you longest
- An Egyptian gallery is beautifully presented and is very much less overwhelming than, say, the British Museum.

Those are national treasures, but the Museum & Art Gallery also covers Birmingham's story and has a section devoted to the Birmingham School of Art.

TLC How about popular culture? Birmingham's contribution to music is Slade and Black Sabbath. Really, what can you say about a city that can't detect the overtones of the second-rate in the expression *B-Side* [the name of the annual Hip Hop Festival, and also a compilation album to represent the best of Birmingham music]? Its best-known comedian is Jasper Carrott. Its most immediately recognisable TV drama has a title like an emetic snack (*Peaky Blinders*) and it gets shunted away on to BBC2.

B Again you're being ridiculous. If you want to go back as far as Black Sabbath, what about the Moody Blues, Spencer Davis or Steve Winwood? Nick Drake, Joan Armatrading? I could give you more lists from the Punk and post-Punk eras, or by genre. In comedy, you clearly haven't heard of Frank Skinner and you're too young to remember Tony Hancock. Birmingham also has the Electric Cinema, perhaps the UK's oldest working cinema, and the Symphony Hall, where the City of Birmingham Symphony Orchestra has an international reputation. *Peaky Blinders* regularly wins awards, including three Baftas.

TLC Sport then. When Birmingham (the only bidder) won the 2022 Commonwealth Games, the organisers wanted to extend the deadline. When did Birmingham last have a top-class football team? And Edgbaston remains one of the leading cricket grounds in the country but Warwickshire seem to be in decline.

B Of course, it would be nice to have sports teams that won all the time, that topped their tables and inspired young people. An Active People Survey in 2013/14 found that participation in sport and active recreation in Birmingham was lower than the national averages, especially for women. So the city is trying to address that issue, by investing in programmes and facilities, while staging ever more high-profile events – in 2017, for example, it held the first annual Birmingham International Marathon and, on 100 miles of closed roads, Velo Birmingham, which will be back in 2019.

TLC Any particular time of year to visit?

B Within the football season, Birmingham's Frankfurt Christmas Market & Craft Fair is one of the great regional attractions. So great, in fact, that I'd strongly recommend that if you go on a Saturday you get there early to beat the crowds, especially at New Street. That said, it's a lot of fun and there's plenty of it. The market/fair runs from mid-November to just before Christmas and its stalls stretch from New Street to Centenary Square. There's a full-scale funfair, an ice-rink and a big wheel at the western end. If you've seen a continental Christmas market you won't be disappointed.

Birmingham City 6 Reading 1
St Andrews, 13 December 2014

Blackburn Rovers

10 Things You Need to Know About Blackburn

1 Blackburn takes its name from the River Blakewater, which runs through (and, in a culvert, beneath) the town. 'Blake' is thought to mean either 'black' or, as in Old English *blaec*, 'clear', an intriguing contradiction. Were the Anglo-Saxons sophisticated enough to use the same word to mean 'clear' and 'black', in the sense of 'absorbing all light'? On the other hand it may have the same root as 'bleak' from the moors where it rises, above the village of Guide. With plans to regenerate the town centre going ahead, the Blakewater might soon emerge from its Stygian tunnel.

2 The other waterway through Blackburn is the Leeds-Liverpool Canal. When this arrived in 1810 the local newspaper looked east as much as west. "There is now a direct communication between this town and Hull," it reported, noting that only "the Corsican tyrant" stood in the way of peace and trade between Blackburn and the continent of Europe. "Not tonight, Josephine. I 'ave to devise a plan to thwart the burghers of Blackburn." At an elaborate opening ceremony, a fleet of 27 vessels bore bands and dignitaries into Blackburn. Commercial deliveries followed, of yarn, tallow, molasses, lead, malt and coal. Why molasses? Perhaps as an ingredient in brewing beer. Imports of raw cotton and coal were balanced by outgoing shipments of processed cloth, and production increased to the point at which Blackburn had 39 mills by the canal.

3 The Canal & River Trust is putting together a Blackburn Heritage Trail. An early entry, on the Daisyfield Corn and Flour Mill, marks the transition from water-powered stone milling to steam-powered rollers. The Daisyfield continued milling until well into the 20th century, finally closing in 1968. It isn't known whether the Trust will extend its PokéTrail to this corner of the canal network.

4 Blackburn may be one of the oldest Christian communities in the

country. The cathedral was consecrated in 1826 but it stands on a site associated with Christian worship since 596. That's before Augustine, the 'Apostle to the English', landed on the Isle of Thanet at Pope Gregory's behest to lead the Anglo-Saxons out of the darkness of paganism. If Christianity was alive in Blackburn, it must have survived independently since the departure of the Romans in the 5th century.

5 Some idea of how early Roman Christianity looked is apparent from what is known of the church that preceded the cathedral on the site. Known as the Old Parish Church and erected 'about 590', it had four gargoyles known locally as Jenny Greenteeth, Old Bloody Bones, Scrat Nell and Hell Fire Sall. The present whereabouts of these sculpted characters are not known.

Jenny (or Jinny) Greenteeth, according to English folklore, was a hag whose pleasure it was to lure small children (or the elderly) to a riverbank and pull them in. Duckweed is Jenny's signature plant, for the way it closes over anything that breaks the surface. Jenny was an unseen menace for the most part, but an account of a sighting in the Liverpool suburb of Fazakerley describes something like a green tree frog with teeth and claws.

Old Bloody Bones was another bogeyman, a creature that lurked in a dark place (a cupboard below the stairs, for example) crouching on a pile of bones. The bones were the mortal remains of children who had told lies.

To Scrat Nell and Hell Fire Sall I can find no other reference, but both are female and neither sounds pleasant. The Saxon church was dedicated to St Mary, as is the cathedral. But they've added St Paul to the cathedral dedication, to keep Scrat Nell and Hell Fire Sall in their places. The later practice of fashioning gargoyles with the face of a church officer must have made it a good deal harder for parents to terrify their children into obedience.

6 Blackburn Central Library is building a collection of photographs known as the Cotton Town Image Gallery. Photographs depicting people, places and buildings in Blackburn and Darwen, from existing collections and from townspeople, have been donated to Blackburn with Darwen Library & Information Service. On view

in the library on special occasions (like September's Heritage Days), these can also be viewed at www.cottontown.org.

7 The town was such a busy centre of the cotton trade that from 1863 it had its own Cotton Exchange. This quickly became a general-purpose civic resource; in 1869 Charles Dickens is said to have given his last public reading there. The building had become redundant as an exchange for traders and manufacturers by the Great War. It was turned into a cinema and has since had a variety of tenants at ground-floor level, but the previously rather grand upper floor of the Victorian Gothic building has been empty for a dozen years. A local charity called Re:Source Blackburn has bought the building and hopes to turn it back into an entertainment venue for Blackburn.

8 Hobkirk Sewing Machines of Darwen Street, Blackburn, is a family firm that dates from 1903. Besides its own ranges of domestic and industrial sewing machines, the company also has what may be one of only two sewing machine museums in the country – there's another in Balham, South London, and the next closest is probably the one in Haarlem, the Netherlands.

9 The Blackburn Beverley, a transport aircraft used by the RAF from 1957 to 1967, may be the oddest-looking aircraft ever built. It was descended from a glider, the GAL50 Hamilcar. The Beverley Association acknowledges that the prototype "was not an attractive or elegant aircraft", and it isn't too proud to pass on the rumour "that bets were taken on whether the aircraft would get off the ground". In the final version the Beverley's fuselage looked like Walt Disney's idea of a flatfish, its tailplane resembled a box-kite and the undercarriage might have been borrowed from a golf trolley. Only 47 Blackburn Beverleys – not so much the Beverleys as the Ugly Sisters – were built.

10 Blackburn is one of the original 12 football league towns. Three more are on the same West Pennines railway line that serves Blackburn: Preston, Accrington and Burnley.

Blackburn Rovers 1 Crystal Palace 2
Ewood Park, 28 April 1969

Blackpool

Blackpool, the Seasiders, the Tangerines, were another of my home teams for five years in the 1960s.

As a schoolboy, I watched Blackpool many times during what proved to be a period of decline. When my family moved to the Fylde coast, Blackpool were a good First Division team; when we left they were a yo-yo team on their way, within a decade, to the Fourth Division.

The same might be said of the town. Blackpool in those days was brash in season and shabby the rest of the year. Fortunately the season, extended by the brainwave of the illuminations, occupied more of the year than the climate might otherwise have allowed. It was the shabbiness that encroached on the town, not the calendar.

I think it's fair to say that Blackpool's heyday as a seaside resort was all but over by the end of the 60s. The holidaymaking habits of the nation were changing. The writing was on the wall in the 1950s, when paid holiday entitlement enabled workers to decide when and where they would put their feet up. Previously, the system of Wakes Weeks had seen entire northern towns shut down (in turn – Blackpool could not accommodate them all at once) and decamp to the seaside; if it interfered with exam schedules, schools declared a week's holiday.

The tradition of Wakes Weeks did not disappear but the destinations changed. Ostend, according to a Manchester travel agent quoted by *History Today*, was "a sort of Belgian Blackpool" by the end of the 1960s. They must have been heady times in Ostend. A Belgian Blackpool...

A Blackburn writer described what Blackpool had to offer the Wakes Week holidaymaker. "It was the one week in all the year when you could escape the drudgery of Cotton Town. A week when new horizons opened up, a week when you glimpsed how different life could be, when you glimpsed what life was like for the wealthy and privileged. It was the holiday week, Wakes Week.

"For many it meant a week at the seaside: golden sands, the

wide blue sea, the cry of seagulls, the stalls, the smell of fried fish, the rides."

As the tide of social history carried mass tourism to more distant shores, Blackpool lowered the bar. By the end of the 60s no-one would have looked along the prom to see what life was like for the wealthy and privileged. Wholesome attractions remained but less salubrious undertones diminished the appeal of the whole: except, at one extreme, to organised crime, where Blackpool is said to have attracted the attention of the Krays.

But for the most part the succeeding decades were characterised by a rearguard action fought by glamour against a rising tide of tackiness. The high-water mark of this struggle was reached in the early years of this century, when a so-called super-casino was proposed for the centre of the town.

The tide has turned, it seems: the casino idea was abandoned and the emphasis now is on heritage as Blackpool seeks to capitalise on its original advantages. The seafront is handsomely remodelled in a major renewal programme, and behind it the town has made a bid to be named a Unesco World Heritage Site.

The challenge for Blackpool (I was going to write 'for a town like Blackpool', but I'm not sure there is anywhere quite like it) is to persuade people to think of it as cheap and cheerful rather than cheap and nasty. Who knows, the pendulum may swing back in its favour. The post-referendum devaluation of the pound, of which there may be more to come, will surely make domestic holidays more attractive again. Blackpool needs to have its image readjusted to be able to take advantage if the day arrives. It may one day be satisfied to be known as a kind of Lancastrian Ostend.

If your team has a fixture there, let Blackpool clasp you to its bosom with the obvious itinerary. Go up the tower, not ignoring the various attractions at its base. Take in at least one of the piers, and walk the promenade between two of them. Inhale the bracing North Sea air, which will buffet your face in vigorous gusts. Try the Pleasure Beach if rides are your pleasure, but don't force yourself – these are serious undertakings. And if you visit during the autumn view the illuminations by tram.

As residents, we enjoyed what Blackpool had to offer but on our own terms. Although it was the nearest big town we didn't visit often. The trips to Bloomfield Road were probably our most frequent outings up the Pool, and they connected us to a bygone era.

My father used to park his car (of which Blackpool and England full-back Jimmy Armfield had been a previous owner) outside his Aunt Edie's house in South Shore. After the match we would knock on her door and have a cup of tea and chat to her. She belonged to a generation that would have taken Wakes Week holidays in Blackpool, possibly by charabanc – as a young woman she had worked in one of the north Manchester mill towns. She had six sisters and three of them, including Edie, never married – a shortage of men after the Great War? Eventually she retired to South Shore, bought a small bungalow and lived out her days there.

As for the United game, one detail remains in my memory. We went, my dad insisted, primarily to see Denis Law, who was one of the wonders of the age. Law was sent off with barely 10 minutes gone for a torrent of foul language aimed at the referee and clearly audible to those behind the goal at the Bloomfield Road end. The richness of the language compensated somewhat for the loss of the prospect of watching Law for the rest of the game.

The United team that day contained not only Law but Bobby Charlton, Nobby Stiles and Pat Crerand, among other notables. Blackpool too would have had one or two internationals on the park: Armfield, Alan Ball, Ray Charnley, perhaps a young Emlyn Hughes, John McPhee, Tony Waiters. My own favourite, and the Blackpool player every urchin kicking a ball about the street wanted to be, was the wonderful Tony Green. Had Green's career survived the injury that terminated it in 1972, when the player was only 25, men would have taken their sons to football matches purely to see him. Not only a genius but also a pleasant and by all accounts even-tempered man, he would almost certainly have rewarded them by staying on the field for the full 90 minutes.

Blackpool 1 Manchester Utd 2
Bloomfield Road, 14 November 1964

Bolton Wanderers

My father was a lifelong supporter of West Bromwich Albion. I followed his lead, though not consistently. I was a fickle child. On that distant autumn afternoon at Burnden Park my allegiance changed every time a goal went in.

My Uncle Ray accompanied us (being a car-owner, he probably took us) and was repeatedly incensed by Roy Hartle, the Bolton right-back. Most teams had a hard man in those days: Hartle was Bolton's. Sure enough, his nickname was Chopper. He died only a couple of years ago at the age of 83. I wonder if many left-wingers sent flowers?

Burnden Park is a vast car-park now, flanked by Asda to the north and Carphone Warehouse to the east. Skirting it, running roughly north to south, is St Peter's Way, or the A666 as the unintentionally whimsical designators of English roads have it.

The modern stadium is miles out of town, close to a junction of the M61. If you're planning to fit a visit in to Bolton's Museum, Aquarium and Archive, or its Steam Museum, or the walking trails highlighting the town's Industrial Heritage, its association with Samuel Crompton and its art, be sure to leave plenty of time to get out to the Macron, or whatever they're calling it this year.

Other attractions include the home (now a heritage centre) of famous steeplejack Fred Dibnah; the Hall i' the Wood half-timbered museum, a 16th century building containing suitably aged furniture and interiors; and the Shree Swaminarayan Sidhant Sajivan Mandal, a Hindu arts and cultural centre where the shrine provides a focal point to what the locals refer to as Bolton's Cistine Chapel.

My own memories of Bolton are more prosaic. After moving from Middleton to the Fylde coast, we occasionally journeyed back to the Manchester area for family events. The two routes available from Preston converged on Bolton.

The better road was the A6, from which the M6 later took its name. This ran through Chorley, Horwich and other smaller towns. It was slow going through the built-up areas but quicker between them.

The alternative may have had a number (the road map now identifies it as the A675) but we knew it as 'over Belmont'. It rose steadily into the moors of the West Pennines, where the radio transmitter at Winter Hill was a rare vertical feature. The village of Belmont was just about the only settlement to cause a driver to slow to 30mph – though in a Morris Minor with four people aboard that was no great imposition.

From this direction, Bolton represented a return to civilisation and it announced itself in two distinct ways.

First, the smell. At one time the pervasive Eau de Moulin would have been so much part of daily life that I would scarcely have noticed it, but after a few months exposed to the bracing fresh air of the Fylde coast my nose had become more discriminating. The smell of manufacturing industry was as much a part of north Manchester in those days as manure is of the countryside. How to describe it? It was the smell of decline, a musty and heavy residue suggestive of the lees left by marinating textiles in chemicals until they were completely decayed. It was by no means as sharp or noisome as the smell around places like Widnes and Warrington but it was far from fragrant.

Second, the leaching of all colour from the urban environment. Bolton, in my mind's eye, was almost entirely monochrome in the early 1960s.

The buildings were mainly black, their brickwork and masonry coated by decades of factory smoke. Perhaps it wasn't actually black: interior designers refer to a shade of brown that is so dark as to be barely distinguishable from black, and this is called wenge; it may be the colour Rembrandt was so fond of.

The roofs were slate grey and the roads, had it been raining, were a slightly slicker version of the same tint.

Most cars were black in those days, advertising hoardings and traffic lights were relatively rare and the only colour I can recall was the orange glow of the street-lamps if we were passing through after dark. Laurence Durrell's description of the Plaka seen from the Acropolis, "like a spilt jewel-casket", comes to mind only as a contrast.

If all this seems a little harsh on Bolton, bear in mind that many northern towns were like that in the era before Clean Air Acts, sand-blasting and, eventually, the replacement of industry by warehousing and logistics. If swift moorland streams, coal measures and a major port had existed on the doorsteps of Oxford and Guildford, they might not have been so attractive.

Bolton Wanderers 3 West Bromwich Albion 1
Burnden Park, 23 September 1961

Bournemouth

I doubt there's a town in this country that has nothing unusual to offer. As a random example, within five miles of where I sit typing you would find: the birthplace of George Washington's bastard great-grandfather; a centre of bog-iron working in the early Roman era; the place of execution of the last English highwayman; and the grave of a feral German child rescued from his snarling and hirsute foster parents by George I. And that's before you think about the National Trust estate, the castle and all the other set-pieces from which you would expect to come away with a tea towel at the very least.

The coast adds a dimension. Bournemouth has formal tourist attractions, large and small. But it also has several miles of golden sand and a promenade along most of them. It helps if the sun shines on your visit, but even on an indifferent day Bournemouth seafront is lovely.

A short distance inland the football ground, now known as the Vitality Stadium, was plain (but somehow less vulgar) Dean Court when I was there. Dean Court stood in a corner of Kings Park, which in turn was some miles to the east of Dean Park. Naturally, a town of Bournemouth's pedigree would have had more than one esteemed dean in its history; but it would help if they could be referred to by name or, as further along the south coast in the case of Rottingdean, description.

Kings Park is at the Boscombe end of the town, and indeed the football club was originally Boscombe FC and later Bournemouth & Boscombe Athletic FC before settling in 1972 on AFC Bournemouth. In my mind's lazy eye the club also flirted briefly with a date prefix – 1972 Bournemouth or something like that, in the way that poor old Darlington are now poor old Darlington 1883, as if they were a brand of bottled ale – but I can find no solid confirmation of this.

The further relevance of Boscombe is geographical. If you're going to a game, go early and park somewhere on the south side of Kings Park. Instead of walking through the park towards the ground, head off in the other direction: the seafront is a little over half a mile away. If you turn to starboard when you reach the front you'll enter Bournemouth via a journey through the vocabulary of southern counties coastal geography.

You'll find yourself first on Boscombe Overcliff, at the foot of which is, of course, Undercliff Drive. Not far along you'll come to Honeycombe Chine, as eccentric a spelling of honeycomb as you could expect to find and one that would make you wonder whether some other derivation is intended – 'combe' as in Ilfracombe or Boscombe. It will also distract you from worrying about what a chine might be.[1] And on reflection, might 'dean' be a variant of the 'dene' used in the North of England to describe a deeply incised and wooded vale running down to the coast?

Boscombe has a fine pier that was renovated in 2008 and won the National Piers Society's Pier of the Year award in 2010. From here to the larger Bournemouth Pier you have a choice of transport: Shank's Pony or the Bournemouth Land Train.

At the Bournemouth Pier end of the line there are conventional seaside attractions. On the pier itself, the usual combination of high-octane naffery, but also RockReef, a kind of adventure playground for children of all ages. This is serious fun – there's even an introductory safety briefing; but after that the choice includes the Leap of Faith, the Death Slide and PierZip, claimed to be the first pier-to-shore zip-wire in the world.

Just beyond the pier is Bournemouth Oceanarium. Inland you'll find attractive parks and gardens, in one of which is Bournemouth Aviary. This is free, run by volunteers and populated largely by rescue birds. But if that gives you an image of pitiable lines of slightly foxed budgerigars or club-footed pigeons, don't let it; the aviary has some fabulous creatures and the idea that the birds have a history adds to the appeal of the place. It's as much a sanctuary as an aviary.

Not far away is another unique Bournemouth attraction: in

---

1 A narrow gulley typically cut through soft rocks by a river or stream making its way to the sea.

the precincts of St Peter's graveyard is the final resting place of Mary Shelley. If you're in Bournemouth for a night match, see whether you have the nerve to visit the church after dark. Elsewhere in the town after dark you may see why the resort once known as the Costa Geriatrica came to be called Bo-Mo by its younger citizens.

By catching the Land Train back to Boscombe you may save yourself enough time to take in the Russell-Cotes Art Gallery and Museum. It's worth a visit for the view alone. If you're at all susceptible to Victorian ebullience you'll enjoy the rest of it too.

The house was a present by Merton Russell-Cotes (the hyphen is a game attempt to reconcile three surnames, don't you think?) to his wife Annie. It displays objets they picked up on their travels, in rooms inspired by those same travels. Hence there's a Japanese collection and a Moorish Room, not to mention four purpose-built galleries. It is a remarkable place.

My visit took place almost 100 years after the completion of Annie's gift. The darkest days of AFC Bournemouth still lay ahead: in 2009, in deep financial difficulties, the club almost dropped out of the league. Their brightest days also lay ahead: now, they are a fixture in the Premier League and play attractive football that is too good for many of their top-flight opponents.

When I was there a dog show was taking place in the park. It seemed to attract a good many more attendees than Bournemouth v Oldham. 'Best Sausage Catcher' would have been the category for the Oldham defenders. They certainly couldn't catch any of the Bournemouth players.

Bournemouth 3 Oldham 0
Dean Court, 8 April 2000

Bradford City

When I planned my trip to Bradford the National Media Museum was high on my agenda. The media has given me a decent living without being unduly exacting in return. Also, Bradford having a National Museum of anything seems like a good idea that should be supported. Surely no-one but a Londoner could argue against a policy of getting things out of London, sharing resources and attractions around the UK.

Since then it has become the National Science & Media Museum. What to make of that? The explosive growth in the media in the past 30 years is largely the product of technology, but that isn't quite what the new name says. Besides, there was technology in the National Media Museum as an integral part of the story. The new label sounds bogus for three reasons:

- First, tacking Science on to the title sounds like a facile attempt to lure as many categories of visitor as possible
- Second, everybody knows where the Science Museum is, and it isn't Bradford, so the words 'pale' and 'imitation' will pop unbidden into some heads
- Third, in the effort to associate Science and the Media the curators might end up with the worst of both worlds. This may not be an exact analogy, but something odd began to happen in the recruitment of sub-editors to publications in the early 1990s. Where previously most of the applicants would have been interested in words, then a majority emerged who were interested in Apple Macintoshes. And here we are, 25 years later, in a world of fake news distributed globally, instantaneously, by 'information' technology.

For the National Media Museum, the writing was on the wall from February 2016 when a press release sneaked out. The transfer of 10% of the collection to the Victoria & Albert was ever so discreetly revealed. If anyone ever doubted that the Government's references to a Northern Powerhouse were empty, offensively disingenuous rhetoric, here was another telling piece of evidence.

Do people need the Royal Photography Society's collection to lure them to the V&A? Of course they don't. Might it help persuade them to visit Bradford? Conceivably. And to the objection that photographs can be duplicated and exhibited in more than one place, that's not the point. It's the blatant theft of prestige and assets from a northern city by a southern one. And if Bradford, where the Museum had only recently returned to an even keel after a period of uncertainty, could not afford the staff to curate the collection, why should not funds (from the Thames 'Garden Bridge' project, perhaps) have been redirected?

When I was there, the Media Museum would have been very good value even if they'd charged for entrance. If you were taking kids (as a parent or, I imagine, as a teacher) you'd probably head for the Wonderlab or the Magic Factory; they might choose the Games Lounge and the Animation Gallery.

I concentrated on the Kodak Gallery, enjoying particularly the sponsor's evasion of the issue of how it missed out on the development of digital photography so abjectly, having effectively invented the technology.

Of the collections, Tony Ray-Jones stays in my mind most clearly – the inexplicable *Bacup Coconut Dancers, 1968*, is unforgettable. Having completed his education in the USA Ray-Jones came back to England and began to document its eccentricities with his camera. "For me there is something very special about the English 'way of life' and I wish to record it from my particular point of view before it becomes Americanised and disappears," he wrote prophetically. Ray-Jones died in 1972 aged just 31.

It was a museum you could easily spend a day in, if you didn't have a football match to go to; or an unfamiliar northern industrial city to explore; or a deep attachment to the Brontës, in which case you would probably be heading east nine miles to Haworth.

I had no such interest, but parts of the Brontë legend are amusing. Charlotte, calling on William Makepeace Thackeray on one of her journeys to London, was not best pleased by his insistence on calling her Jane Eyre. Asked whether she liked London, she replied: "Yes and no."

I had parked on one of central Bradford's peripheral dustbowls – we're going back a little here, but not distantly – in the evocatively named Canal Road and Mill Street area and walked through the city centre.

The route into the city goes through Forster Square railway station, which was once the city's main station but is now restricted largely to trains serving Yorkshire destinations. The escarpment of Cheapside looms ahead, but the footpath takes you left through a small pedestrian precinct and up alongside the Midland Hotel and abruptly you're in the city centre.

When I was there, that meant the immediate prospect of a vast building site. Westfield, known locally as Wastefield, bounded by Lower Kirkgate, Church Bank, Well St and the A6181 was under development. It was a bleak scene, despite a certain amount of list-less Saturday activity. The dominant colour of the building site, of the city behind it and of the sky above was grey. It would have taken a Pantone obsessive to have done justice to the view. From a brow above the site, Bradford Cathedral (a parish church until 1919) looked down on the earth-moving money-spinning Mammon motive in action.

In a more advanced state of completion was the piazza called Centenary Square in front of the City Hall. The photograph taken by Google Earth's satellite shows something that looks like a par-tially reconstructed cranium recovered from an archaeological dig. On the ground, it's a modern city centre square albeit with a rather motley collection of buildings on its periphery.

In front of Nando's, at the base of a building that wouldn't be out of place on a Mediterranean promenade, a jazz band – instru-ments and suits glittering in the gloom – was taking a break. To the east, a magnificent northern City Hall expresses the satisfaction of the city's Victorian fathers in their achievements in a peculiarly Italian way. An annual horse-race around the square would not be inappropriate.

On the south side, the Bradford & Keighley Magistrates Court presents a face like a radiator grill behind which, presum-ably, a great deal of heat and energy is generated. The west side is largely open and gives on to the inner ring road and, beyond, the world-famous Alhambra, the Central Library and the National Media Museum as was.

Other attractions of central Bradford? The cathedral, the oldest building in the city if you overlook the three phases of rebuilding, is worth a visit. Pay particular attention to the windows: there's an unusual feminine theme. Women are prominent in many of the stained glass windows and nowhere more so than the West Window, which depicts the women of the Bible. Saints and martyrs also feature, but especially northern saints.

The pub I chose for lunch was undistinguished and I forget its name. Likewise the only shop I can recall was the Oxfam bookshop, which was uncommonly good. And, of course, the football ground, where an Oldham win is always worth a recommendation.

Bradford City 2 Oldham Athletic 3
Valley Parade, 5 April 2014

Brentford

Asked to name a waterside London football club, most people would say: "Fulham." Strictly speaking they would be right, but you could make a decent case for Brentford too. Griffin Park is barely a quarter of a mile from the Thames. It's about the same distance from the River Brent, which is canalised here and is effectively the southern end of the Grand Union Canal.

That puts the magnificent parks of Syon and Kew Gardens within easy reach, too. In other words Brentford, an unassuming corner of West London, is in a pretty smart neighbourhood.

Where the parks are concerned you might need several days to do justice to both. If you have to choose, Syon is English country house territory, interesting interiors lovingly restored and with a genuine sense of being lived in, and Kew Gardens has, according to *Time Out*, "loads to see here, whether you like green stuff or not".

A novel if slightly expensive way to approach Brentford, at any time of year, would be to take the London Overground to Kew Gardens. The station at Kew Gardens is a strange, exotic place, like an alpine plant in Transport for London's austere rockery. From there it's just a few minutes on foot to the Royal Botanic Gardens. The most direct arc through the Gardens would take you past the Palm House, the Hive, the Orangery and Kew Palace; it wouldn't be an enormous diversion to take in the Temperate House and the Treetop Walkway. At the Elizabeth Gate you come out on to Kew Green, from where it's no great distance to Griffin Park.

On the way, almost immediately over Kew Bridge, are two of London's more unusual museums. The first is unmissable at the foot of its 61-metre Italian tower – the London Museum of Water & Steam. 'Water' refers to municipal supply and disposal, 'steam' to the means of powering the pumps to draw the water up and move it around.

Some museums can be a bit dry; not this one. All its rooms and machine halls are redolent of pumping stations and water networks: flaking plaster, arches, exposed brickwork, huge columns, pipes and dials. The opening gallery introduces Thomas Crapper at an early stage and doesn't look back. A wall of appliances, boilers and ceramics towers over a layout of working models, backed by exhibition space in which the processes of water supply, distribution, treatment and disposal are explained.

Here the illustrations – especially period cartoons and clippings – are consistently attractive and often memorable. In one drawing captioned 'Before and after Cholera' a pretty apple-cheeked maid becomes a grey-faced invalid. In another, Death rows casually along the Thames. Cut-away models of homes through the ages demonstrate the growing sophistication of domestic water supply – and the increasing propensity to waste water.

Most of the rest of the galleries house the engines that pumped the water. Those from the steam era range from elegant precursors of locomotives to behemoths that disappear through the ceilings (and in one case, vertiginously into the Artesian depths of the earth as well). The collection includes the largest working beam engine in the world. The shift into the electronic era is reflected not only in the greatly reduced size of the engines but also in the blandness of their environment, not unlike the control rooms through which Bond villains planned to achieve world domination in the early films.

Outside there's an area where children can play (whether they realise it or not) with a water-wheel and an Archimedes Screw, and a narrow-gauge steam locomotive runs around the site at weekends. Inside, don't miss the café: the coffee is very good and the walls are an extension of the museum. There's also a small garden at the northern end of the site.

A little further along the road towards the football ground is The Musical Museum. Ordinarily my preference is to saunter around a museum at my own pace; here, though, it's probably essential to take the tour. The exhibits are automatic musical instruments – recorded sound from the era before phonographs, gramophones, radio etc. The tour guide makes them work and tells their stories. In the case of one pianola, he or she will invite you to have a go. In a self-playing piano, you may think, that would be a rather passive activity – but this is a pneumatic device and someone has to pump the bellows.

The tour can take about an hour and a half, depending on the age and attention span of the visitors. It culminates in a theatre with a performance of Wurlitzer music. You will be astonished at the variety of instruments that were automated and/or imitated, especially in the late 19th century and through to the early 1920s – pianos, of course, but also organs, percussion, brass and violins. The Museum has two types of violin-playing machines. In one, a single violin is 'played' by four rosin-covered wheels manoeuvred on to the strings by electromagnets; in the other, three violins with one string each present themselves in turn, pneumatically, to a rotating circular 'bow' – the fourth string is impersonated by an in-built automatic piano.

Don't be deceived by the name. It may sound like a narrowly specialist museum, but the exhibits and the narration carry interest well beyond the production of music: silent films, the history of automata and, with the importance of punched rolls of paper, early computer technology are all corollaries. Overall, it's a nostalgic hour or two spent in the parlour of social history.

Brentford 2 Oldham 1
Griffin Park, 28 March 1998

Brighton & Hove Albion

Among football fans, it's no small thing to complete 'the 92'. But the formal 92 Club has strict membership rules. To gain entry you must have seen a competitive game at the *current* ground of every league club.

Brighton & Hove Albion will have tested the dedication of members. The Seagulls have moved twice in the past 20 years. I have never been to their current home, near Sussex University at Fulmer, but I wouldn't qualify for membership for any number of reasons and in any case, I'm still recovering from a day at their previous pied-à-terre.

The Withdean Stadium... Where to start? Apparently it was the fourth worst football ground in the UK, according to *The Observer* in 2004. The three beneath it must have been something to see. Not that it was ugly, just ramshackle.

I set off in good time but could find neither the stadium nor the Park & Ride. I parked on the street and rode in a taxi. I know, it's a bit Bake-Off to arrive at a football match in a taxi, but time was ticking away.

The taxi delivered me a couple of minutes after kick-off to a most unlikely football venue. It was as though the Goths, rather than sack Rome, had annexed a leafy corner of it to watch sporting contests. With the fans, horny-handed sons of toil, shut away in their improvised accommodation, young ladies in pristine white skirts strolled out to the tennis courts. Ahead of me, a leisure centre opened its doors for the afternoon leisure-seekers.

The visiting supporters' end was on the other side of the leisure centre down what looked like a service road. The ticket office was a Portakabin. The turnstiles had a provisional air, as though they might have doubled as transportation for homing pigeons.

Having recently paid for a taxi and stuffed my wallet back into the first available pocket, I was searching for it as I approached the turnstiles. And so I found, almost immediately, that I had a debit card belonging to S, who had handed it to me "for safe keeping" in the pub where we had had lunch. The arrangement had been that I would go to the match and she would go shopping and we would reconvene at the hotel on Regency Square at 5.30pm. Since I had her card, S was going to be heading for the shops with whatever loose change she had in her pockets and her bag. That would almost certainly be less than £5; she rarely bothered with cash.

On a relatively warm spring afternoon a chill ran up my spine. When they told me at the gate that the visiting supporters' end was full, I actually considered going back to the town centre to look for her. Emitting steam, she would be easy enough to find. But a steward, registering at least part of my predicament, recalled that someone had left a ticket someone else had been unable to use and it was mine if I wanted it. And so, in possession of debit cards for two and abundant cash, I watched the match in return for a donation dropped into a collecting bucket.

At the Withdean Stadium, football was a field event and a running track surrounded it. The stands around the track, around the pitch, were taken down at the end of each season and put back for the next. There's a story that in one interval they were used at an Open Championship.

The West Stand, allocated to away fans, ran along a tangent at the crown of the running track's bend. That made it quite a long way from the goal at its own end of the ground, let alone the far end. Brighton fans acknowledged that this was the poorest visiting accommodation in the league, especially when they were forced to use it – the arrival of Portsmouth, entitled for a cup-tie to 15% of the seating by FA Cup rules, saw rearrangements that left home fans in tenancy for the day.

Watching Oldham Athletic crumble at a distance was no less disappointing than being able to see the process clearly. Plus I had the prospect of having to explain later why my possession of S's card was not entirely my fault. Whether I'd ever find the car again began to look a very minor concern. It was an afternoon in the Slough of Despond.

S was furious. I could hardly regard myself as solely responsible for the fiasco but she wasn't inclined to be so generous. When I found her at the hotel she had been there for most of the afternoon. She had tried window-shopping, she said, but Brighton had taunted her by constantly presenting her with treasures she could not buy.

She never saw much point in walking purely for the sake of the scenery, and sitting at a café table watching the world go by was beyond her resources. She had returned to the hotel as much to hide her shame as to pass the time without incurring any expense. She had 66p in her pockets.

I made it up to her by immediately taking her to the Palace Pier and funding her 2p coin-cascade habit. Quick to anger, S was equally easily pacified. With the luck she enjoyed that Saturday evening, the 66p of earlier in the day would have kept her entertained for most of an hour. She could also have visited the Museum of Penny Slot Machines, for free, but S no more went to museums than she carried cash.

The Brighton Museum & Art Gallery would have also been beyond her, requiring money for a ticket. The Old Police Cells Museum was free but was available only to booked parties. Perhaps she had a point.

Or she could have gone to contemplate Brighton Pavilion, memorably described by 19th century wit and liberal reformer Sydney Smith as looking "for all the world as if the Dome of St Paul's had came down to Brighton and pupped".

We walked back through the Lanes where the shops stay open late and made some entirely unnecessary purchases, just because we could. By dinner, equilibrium was restored.

Brighton & Hove Albion 3 Oldham 1
Withdean Stadium, 18 April 2009

Bristol City

At Bristol City's ground, Ashton Gate, towards the end of the 20th century, spectators at the visiting supporters' end sat on wooden benches. Leaning or shuffling backwards, they would find their backs coming into contact with the knees of the person behind. This added little to either party's enjoyment of the game.

"The end of wooden seats on soccer grounds?" a publication called the *Football League Review* had wondered aloud in its issue for the week ending 11 March 1967. The answer, almost 30 years later, was clearly a resounding "No".

Leicester City's "experiment in comfort" was the occasion for the *Review*'s question. Filbert Street had become the first football stadium in the country to install plastic seats... Sorry, not plastic, but British Resin Products' Rigidex high-density polyethylene.

The *Football League Review* was a free insert in football programmes in the late 1960s. Declaring itself *The Official Journal of the Football League*, it recalls simpler if not more innocent times. One issue inadvertently printed a picture of a player cheekily flashing for the camera in a Millwall team photograph. With that sort of thing getting past them, the staff couldn't be expected to give much time to what later became known as the marriage of form and function. With plastics, excitement at what might be done trumped aesthetic anxieties.

(A decade later, at the start of my career in journalism, plastic seating coincided with another growing enthusiasm: computers. One of the first stories I was given to work on, as a junior reporter with a weekly magazine for computer programmers, was the rumour that the seats in McDonald's were designed by computer. There was still something sinister in the idea of any such use of computers; and rightly so in this case, because the implication was that the seats would become uncomfortable after 30 minutes, so that diners would not linger, being untidy and taking up space.)

In the 1960s there was great enthusiasm for plastic and taking it into a sports stadium was a natural step. Although stands (so

called, perversely, because that was where spectators sat down)
were generally covered, plastic would have been more easily maintained than wood.

Seating, not then mandatory, was a neglected aspect of accommodation at football grounds. Comfort was even more neglected.
Not that the spectators were being discriminated against: the
managers, trainers and solitary substitute in the dugout were also
given unyielding benches to sit on, and if they leapt up in excitement they risked braining themselves on the corrugated iron or
slab concrete roof.

Besides, football was a winter sport and a degree of discomfort was taken for granted. Perhaps the reasoning was fair: on a
cold February night at Leyton Orient, a bit of cushioning under
your backside wasn't going to make much difference.

The terracing at football grounds was fairly standard: concrete
steps with, at intervals laterally and down the sweep of the terrace,
metal bars mounted on legs set into the concrete. People arriving at
the ground early tended to congregate around these bars. They gave
you something to lean against and, by way of a slight bonus, made
the people in front one step lower than anywhere else, giving you a
better chance of an unimpeded view.

A very distant and perhaps unreliable memory of Spotland,
Rochdale, presents me with an image of cinder banking rather
than concrete. This may be an Oldham supporter's natural inclina-
tion to denigrate Rochdale.

The possibility of a tall person's head being in your way was
only one kind of obstacle. If you were under cover, the pillars holding up the roof were a regular nuisance. I believe this still happens
at Goodison Park, Everton, along one side; and at Fulham, where
my brother-in-law has been a regular all his life, he and his mates
would use the stanchions to locate each other.

Cantilever roofs have resolved the impeded view problem but
some grounds still present quirky challenges. Visiting supporters
are almost invariably accommodated behind a goal and often to
one side of the goal, towards the corner. At Carlisle United they are
put into one of the long stands down the side of the field, but this

structure extends perhaps 15 metres beyond the goal line. If the away team takes its full allocation of seats, many of the fans will be peering at the game from a very acute angle and at a great distance. This stand, by the way, is the same distance short of the goal line at the other end of the pitch. It's as though the stand was built and the pitch was subsequently shifted 15 metres to the south. Brunton Park, Carlisle, is a pleasant, homely ground. A footloose stand is just one of its many charms.

Cinders, stanchions, benches and entire stands displaced... They're light years from the experience afforded the contemporary elite among football watchers. Corporate hospitality is in a different league.

Those lines of boxes, as at a theatre but glazed against the possibility of inclement weather, now routinely constitute a mezzanine level inlaid into the face of the stand. Within, you'll find tables, chairs, a bar and a pre-match dinner; in front, a couple of short rows of seats.

Anyone who has ever attended a baseball game in the USA will have been first startled and then delighted by the readiness with which beer and hot-dogs are delivered to you where you sit. Here in class-ridden Britain, those privileges do not yet extend to the hoi-polloi. But the fare in the hospitality booths is a good deal more varied and impressive than watery beer and spongy wieners. And the view is of a football match.

Will vendors ever bring beer and Pukka pies to football fans in the cheap seats, as it were? Probably not. The growing comfort of football stadiums has accompanied a deliberate policy of sanitisation as the game has tried to rid itself of hooliganism. Drink especially has always been associated with trouble at football grounds. It may be on sale, but usherettes with trays of it would be a step too far. Besides, beer and Pukka pies aren't aspirational.

There's another, rather more fanciful case to be made against treating the mass of football supporters too well. The game is not sure it needs them, except to buy replica strips and satellite TV subscriptions. There's a clue in the insulated nature of the corporate hospitality booth. Football is turning into a game enjoyed primarily on television. The booth is a half-way house; you're there at the game but are subtly distanced from it by the attendant home comforts of food, drink and warmth and by the absence from your immediate vicinity of sweaty, foul-mouthed examples of your fellow man.

With glacial stealth the game is gradually excluding behaviour that has been regarded as unacceptable elsewhere in society for decades. Eventually, the Augean Stables will be cleansed, Pimms will be the beverage of choice and football will be played to the accompaniment of canned crowd noise.

Bristol City 2-2 Oldham
Ashton Gate, 18 February 1995

Bristol Rovers

It is odd that a city of the status of Bristol should have two such consistently ordinary football teams. In the past 100 years Bristol City have spent just four seasons in the top flight, achieving a best place of 13th and winning the Anglo-Scottish Cup. The highest finish Rovers ever achieved was sixth place in the second tier, in the 1950s.

Rovers are perhaps the more colourful of the two clubs. They have not one but two nicknames – the Gas and the Pirates – and each is a cut above the workaday artlessness so common among other clubs. Even better, Rovers started life in Victorian times as the Black Arabs and at the time of writing were owned by a Qatari family. It's an elaborate pedigree.

My common-law brother-in-law went with me to Bristol Rovers. He also did the driving, but he can't be blamed for the fact that we arrived late.

We left the M4 in the vicinity of Hungerford to look for lunch. From there, we decided, the journey would be more interesting off the motorway.

So it proved. We approached Bristol on the A4, which took us close to Avebury. Andrew had never been. Everybody should go to Avebury, though not all at once. In the same way that I regard it as my duty as an uncle to take my nephews (invariably nephews) to an Oldham Athletic match (and none so far has asked to go to more than once), I can think of few more valuable services I can provide than to show people Avebury. We turned off the A4 and followed the signs.

From this direction you are given no idea what to expect and Avebury retains its element of surprise. The lane takes you towards the village and then sweeps you round a 90° bend to a car-park. Thus eventually you approach Avebury on foot, along a path with the cricket field on one side and scrubby trees on the other.

Quite abruptly you're over an earthwork or dyke and into

a field of standing stones. Sheep may be casually grazing at their bases, and people equally casually wandering among them. You'd only need the most fleeting acquaintance with the restrictions of Stonehenge to know how astonishing this is. And nobody shouts at you. If you strayed on to the square at the cricket field they'd make more fuss.

The stones have a louche, malingering air, as though waiting for a sculptor to turn them into something recognisable. You will notice, though, that those to left and right are arranged in an arc, following the inner line of the earthwork. This feature forms a circle around the village; two roads intersect at a slightly offset crossroads where the Red Lion stands. There aren't stones all the way round. In fact there isn't a full complement of megaliths where traces of a full arc remain, but markers indicate where other stones would once have stood.

The stones were put here in about 2,500 BC, perhaps a little before work began at Stonehenge. It's believed there was a large outer circle and two small inner circles. Quite what it was all about is unknown, but that's part of the appeal of such places, isn't it? You can supply your own story.

This diversion meant that by the time we were close to Bristol Rovers' Memorial Stadium, kick-off was near and parking was hard to find. After a slow and abortive circuit of adjacent residential streets, we found a space perhaps half a mile from the ground and made our way there at a very brisk walk.

We needn't have bothered. The ground was more interesting than the game. Its rugby club heritage was obvious and no two sides looked either the same or even related: one long stand, one short stand flanked by standing areas, one shed and, for the visiting fans, a kind of marquee. There was plenty of room in the marquee and, indeed, around the rest of the ground.

Bristol Rovers won 1-0. For Oldham, this was the fourth game in what became a series of 12 matches without a win. In 10 of them the team failed to score. In a dozen games, from early February to the end of March, Oldham gained four points and scored three goals. At the club's end-of-season dinner nobody was impolite enough to mention this. Thanks to an unusually good first half to the season, Athletic were safe for another year.

As we walked back to where we had left the car the mood among the home supporters was buoyant. Bristol Rovers needed the points; I found myself able to be pleased for the young lads skipping home with their dads, looking forward to the next match with renewed hope. In the event Rovers were relegated.

Andrew and I made our way to Clifton and located the Rodney Hotel. We found somewhere to eat (where we were the oldest diners, by decades) and reviewed the day with satisfaction.

The following morning was grey and cool. We set off to look at the Clifton Suspension Bridge, and once there it would have seemed disrespectful not to cross it. What had looked like a woodland path running alongside the river back towards the city proved to be a railway line, but eventually we found a path and followed it to where the River Avon turns east and a bridge takes you on to Spike Island.

Approaching Bristol from this direction makes it almost impossible to avoid the *SS Great Britain*. We were looking for a coffee rather than a relic of the Golden Age of Steam, but Andrew was an engineer and his enthusiasm for the exhibition was infectious. If you plan to go, don't be discouraged by the website, which tends towards the infantile; but if you can, take an engineer to show you round.

Also in the docks area you'll find the eclectic M Shed, a very distinctive perspective on Bristol; We The Curious, a thoroughly modern science museum; and the Bristol Aquarium, described by one visitor as "the perfect size if you only have an hour or so before a football match".

Up the road in the University area there's another group: the Bristol Museum & Art Gallery, the Red Lodge Museum, the Georgian House, the Earth Sciences Museum and more.

If sherry or cocktails are your poison, Harvey's Cellars behind the Hippodrome has art on the walls and artefacts at the back, although calling this the Harvey's Wine Museum may be gilding

the lily. And if you have the time, an app-based Banksy Walking
Tour takes about two hours.

Bristol Rovers 1-0 Oldham
Memorial Stadium, 19 February 2011

Burnley

At sporting events overseas, spectators release animals or other objects on to the field of play for comic effect. In rugby union, cockerels have been let loose not only for the French XV's home games but also at Twickenham, Lansdowne Road and Murrayfield. US supporters throw a catfish (dead and gutted to avoid unnecessary mess) on to the rink to widespread delight during the Nashville Predators ice-hockey contests. In the UK, we confine ourselves largely to unsolicited comments.

Most football grounds will have at least one loudmouth among their regulars. This man (it is always a man) loves the sound of his own voice and has no doubt that thousands of other people share his affection.

The upper limit to his idea of his popularity will be determined not by the capacity of the stadium but by his timing; a football crowd generates a good deal of ambient noise, the kind of background rumble that arises from a nearby motorway. Even when there are no songs being rehearsed, no chants being intoned, neither drumming nor vuvuzelas, a large crowd will rarely be entirely silent. Something unexpected or shocking – an outbreak of sportsmanship, for example – might be sufficiently jaw-dropping to produce a silence of startling clarity. Into that, a totally insensitive loudmouth can project his inane comment across an entire stadium.

The comment need not be inane. Sometimes it will be moderately funny, and a regional accent is rarely a handicap.

I was at a Heart of Midlothian home game against Motherwell when play was interrupted for an injured Motherwell player to receive treatment. The Hearts goalkeeper kicked the ball into touch, the kind of gesture that seldom fails to provoke warm applause. The ball came into the crowd close to where I was sitting. As the clapping died away, a Motherwell player came over to take the throw-in. The ball was lobbed towards him, and as it described its leisurely arc a voice behind me called out: "Hey, son, you're fucking ugly, by the way." The player was just sufficiently distracted to take his eye off the ball, which went between his hands and hit him on the nose.

The casual, conversational quality of the insult; the familiar, even friendly form of address; and the gratuitous, emphatic vulgarity... It was very funny. As is so often the case, however, the laughter that greeted the remark persuaded its perpetrator that he was the Oscar Wilde of the Wheatfield Stand and he continued to bellow increasingly mindless and offensive insults for the rest of the game.

On reflection, Oscar Wilde is too recent. Classical references are more appropriate. In Greek mythology two figures in particular were known for their ability to project vocally. One, Stentor, was known for nothing else. He would be completely forgotten were it not for the use of his name in an adjective, 'stentorian', deployed since the 17th century to indicate an unusually powerful voice. Stentor was a herald at the Trojan War and according to Homer had a voice capable of matching those of 50 ordinarily mortals combined.

The more interesting foghorn from those times was another warrior from the Greek side at Troy. Menelaus, the brother of the Greek leader Agamemnon, is referred to repeatedly by Homer as 'Menelaus of the loud war-cry'. This may be history's first instance of a man's bark being worse than his bite; certainly of an empty vessel making the most noise. It was Menelaus of whom Paris made a cuckold by running off with Helen. Yes, this was the Helen subsequently known so widely as Helen of Troy that her previous life as Helen of Menelaus is generally forgotten. Menelaus was married to the most beautiful woman in history and he lost her. What might his war-cry have been? "D'oh!"

The cry from the terraces at Burnley on that distant day in 1968 was delivered in a broad East Lancashire accent and with distinct relish at the unsavoury details of its imagery. As Burnley toiled to break down an obdurate West Bromwich defence, a man in the crowd bellowed: "They're like black'eads – you've got to squeeze 'em out!"

He was only half right. As the game wore on – and on, and on – Albion defenders were like blackheads more in the sense that they appeared to multiply and any aggressive threat from the visitors melted away completely.

West Brom's strategy that day was probably dictated by other concerns. They saved energy at Burnley and key players were sheltered from potential injury. West Bromwich, dourly unambitious at Turf Moor, faced an FA Cup replay at Liverpool a few days later. Liverpool were on the verge of becoming one of the dominant clubs in all of Europe; they might have been expected to be more adept at squeezing a blackhead than Burnley.

In the event, though, the replay at Anfield finished 1-1 and 10 days after that West Bromwich won a second replay 2-1. Albion went on to win the FA Cup that year, beating Everton 1-0 in a final memorable only for it being the last time West Bromwich Albion won a trophy.

The result at Burnley did not lie. It was as dull a goalless draw as you could wish to avoid. Not the least remarkable feature of the scoreline was the fact that the previous meeting between these two clubs, not four months earlier, had finished 8-1 in West Brom's favour. Not much squeezing out needed on that occasion.

Burnley 0 West Bromwich Albion 0
Turf Moor, 6 April 1968

Burton Albion

Night is close when Modwenna and her two companions reach the river. They are aware of it first through their feet. As the ground becomes softer, water pools around their soles. In the deepening gloom, Modwenna hears a breeze sighing through reeds. Barely able to see the river they have no means to judge its width. The three women retrace their steps into the forest, where the land rises gently and the earth is dry and firm.

They have passed no habitation for more than a league[1]. There is no evidence of human activity here, certainly no indication of a crossing-point. Modwenna declares that they should make camp in the trees rather than stumble about in the dark, and be as comfortable as they may. Lazar and Althia, companions in name rather than rank, do as they are told.

The women, pilgrims bound eventually for Rome, carry with them much of what they need. This is not their first night in the open, in the woods. Besides, their needs are modest. Modwenna is an Irishwoman of some nobility but she has turned her back on privileges bestowed by birth and confirmed by marriage. Lazar and Althia, her sisters in Christ, are bound to her by ties of family and duty older than the church.

The morning brings bright sunlight, though not to Althia. At some time in the night – or possibly the previous evening, as they approached the river in the gloomy half-light – her eyes have become clouded. Modwenna and Lazar look into them and see swirling mist in the pupils instead of a depthless coal black and the sparkle as of a distant planet. Althia is effectively blind, and very frightened.

The three women have experience of sight loss but only among their elders, and usually after gradual degeneration. They pray, fervently. Modwenna then rises and, following a track made by animals, makes her way to the river's bank. She hopes to find clean, fresh water, in which hope she is disappointed – the river is

---

1 About three miles.

wide, turbulent and heavy with sediment. But the movement of the water suggests to her what she needs to do.

Modwenna instructs Lazar to stay with Althia. She will follow the course of the river southward, against the flow. Already broad and unfathomably deep, it can only get broader and deeper downstream. Such a noble river must sustain communities, she reasons; she will return with fresh food and water and, perhaps, a cleric with some knowledge of herbs.

Help proves to be closer at hand than she could have hoped. Skirting the woodland, she walks barely 400 paces before a water meadow gives her a clear view of the river itself and of the far bank. On the other side stands a settlement clustered around a hunch-shouldered Saxon church.

Modwenna makes her way cautiously across the river meadow to the bank. Here the habit of command serves her. Across the river, perhaps 60 paces away, a peasant at work scraping a hide appears to be using the water to soften it; Modwenna calls out to him and within a short time she is ferried across the river, in a craft made of animal skins stretched over a wooden frame. The peasant is not permitted to return to his hide. Modwenna commandeers him and not long afterwards returns across the river with fresh water, fresh fruit and the prayers of the priest, whose knowledge of specifics is less than her own.

Althia is treated with water from a well rather than from the river; with fruit, damsons predominantly; and of course with prayers from a growing number of souls. The congregation of the church of St Peter, which later gives the village of Stapenhill its name, add their own ambiguous desiderata. Modwenna and her companions establish a camp set back from the west bank of the river, but not before youths from the village dig a well for them. The site is less convenient where maintaining a supply of food is concerned, but from the villagers' point of view it effectively isolates the pilgrims while Althia's sickness takes its course.

The National Brewery Centre's museum makes excellent use of quotations on the panels that tell you what you're looking at. An example: "One no sooner enters the town of Burton than he begins to be oppressed by a sense of brewery on the brain." The comment is given no attribution beyond being that of "a visitor [evidently male] to Burton in 1882". But the observation holds good 135 years later.

The valley in which Burton upon Trent stands contains layers of sand and gravel up to about 20 metres deep. As water has seeped through these layers over the millennia it has picked up minerals. In particular it has high sulphate, magnesium and calcium content, and is correspondingly low in sodium and bicarbonate. That, apparently, makes it perfect for brewing beer. Burton beer is known for a dry, slightly sulphurous scent that has passed into the lexicon of brewing as the 'Burton snatch'.

Through the north-west corner of the football ground, three brewery storage tanks are visible. As the sun sets it gives them a copper sheen; it playfully repeats this trick of the light later, on the base of the clouds. Perhaps through the power of suggestion, there's a distinctive smell on the air too.

The skyline throughout the town is distinguished by brewery architecture. If it isn't the modern, silver cylindrical towers it's the traditional pyramidal roofs topped by ventilators at the apex. Some chimneys survive, though like the rest of us they are mainly non-smoking.

Such buildings tend now to belong to trading estates. The area between the Three Queens Hotel and the stadium is business park territory, here in the traditional low-rise warehouse style, there in converted industrial premises, some more ad hoc than others.

You get a sense of a town that takes a quiet pride in itself. A Burton Civic Society Award plaque on an otherwise unremarkable terrace makes you look more closely: the French word 'remarquer' means 'to notice'. In this spirit, I notice the humour of a pub on Wetmore Road called the Wetmore Whistle, sadly abandoned, and, on the slope of a railway bridge, a yellow wildflower with flowers like a snapdragon and flimsy, whispy foliage.

The approach to Burton from the south on the A444 is one in the eye for anyone who regards the New World habit of driving great distances at the drop of a hat as anything other than ridiculous. Of course they will drive long distances – there's nothing to stop for in between. In this country, we have compelling distractions every couple of hundred yards.

On the A444 they are the Historic St Michael's Church, followed soon by a sign (not hidden by trees) for the National Forest and then a brown sign of the kind that normally directs you to an ancient market town, a heritage site or a motte and bailey castle – but this one reads: 'For furniture superstore follow A444'. Opportunism with a rhyme.

The Three Queens prove difficult to locate. Looking for Bridge Street, I drive the considerable length of Uxbridge Street, which introduces me to Burton's ethnic diversity but gets me no closer to the hotel. Eventually a cyclist gives me directions with the precision that only a man reliant on the strength of his legs for his knowledge of an area could give. His directions are spot-on.

The three queens are Mary, Elizabeth I and Anne. The accession to the throne of Elizabeth II gave the landlord a problem that he resolved by changing the name to The Queens, but new owners have reverted enthusiastically to the earlier triumvirate.

They apply no such sense of tradition to the interior of the bar. It is an exhilarating confusion of styles. Swirling carpets recall the 60s and caramel leather sofas the 70s. On the walls, *trompe-l'oeil* wallpaper pretends to be bookshelves, brickwork, chocolate-coloured wood panelling, wine labels and bottles. The radiators are painted streakily in the same odd chocolate colour. An exaggerated Norman arch motif recurs, faux-Tiffany lights illuminate window sills of great depth, Art Deco wall-lights shed an agreeable glow on a mosaic bar. Modestly framed pictures of the queens line the walls except where a vast television regales the clientele with what may be a version of MTV for the over-50s.

Fed by donations, watered by the well, Modwenna, Lazar and Althia settle into their isolation ward. Modwenna treats Althia by bathing her eyes with water several times a day, and in another sense by giving her the best of the food the villagers provide. That means fish, for the most part, vegetables and woodland fruits. With Lazar she prepares and plants a small vegetable garden in the rich alluvial soil. The villagers scoff, warning that it will flood.

But the vegetable plot may be irrelevant for another reason. Althia's sight begins to return. After a month she is able to walk short distances unescorted. After six weeks they begin to make plans to resume their pilgrimage.

On Saturday morning an open market sets up in the square in front of the Market Hall. The Burton Brewery Trail doesn't take you quite that far down the High Street but it isn't an enormous diversion to get to the town's historic core – the former site of the abbey, around St Modwen's and the Market Hall (the Catholic church is also dedicated to Modwen, although she shares it with St Mary).

Many of the shops are open at 9am. St Modwen's opens at 10am, as does the museum attached to the National Brewery Centre. St Modwen's is free, the museum not so. £9.95 might strike you as a bit steep for a museum, especially one as limited in its subject matter as this. But the ticket also buys you a pint and three tasters, which brings the price back into the realms of the reasonable. When you reflect, after your visit, you might even regard it as exceptional value.

The early halls walk you through the processes and techniques of brewing. Who would have thought there was so much to malting? And it's another of those discoveries that elevate your regard for primitive people and their boundless ingenuity. It's easy to imagine that barley might have been allowed to germinate by accident, and the process arrested when the farmer saw what was happening. But he/she would then have had to say to him/herself: "Hmm, this grain might not be spoiled. I'll cook it and soak it in very hot water for a while, to see if I can retrieve the situation." And with a little natural yeast mouldering on the pots, the beginnings of a brew would result and life would never be the same again.

It's a museum with plenty of variety. There are spectacular models: of steam engines (one or two life-size); most exceptionally, of Burton in the early 20th century, a vast and beautiful model that occupies most of a large room; and making the point that Burton's product reached across the globe, of ships at dock (in Horninglow, a couple of miles up the road on the Trent-Mersey Canal, and at Calcutta, on the other side of the world).

Modwenna, Althia and Lazar left their camp, crossed the river and gave thanks at the church of St Peter. With the good wishes of the villagers and as much food and water as they could carry, they set off towards the south, aiming eventually for Tamworth, in the heart of Mercia.

The three women made good progress along the eastern bank of the river. But they had hardly covered two leagues when Althia began to complain of dizziness. They rested, drank some water and moved on. Almost immediately Althia's dizziness became something more sinister; although midday still lay ahead, Althia felt herself overwhelmed by darkness. Her sight was failing.

Modwenna bade her lie down and she bathed her sister's eyes. Althia was weeping with frustration and fear, and her salt tears mingled with the well-water and ran down her cheeks. The bathing had no effect, nor later when Modwenna repeated the treatment. As late afternoon approached, the women decided they must go back to the village.

After the exultation of the morning – a celebrated departure, a pilgrimage resumed, the good wishes of new friends ringing in their ears – it was a mournful return. The track was no more difficult, but the necessity to lead Althia slowed their progress. Eventually, reaching the precincts of St Peter, they were unable to bear the sympathy of the villagers and asked to be ferried back to their camp.

The following morning, with fresh water from the well to drink and to use as a salve, Althia's sight returned.

The National Brewery Centre's models are not universally impressive. The exhibit explaining the chemistry of brewing is dominated by a mannequin that looks spookily like TS Eliot. As you approach, a motion censor sparks it into fitful movement. The poet/biochemist, test-tube in hand, shudders fractionally before stopping, as though exhausted. Perhaps he is; after all, he has been dead 50 years or more. Or perhaps he is discouraged by his repeated failure to make any progress in synthesising isinglass, despite years of creaking to and fro. A sign notes that the windows in the original lab would have been whitewashed, to prevent anyone discovering what was taking place within. I prefer to think the purpose would have been to protect the chemist's dignity.

There are elements of a conventional small town museum, but as with the rest of the displays they are beautifully – in some cases lavishly – produced. We learn how St Modwen arrived and how Wulfric Spott (or Spot) founded the abbey on which Burton's fortune was eventually based. A geological cross-section of a well will give geologists and model-makers great pleasure.

The museum also has horses, steam trains, historic vehicles; art and graphic design; chronology, from the days before Burton existed; and more beer mats and inn signs than you could shake a cocktail at.

Did I take the National Brewery Centre up on its offer of a pint and three tasters? I did not. This is the town, let's not forget, that despite its natural advantages produced some of the most indifferent beers in history, and might still be doing so were it not for the much mocked and maligned greybeards of Camra. Whatever I drank in Burton, it would carry the aftertaste of Double Diamond. Would I go to London and seek out a pint of Watneys Red Barrel? Of course not.

In the following weeks Modwenna and Althia conducted simple experiments. While Lazar tended the camp and looked after the vegetables, Modwenna and Althia set out on measured expeditions.

They discovered that Althia's sight began to deteriorate not at a certain distance from the camp but at an interval of time since exposure to fresh well-water.

They confirmed this by remaining in the camp but rationing the treatments. If half a day passed without Althia's eyes being bathed in fresh water from the well, her sight began quickly to fade. Water stored and carried in sacks or flasks of various materials had no effect. Food and drink appeared to make no difference one way or another. They concluded that Althia had no alternative but to stay close to the well.

Modwenna detected the will of God in what was happening. She and Lazar declared that they too would stay, and that between them they would found a religious community on the west bank of the river. They embraced and wept at the surfeit of love they felt for each other.

The charity shops of the town are staffed by ladies who might be priestesses of the cult of Modwen. One talked to me about her fear of spiders, a subject that arose from a conversation about housework. To overcome it, she had visited a phobia workshop where she had held a tarantula on her open hand.

"It was all right as long as you didn't agitate it," she said. "So you held it for a while and then put it down very gently."

"What if it tried to escape?" I asked.

"Well, I expect you bring your other hand down on it very quickly and firmly," she replied.

A phobia workshop is the kind of thing a saint's devotee would do. They are, after all, God's creatures, and we should be capable of living with them.

It was never Modwenna's intention to promote the mysterious properties of the water in any way. For all she knew, they applied only to Althia and her particular problem. But word flowed upstream and down, and ninth-century traders carried the news far afield.

Just over midway through the century, a young boy arrived with symptoms that would now be recognised as Crohn's Disease. Whether the water cured him or not is arguable; he suffered from poor health most of his life but that did not prevented him being remembered as Alfred the Great. The reputation of the settlement opposite Stapenhill was assured.

Modwenna stayed there for seven years. When she founded a church (dedicated to St Andrew) on an island in the river, the community began to grow around it and the name of Burton entered the historical record (replacing 'Mudwennestow', which means 'Modwen's holy place'). Modwenna did finally reach Rome, having left Althia in charge, and on her return to Britain she worked as a missionary in Scotland. When she died, aged 130, near Dundee, silver swans accompanied her soul to heaven.

In another charity shop the books were arranged bustrophedon, which is to say in the way a farmer would plough a field. They started with A at the top left, worked their way across to J and then began on the next row to head left towards M, and so on.

Saturday morning was a busy time in the charity shop sector. The Christian aspect was apparent in one of life's timeless victims bending the ear of one of the helpers about how Jesus was helping him turn his life around. "I'm not having you on," he insisted at intervals.

Burton Albion 2 Birmingham City 1
Pirelli Stadium, 18 August 2017

Bury

Bury, you might say, is the South Kensington of North Manchester. But the association in the sentence of 'south' and 'north' is confusing and clumsy. Besides, the comparison is unjust and could easily be the other way round: the number of museums, galleries and heritage sites per square kilometre in Bury may be higher than anywhere else in the country, South Kensington included.

The immediate prospect from Bury's Metrolink station isn't promising unless you happen to be looking for a bus-stop. Still, if you've got that far you've learnt an important lesson about Greater Manchester's tram network. If you feared there would be a stop every 100 metres, and more delays at contrary traffic lights and roundabouts, you now know better. Beyond Manchester Victoria it is effectively a suburban commuter railway, and the trams swish along briskly between stations. Confirmation that they are proper railway stations is found at Bury Transport Museum, where the old London Midland Scottish crimson lake station nameplates decorate a wall.

Transport is a dominant theme in Bury. The Transport Museum is free and run largely by volunteers who give it a friendly, personal touch. It has everything from early bicycles to a collection of buses, with advanced technology in a series of interactive displays.

The layout is simple: a central display area with vehicles, engines, rolling stock etc, flanked by two 'platforms' with smaller displays, models and a reconstruction of a goods manager's office.

For me, the colours were the most evocative aspect of the museum: the crimson lake of the LMS livery, the two-tone Yelloway coach and the cowslip yellow of the old Manchester bus-stop signs, which told you which side to queue. Would the bus have hurtled past if the queue formed on the wrong side? Or, worse yet, no queue formed? Who'd want to risk it?

The coach, incidentally, contains the Yelloway Motorcoach Museum, which may be the cutest such attraction in the UK.

Another highlight is the working model of the Bury section of the East Lancashire Railway as it was in the 1940s – the model itself is almost 30 years old, and it blends in well.

The East Lancs Railway itself is just across the road, at Bury Bolton Street station. The line runs 12 miles from Heywood in the east to Rawtenstall at the northern terminus. Steam engines and diesels pull multiple units or corridor carriages through the industrial past. The railway operates a regular timetable throughout the year: weekends through the winter, and Wednesday to Sunday (plus Bank Holiday Mondays) from April to September.

The other focus of museums in Bury is Moss Street, where the Fusilier Museum and the Bury Art Museum & Sculpture Centre are across the road from each other.

The Fusilier Museum houses the collections of the XX Lancashire Fusiliers and the Royal Regiment of Fusiliers. There are more than 300 years of military history here, but the museum is as much about individuals, and not always soldiers – one display celebrates the devotion of a wounded officer's wife. The Royal Regiment of Fusiliers marks its 50th anniversary in 2018. The museum has a new exhibition and an artist-in-residence to mark the event.

This is Bury's Cultural Quarter. When did ordinary English towns begin to have quarters? The answer may be Birmingham's Jewellery Quarter, said to date back 200 years. London's South Bank is now referred to as a Cultural Quarter by estate agents, which looks like a case of gilding the lily. But Sheffield takes the biscuit, with five quarters and six more districts that might be mistaken for quarters. A Cultural Eleventh doesn't sound quite so trendy and French; in fact it sounds like the last kid to be picked in a playground football match.

The Art Museum & Sculpture Centre is a worthy focal point in the Cultural Quarter. It has some great British artists of the past: Turner's *Calais Sands at Low Tide*, Constable's *Hampstead Heath*, two Epsteins including a bust of George Bernard Shaw; and some spectacular modern pieces. In May 2018 the ground floor space was devoted to the 25th anniversary of the Irwell Sculpture Trail. A lamp circled an assemblage of moulded figures around a 19th century pagoda in bone and ivory, casting mesmeric shadows on to the walls.

In the museum section of the building, a class of primary school children was listening to a lively presentation on life in Bury during the war. In the next room, recruitment posters dating from World War I asked especially for men with a trade. A general appeal for recruits to the artillery promised training "at Lytham St Annes, where everything possible will be arranged for their comfort". It sounded like the senator's line in *The Outlaw Josey Wales*: "They were decently treated, they were decently fed and then they were decently shot."

Other things to see in Bury:

- The statue of Robert Peel, born in Bury, twice Prime Minister and regarded as the founder of the Conservative Party. According to one story, the statue once adorned public conveniences and the great man's hand gesture indicated the men's entrance.
- The only visible remains of Bury Castle are foundations in Castle Square, in front of the Castle Barracks and Armoury.
- Bury Market regularly wins awards. It was the National Association of British Market Authorities' Market of the Year in 2006 and has picked up more national and regional awards since then.

Bury 0 Stoke City 2
Gigg Lane, 26 December 1961

Cambridge United

The name of Cambridge echoes down the world's corridors of learning, in time and space, amplified by the tireless work of great scholars. Too many to name, they are giants bestriding many fields: science, statecraft, sport, stand-up... 50% more Nobel prize-winners than Oxford, or so it's said.

Then there are the famous sights: the architecture, the Backs, the Mathematical Bridge... and Parker's Piece, where the rules of modern football were first applied in 1863. They outlawed 'hacking'. Yes, seriously.

Yet all I have to offer from the two or three occasions I've been to Cambridge, to look round, visit friends and feel inadequate, is the pub dinner I had on the Tuesday evening of this League Cup tie.

It too was a Thai. In a simple boozer on the Newmarket Road, they were serving Thai food in 1992. It's barely imaginable even now; and yet somebody not only imagined it but brought it bravely to market. And people swallowed it.

I can't remember the name of the pub. I wouldn't want to, except perhaps to be sure of avoiding it in future. And that shouldn't be too difficult: Cambridge must have scores of more enticing places to eat.

The Fitzwilliam Museum's Courtyard Café, for example, not only serves a variety of nourishing meals but also has a fine museum attached. However, it closes at 5pm on a Tuesday, as do the Museum of Cambridge, the Centre for Computing History, the Museum of Classical Archaeology and the Sedgwick Museum of Earth Sciences.

The Polar Museum closes an hour earlier, and at 4.30pm the Museum of Archaeology & Anthropology and the Whipple Museum of the History of Science shut their doors. Not all of them, in any case, serve what you might call a square meal.

It begins to look as though a day of cultural exploration in Cambridge followed by an evening of more proletarian pursuits will leave a hiatus of at least two and a half hours. On a December night, it won't just be beer goggles that make a random pub on the Newmarket Road look more impressive than might otherwise be the case.

My previous experience of Thai cuisine had been inauspicious. It began in January 1982 when a Thai International Airways Royal Orchid Refresher Stop found me in Bangkok for two or three days on the way from London to Sydney. Fetching up exhausted at the Hotel Erewan, I couldn't sleep and so set out into the night to eat. As I left the hotel – on foot – I was harangued by a taxi driver who demanded through his wound-down window to know why I was walking. Meanwhile a man fell into step alongside me, offering to guide me to "an exciting spectacle". Ignoring the taxi driver, I explained to the tout that I was tired from a long flight. To his credit, he was adaptable and creative. "Ah, you want massage!" he said.

Shaking off my pursuers I inadvertently turned right out of the hotel, away from the city centre, instead of left towards it. Disorientated by jet-lag and in an unfamiliar city, I didn't realise my mistake for some time. Perhaps it was the difficult crossing of a building site where a freeway was taking shape; perhaps the steady diminution in the number of street lamps; perhaps, eventually, the complete absence of commercial premises alerted me to the possibility that I was lost.

And then, like Grace Darling waving a lantern to bring me into a safe haven, a lamp above the door of a restaurant appeared. On a stool beside the doorway sat what I took to be a child wearing a sombrero. As he stood to usher me inside it became clear that he was a dwarf. Simultaneously a sticker in the window caught my eye: this establishment would honour my Royal Orchid Refresher Stop meal voucher. And there were people – locals, presumably – eating. Although the restaurant might have been designed by Stanley Kubrick I entered it with confidence. Besides, finding another in this neck of the klongs was unlikely.

The menu was almost completely indecipherable. The names of the dishes were rendered in Western script but no accompanying descriptions. I ordered something called Phat Prik on the basis that the Anglicised version made something close to sense.

It proved to be thinly sliced, undercooked beef on a bed of lettuce that might have been washed in Daz. I can't remember what I ordered for dessert, but it failed to take the taste away.

When the time came, my voucher was greeted with such enthusiasm that I supplemented it with a large tip, and the doorman took off his sombrero and drove me back to the Erewan.

After that I gave Thai food a wide berth for many years until, weakening in 1989, I went with friends to a Thai restaurant in Clerkenwell and had a glass of beer tipped over me by a maladroit waitress.

Why would an English pub serve Thai food? The *Financial Times* explored the topic in a feature in 2009 (and the date suggests that the pub I ate in was truly a trail-blazer). A publican explained that his customers were happy with sausage and chips at lunchtime but wanted something better in the evening. In 1988 he employed a Thai chef on a trial basis and never looked back.

What catches the eye there is the sense of entitlement implied. When did the English decide that gristly pies, watery cauliflower cheese and tepid fish and chips were inadequate evening fare? What happened between 1pm and 7pm (or, for that matter, between 1980 and 1990) to cause people to want and expect something better?

In the small town in which I live now there are two Thai restaurants (10% of the total), and three local pubs have dabbled with Thai at one time or another. It is no longer unusual, although a well-outfitted Thai restaurant is still exotic. Phat Prik still appears in a variety of guises, but I can't say whether the dish I ate in 1982 was a good example. It isn't the kind of mistake you make more than once.

And the football match? Oldham had been League Cup finalists in 1990 and they went to Second Division Cambridge United as a top-tier team. Perhaps the pre-match meal disagreed with them.

Cambridge United 1 Oldham 0
Abbey Stadium, 1 December 1992

Cardiff City

This guide has carefully steered clear of the tempting territory of restaurant reviews.

Of course, people pitching up in unfamiliar towns will be interested in where to eat, but (with one or two exceptions) they won't find the answer here. For a number of good reasons:

- First, restaurants come and go; pubs too, or they change hands and change character. The World Wide Trough is a far better source of up-to-date reviews, menus and immoderate criticism posted by trolls
- Second, with the best will in the world I would rarely be in a position to comment on the qualities of more than one restaurant. Blameless but overlooked, all other restaurants, pubs and bistros in the town in question would by implication be discriminated against
- Third, restaurant reviewing is a serious business. In the modern vernacular, you'd need some chops to do it. My own culinary preferences, especially on a Saturday afternoon, run hardly any further than a cheeseburger. That's not necessarily a third strike against the idea of reviews: I could have applied a grading system for cheeseburgers in each town. At the bottom of the scale would be the appalling putty patties of the Casey Jones franchise from the days of British Rail. In the modern era, 'artisanal' burgers may be the evolutionary peak of the genus. And the marketing that encourages us to eat them pink is the peak of a different kind of bovine product.

Despite all of the above, I'm going to make an exception for Cardiff. Friends showed me round the city and took me to lunch chez Madame Fromage, in the Castle Arcade. Madame, whom I picture knitting cheesecloth or muslin as she sits sternly at a cash register, runs an exceptional establishment. I recommend it with no hesitation but also with no implied criticism of any of the places in Cardiff that don't sell the world's finest Croque Monsieur.

There are reasons to be optimistic about Madame's longevity.

Cardiff's Victorian arcades are themselves survivors. Beautifully maintained and stylishly elegant, they link the streets of the city centre like a series of stations on the Moscow underground. They thrive in the face of such bland modern competition as the St David's Centre, in which (like Toronto or a Las Vegas casino) you can spend hours without experiencing the outdoors.

Within their ornate passages, independent traders defy the ruins of time. Spillers Records, in the Morgan Arcade, goes back to 1894 and describes itself as the oldest record shop in the world. Elsewhere there are shops devoted to stringed instruments played with bows, board games, fancy dress, jokes, books and buttons. There is intricately cast and painted ironwork, glass and bunting. Cardiff calls itself a young city but its arcades are a bequest in a will written generations ago.

The 'young city' tag is something of a conceit anyway. Cardiff promotes itself as a 'cool, cosmopolitan capital', an image at odds with the stuffier aspects of the heritage business. But when it declares, to emphasise its youth as a city, that it was either a 'small market town' or 'a fishing village' in the 1300s, it is disingenuous. First, most places were either small market towns or villages in the 14th century (and some were even smaller by the 15th, thanks to the Black Death). Second, Cardiff was a small market town (and a fishing village) with a substantial Norman castle attached.

I didn't have time to look round the castle. From the outside it looks more ceremonial than military, and indeed much of it dates (like the Arcades) from the Victorian era. Castell Coch, a few miles northwest of Cardiff, has some of the character of a Disney fairy-tale castle but Cardiff Castle itself isn't entirely devoid... Sure enough, a few days later Prince Harry and his then bride-to-be were there. Among the people they met, according to reports, were two local sisters and their dog, loyally named Camilla. The dog, a spaniel of some kind (a King Charles, probably), looked utterly miserable despite (or perhaps because of) the tiara it wore and the pushchair in which it sat.

Back at Madame Fromage there was an equally enthusiastic crowd. We queued for a while for a table to become available

– it's a good sign, especially for such a late lunch. The Cardiff City/Sunderland game had kicked off at 12.30pm and was over by 2.20pm, for the convenience of Sky subscribers. It was almost 3.30pm, then, when we sat down to eat.

The timing inconvenienced me only to the extent that I had little time for sightseeing before the game. Still, a trot round the Cardiff Story museum in the Old Library was a good start to the day.

It was disconcerting at first: the Cardiff Story is told in a single large room through multiple screens and projections, and many of the displays are above eye level on boards reaching up to a very high ceiling. The initial impression is overwhelmingly confusing. But when you start to focus on one thing at a time it's great fun. There are cityscape models on which buildings light up in response to a pressure pad; a game takes you through the three successive means – pack animal, canal and railway – of getting coal to the docks; there are things to play with all over the room. It isn't a large museum but it's free and very engaging.

I might apply the second adjective to Cardiff City Football Club too. Beneath the stand, in the time leading up to the match, the club organised activities for kids. There was a Target Golf game, and Kick a Football through a Doughnut, and basketball. Roaming through the family groups was an unusual mascot in a spherical blue suit with prongs; it looked as if it might represent the flu bacteria sweeping the country. Youngsters were invited to hit it with an inflatable hammer, although a hypodermic loaded with vaccine would surely have been more effective. This strange creature appeared again during the half-time entertainment, doubling as a surprisingly mobile goalkeeper alongside the more conventional Cardiff bluebird mascot.

After the match and after lunch there was time only for the most cursory glance at:

- The National Museum, for art and natural history
- The Central Market, approached in our case through the church-yard of St John the Baptist, over numbered paving stones indicating last resting places

- The Brewery Quarter, tangentially, and Chippy Alley
- A statue of Aneurin Bevan, in a disconcerting pose that suggests the founder of the NHS might jump off his plinth at any moment to berate those who neglect his creation
- Hints of other Cardiff specialities – a Centenary Trail, for example, and Art Deco at the railway station and the Hilton.

On an earlier visit I had walked across the barrage from Penarth as far as the Scott Memorial – Captain Scott's last expedition to the Antarctic sailed from Cardiff in 1910. At the Cardiff end of the breakwater, you'd find the revitalised waterfront with the National Assembly for Wales building, the Norwegian Church art centre and much more, plus many places to eat and drink.

Another day, perhaps – though not in the near future for Sunderland fans. Although inconvenienced to the tune of 12 hours on a coach after setting off in the small hours, they turned out in large numbers – 900 was the estimate. A 4-0 beating confirmed their team's place at the foot of the league table. They won't need to make this journey again next season. 'Long-suffering' seems a barely adequate description.

Cardiff City 4 Sunderland 0
Cardiff City Stadium, 13 January 2018

Carlisle United

The magazine that gave me a start as a trainee reporter was printed in Carlisle. When our printers invested in new equipment they invited us up to watch our magazine coming off the presses, but nobody went. From our offices on Dean Street, Soho, opposite the Sunset Strip, we affected a metropolitan scorn for the distant north.

We should have been less snooty. Whatever Carlisle was like in those days – the late 1970s – the presses would have been something to see. The new machinery our printers wanted to show off was found, on delivery, to require 12ft more space than the units it was to replace. With no room to spare in their workshop they knocked out an external wall at the back, opening out into a yard or delivery bay. That allowed them to get most of the machinery in, and they put up an awning to keep the rest dry. With a little more ingenuity, perhaps, they could have printed straight into the backs of trucks.

Almost 40 years later I set off on my first visit to Carlisle expecting very little. It might be interesting, I thought, to see whether the Oldham fans would chant: "Dirty northern bastards" at the first sign of foul play from the home team, but beyond that I had low expectations. How wrong I was, and had been for almost 40 years.

Carlisle shares its charms with you hesitantly, like a winsome spinster unsure of the effect she's having. Perhaps the novelty of trying to attract visitors is too recent; Carlisle will have spent most of its history trying to fend them off. Many unwelcome and unbidden folk must have crossed the Eden here bent on conquest or, at least, pillage. There's no sign of Hadrian's Wall in the city, but the castle is a stern reminder of a disputed frontier.

Unfortunately I can offer no useful account of Carlisle Castle. I approached the castle grounds fully intending to look the place over but allowed petulance to turn me away.

As I neared the desk to buy a ticket, I paused to look around. Into that brief gap stepped a young couple also intent on visiting the castle. They had not, strictly speaking, jumped the queue; and I was in no hurry. I prepared to take my turn.

My turn, it transpired, would be delayed while the man selling the tickets sought laboriously to sell a subscription to the National Trust. "Two tickets?" he began, redundantly, unless he thought the old fellow dithering in the background might be their grandfather.

"Yes," the young man replied.

"Are you regular visitors to National Trust properties?" he asked.

"Now and then," the young man replied noncommittally. His companion slid her arm into his.

"If you joined you could walk straight into all of them, hundreds of places," he smirked. "And it would only cost you about a fiver a month."

"Each?" said the young man, who may actually have been considering it.

"No. A joint membership would work out at quite a bit less..." There was a pause while he consulted something out of sight: possibly a computer screen but more likely a Post-it note. "It's worth about a 15% discount, or life membership to young people of your age would bring it down to no more than a couple of quid a month, pro rata."

I had the impression that he was gabbling, if not making it up as he went along. Since he gave no sign of having noticed me, I moved off to browse the goods in the souvenir shop, simply to be doing something.

From the shop I could follow the conversation as it progressed, increasingly one-sided, towards its inevitable failure. The number of NT properties, which it insists on referring to as 'special places', turns out to be 500; free parking is widely available for members; a magazine will drop through your letterbox three times a year.

At last the young couple made good their escape and the counter became free. The would-be Membership Secretary looked up and smiled encouragingly as I approached. A member would have flashed a pass and walked in; I was another potential recruit. Before he could begin, I said: "I changed my mind," and left by the door I'd come in. Without a backward glance. It's like a version of the Prometheus and his liver story: I regularly cut off my nose to spite my face and then grow another one.

Fortunately Tullie House, a short underpass away from the castle, is an excellent local museum and gallery and nobody tries to sell you a season ticket.

You know it's something special from the approach. On the castle side there's a passageway whose floors and walls are lined with artwork of a style best describe as challenging. Prominent is a stone on which is engraved an ancient curse directed at border raiders known as Reivers. It gets you into a receptive frame of mind.

But the Tullie House has many mansions, and you will find something to suit your tastes. A substantial gallery is devoted to the Roman frontier; the aforementioned Reivers have a space to themselves; and the layout of Carlisle through the Ages is attractively done. The art gallery occupies much of the ground floor, and in the original Tullie House building there's a separate room for the Pre-Raphaelites. And the presentation of the past is not restricted to indoors: Jacobean and Roman gardens complement a patio area on the south side of the building.

To the southeast is Carlisle Cathedral, a wonderful building with many highlights. My favourite is a pair of runic inscriptions, two of only 17 such records to have been found in mainland England according to the cathedral publicity. One translates as: "Tolfink wrote these runes on this stone," which seems barely worth the effort on Tolfink's part unless the stone were originally attached to a magnificent piece of public sculpture, sadly lost. The other is even more economical: "Reginald," it announces, mysteriously. They date from the 12th century.

The Cathedral's Romanesque Project aims to produce a 3D model of what the building would have looked like in 1133, when it was given cathedral status. Meanwhile the Cathedral offers plenty to look at and admire. An exhibition in the Treasury displays finds from archaeological excavations on the site, from the late 19th century onwards.

I should also give a brief plug to the Cathedral café, branded as the Prior's Kitchen. I ate Saturday lunch there in the vaulted undercroft that was originally a monks' refectory. The establishment offers vouchers, encouraging you to treat someone to a good meal in unusually historic surroundings.

And from the Cathedral it is barely a stone's throw to the city centre, where Castle Street meets the pedestrianised precinct that runs from Rickergate in the north to the wonderfully named Botchergate in the south. Was 'botcher' a recognised trade in the Middle Ages?

I had a look round one more Carlisle museum. The Guildhall Museum occupies the upper floors of the city's last remaining medieval house. Each of Carlisle's eight trade guilds – no mention of the botchers – had a room there, and their separate specialities give the museum an attractive and varied character.

This, it turns out, applies to the city in general: and if something in front of you is at all disappointing, turn round and you'll be sure to find something better. This is apparent from the moment you leave the railway station and encounter the immense oval bastions known as The Citadel. The two sturdy towers were built in the early 19th century to a design originally produced by Thomas Telford. The West Tower is open to visitors.

The journey to and from the football ground is another case in point. On the way, starting from the city centre, you'll go past the bus station which since 2015 has had its own YouTube video. Entitled *An Hour at Carlisle bus station*, this strange production is mercifully 49 minutes short of the full hour. Then you're on to the tree-lined Warwick Road, with equally leafy residential streets arranged in a series of geometrical shapes to the south. Appropriate to a game that traditionally starts at 3pm, the football ground is at exactly 3 o'clock if you view Carlisle as a clockface.

After the game I headed north towards the river. Here the path skirts the playing fields of the Newman Catholic School and takes you across the Eden by a footbridge and into Rickerby Park. The river's meanders make this a longer route but the park has compensations. Formerly an estate, it became a civic memorial to the 10,000 men and women from Carlisle who died in the Great

War – the cenotaph of Shap granite is a central feature. The park has small ornamental gardens and extensive country estate parkland alike, with the river forming its southern boundary.

On the other side of the bridge that carries the A7 to Scotland there are more green spaces at Carlisle Cricket Club. A game was in progress and I stopped to have a drink and to enjoy the overlap in the seasons. On a warm, sunny evening, after the last football match of a successful campaign – relegation narrowly avoided once again – it was another fine advertisement for Carlisle.

The following day was grey and cool, with rain in the air. This was more the Carlisle I had expected, but my plan was to leave the city and go to see something of Hadrian's Wall.

Carlisle's geographical proximity to Hadrian's Wall proved to be something of a tease. On a Sunday morning, close to summer, it wasn't possible to reach Hadrian's Wall from Carlisle by public transport. And if I'd wanted to push the boat out by hiring a car, the car-hire offices at the railway station were as silent as the mile-castles. Left with no alternative, apart perhaps from hailing a taxi, I took the train to Haltwhistle and walked to the Wall from there.

A persistent drizzle had set in. I was carrying more than I needed to be, because of course there is no longer any provision for left luggage (or 'suspicious objects' as it would now be known) at railway stations. Still, I was in the fresh air, getting exercise and not very far from a World Heritage Site. Also the path from Haltwhistle followed a gurgling Cumbrian beck in which dippers dipped and where wagtails flicked their tails.

The path eventually emerged into open country, as though the Romans had scorched the earth on their side of the Wall, hoping perhaps to make invasion look less attractive to marauding Picts. With no protection from the wind and rain and the Wall still not in sight, I began to question precisely how much I wanted to visit it. The map indicated no shelter, neither pub nor visitor experience, within five miles. The Wall itself was a mile away. I crossed a road, struck off along a farm track and at last found my way barred by ancient masonry.

At first I was uncertain whether I had actually arrived at the Wall. A little over 6ft high, it was a single course of stonework not totally dissimilar to the field boundary walls that ran into it, confining sheep. The only remotely military feature was something that could have been mistaken for a firing-step set into the stone about a third of the way up. I was considering scaling this wall and continuing northwards when walkers appeared, moving from left to right and vice versa along its length. The mist parted and to the east the Wall rose to ascend a crag.

I turned to head west, the direction of the Roman fort/English Heritage Experience Site at Birdoswald. It was vaguely in my mind to walk there and hope to find a taxi to take me back to Carlisle. But Birdoswald was several exposed miles away, whereas the path back to Haltwhistle was nearby and sheltered, and there was a pub at the station. I was silent for a moment before an altar to Mithras, identified and admired a vallum and headed south again to rejoin the waterfowl by the Haltwhistle Burn.

My original plan for the weekend had been to take a bicycle – I had gone as far as booking space for it on the train. Perhaps it would have helped in reaching the Wall; on the other hand, I would have boarded the train home drenched and exhausted. It's a pity not to be able to rely on public transport, especially to reach World Heritage sites. But it isn't entirely devoid of comfort to find that the 21st century is slow to arrive in some parts.

Carlisle United 0 Oldham 1
Brunton Park, 26 April 2014

Charlton Athletic

The Charlton entry takes us back to the old days of the Valley, before the club roamed the wilderness (or, at least, the parks of Selhurst and Upton) for a while in the late 80s/early 90s.

I was working in the West End at the time. Charlton was no great distance to travel to watch a football match. But I hesitated for two reasons, both feeble.

The more substantial objection, that November 1979 was unusually cold by day let alone by night (when the game would be played), was easily dealt with. Football is a winter sport. In moments of absent-mindedness I was apt to wax lyrical on the subject. Football on a cold winter's night is a bonding exercise; the misery of frozen feet and fingers represents an ordeal by endurance without which, in another context, the hero cannot hope to win the maiden.

The second objection hinged on psychological and practical considerations. Charlton is in Southeast London. I was living at that time in Highbury, in North London, and had absorbed the North Londoner's apprehension about civilisation south of the Thames.

Does anxiety about South London still afflict the rest of the capital? Can it be a coincidence that, of the places people will readily cross the Thames for, most are barely 100 metres from a bridge: Borough Market, the Globe, Tate Modern, the National Theatre, the London Eye etc? It looks very much as though people will dip a toe into South London, but they seem to feel more comfortable knowing they can easily get back.

If they were to venture further south, their maps would not say: "Here be dragons." On the other hand, those same maps reveal a practical complication: the distortion of geography in South London. Places are hard to find and even harder to get to. Public transport connections between them and the rest of the capital are utterly baffling.

A glance at a map of rail connections reinforces the point.

The major rail termini for lines heading east, north and west out of London lie on an arc from Fenchurch Street in the east to Paddington in the west. Domestic mainlines run out from them at regular intervals, like the spokes on a bicycle wheel. I say 'domestic' because the elevation of St Pancras to international status complicates the picture, but Paris, Brussels and now Amsterdam are sufficiently exotic destinations to constitute the exception that proves the rule. For the most part there is elegance and logic in the arrangement.

The main stations even lie on or very close to the same Underground line. A traveller – 'customer' in the rail industry's parlance – heading for, say, Stevenage, would need only a basic knowledge of Home Counties geography to narrow the choice of termini down to Kings Cross or St Pancras. He or she could then set out for the Circle or Metropolitan Line and expect to go straight to the appropriate station.

Compare this neatness with the chaotic layout of railway lines south of the river. Here, instead of spokes on a wheel, the lines criss-cross one another like a cat's cradle constructed by excitable kittens.

It is disorientating, to begin with, that two of South London's more important termini are in fact north of the river: Victoria and Charing Cross. This makes it difficult to know what to make of outliers like London Bridge and Vauxhall, while other north-bank southbound stations like Blackfriars, Cannon Street and Holborn Viaduct are inexplicable.

And of the stations south of the river, only Waterloo is at all well-connected on the Underground. A case might be made for Vauxhall on the Victoria Line, or London Bridge on the Jubilee and Northern Lines, but where do trains from those stations go? Precisely. Only a public transport geek would know[1]. (A Russian geek, by contrast, would be able to explain the origin of the Russian word for a railway station. In the Victorian era, people building railways came to Britain to learn how it was done. The Tsar's delegation duly came and was given guided tours of some of the

---

1 South and west. Vauxhall is one of the few logical points on the South London network.

nascent network's principle features. After a visit to Vauxhall, no doubt to study bogies or wheel-tapping, it returned to Holy Russia under the misapprehension that the word for a railway station was Vauxhall; which entered the Russian language as *voksal*.)

Charlton, then, presented problems. According to Wikipedia, it is served by trains from Charing Cross and Cannon Street. Finding the times of those trains would be the work of seconds at www.nationalrail.co.uk. But neither Wikipedia nor www.nationalrail.co.uk was available in 1979.

What was available was a telephone enquiry service in which the word 'service' would provoke a hollow laugh.

First, you would hold for many minutes, listening only to a ringing tone, with no indication that your call was of value to anyone, nor of your position in any notional queue, nor with soothing though repetitive music to pass the time.

At last a surly operator would respond to your enquiry about trains to Charlton with questions to which the answers were unknowable. Where did I want to leave from? From wherever trains left for Charlton. What time did I want to leave? At a time that would get me to Charlton for about 7pm (evening games started at 7.30pm in those days – the fetish for 7.45pm kick-offs, with 15 minutes for half-time, is a relatively recent development).

Like a GP who will only field questions about one condition at a time, the rail enquiries operators were loathe to impart any more information than they had to. Eventually mine suggested a train that departed from London Bridge at a time that seemed vaguely suitable. The train may well have started its journey at Charing Cross, a short walk from my office, but that was not a conversation the operator was going to get into. If I was going to quibble about the starting point I might want to change the destination, and then where would we be? There were other callers he needed to obstruct in a well-practised, borderline rude manner.

I rang off and prepared to tackle the next challenge: how to find London Bridge station.

In the days before the eastern extension of the Jubilee Line, itself the newest on the Tube map, London Bridge was accessible by

Tube only on the eastern branch of the Northern Line. There were probably buses but finding out about them took real dedication. A Central Line train east from Tottenham Court Road, then, and a change at Bank. There was nothing complicated about the journey, except that in the time it took I could as easily have been at home in front of a fire.

To be quite certain that I wanted to go to Charlton I tossed a coin. Its verdict was that I should go. To try the best of three would have been to hold the laws of chance in contempt. I left work at the usual time, had a fortifying pint or two with my colleagues in the Crown & Two Chairmen and made my circuitous way to Charlton.

The match provides two clear memories. The first is that Oldham, having taken the lead with a thunderous shot from former Charlton favourite Vic Halom, began to push the ball about with increasing confidence and looked well in control. But pushing the ball about was not their natural game. Muscular endeavour was more their forte. Exceeding the limits of their competence, they began to lose the ball with increasing frequency and were eventually overwhelmed by Charlton.

The other memory was the temperature. According to Met Office records, the temperatures by night in mid-November 1979 often fell below -5°. The visiting supporters' end at the Valley was open and exceptionally cold. Napoleon would have thought twice about taking it on. When, at half-time, the operator of the kiosk selling hot drinks and burgers and so forth wanted to pack up and go home, the police left the visiting supporters to their own devices for a while and marshalled the kiosk owner instead. He stayed open. Cases of hypothermia and frostbite were almost certainly avoided through their decisive action.

Charlton Athletic 2 Oldham 1
The Valley, 9 November 1979

Chelsea

The Design Museum isn't far from Stamford Bridge. That puts it a little way off the beaten track where many tourists to London are concerned, but it's well worth a visit. Besides, you could make a case for Chelsea being the UK's most trendy or design-influenced club.

The Design Museum used to be the Commonwealth Institute. If you ever went to Earls Court from the West End by bus you may have noticed it, the flags of many nations fluttering like an upmarket Butlins. Reminders of its previous occupants are set into the paving stones on the approach, and outside is one of those pavement fountains from which jets ascend in response to unseen stimuli. Waiting for an old friend with the appropriately West London name of Barnes, I was watching this fountain and wondering what, in the absence of children, it was doing there; and then a party of schoolchildren (early to mid teens) arrived and the question became moot.

The exhibition we went to see was called 'California: Designing Freedom'. According to the promotional blurb it would "pick up the story" in the 1960s with peace, love, pot and protest, and chart "the journey from the counterculture to Silicon Valley's tech culture". In the event it did not so much pick up the story as lose threads successively, like Theseus having a senior moment in the Labyrinth.

The exhibition had little structure, thematically or chronologically. Barnes, no stranger in his younger day to experimental psychodaelia, wondered aloud whether the curators might have had impaired attention spans when they were laying the show out.

Some parts were more disappointing than others. The area devoted to Hells Angels, for example, cried out for the sobering contemporary reference Altamont could have supplied. Instead we got leather jackets and a couple of hogs, then and now, with the Captain America chopper from *Easy Rider* to make the point that style was at issue here, not substance nor reality.

In the background Mario Savio's speech spooled around a perpetual loop. Anyone who has previously only seen the speech on paper would be excited to hear it spoken. It was an extraordinary, era-defining improvisation by a 21-year-old activist who came to represent one significant strand of the 1960s' legacy. It's worth quoting, perhaps especially now, when globalisation has so dramatically extended the size of the hopper on the machine he described: "There's a time when the operation of the machine becomes so odious, makes you so sick at heart, that you can't take part! You can't even passively take part! And you've got to put your bodies upon the gears and upon the wheels... upon the levers, upon all the apparatus, and you've got to make it stop!" The venue was the steps of Sproul Hall, Los Angeles, now renamed the Mario Savio Steps. The occasion was a civil rights protest on the Berkeley campus of the University of California. The direct result was Savio's arrest (with 800 others) and his subsequent sentence of 120 days. Whether there were any longer-term consequences is a matter of opinion.

In a West London museum 53 years later, the speech lost a small part of its power with each repetition. By the time you passed to the other end of the main hall, where it was drowned out by other sounds of Californian origin, you'd ceased to notice it anyway.

Bleaching all the colour from a significant cultural artefact is no small misdemeanour. The exhibition organisers could have made the speech available to individuals through earphones; or, like the growling tones of Richard Burton outside the Dylan Thomas Museum in Swansea, they could have located it such that it didn't have to compete with everything else.

Their failure to consider the content of the speech, to assess its significance and handle it with care was symptomatic of the weakness of the exhibition. Perhaps by accident, it symbolises the wider contribution of California. While the main cultural exports were jingly-jangly electric guitars and mild intoxicants, all was well. But California has found itself directing much of the world's economic and psychic traffic and its experience with freeways has proved a poor model.

One of the threads the exhibition conspicuously failed to pick up was the development of "Silicon Valley's tech culture". We need to go back, appropriately enough, to the late 1960s for the start of the end of the world.

In those days, away from the West Coast counter-culture, the centre of the computer industry was on the East Coast of the United States: IBM in New York State and Digital Equipment and Data General in New England. The purpose of computers in those innocent times was to take on some of the donkey work associated with the more tedious business functions: bookkeeping, especially. Away from work, people made their own amusement or, when they were pushing the boat out, went to the cinema. Black-and-white television, radio and events known as concerts were also options.

Fast-forward 50 years. The computer industry has permeated business at all levels and in most roles, and has long since spread beyond it. Barely recognisable as computers, devices have colonised homes, vehicles, pockets, wrists etc. There are even implants, no longer restricted to animals but increasingly proposed for humans.

The relief of hard-pressed office staff and the increased efficiency of industry is more or less accomplished; in that context, computing is moving on to the next level, where it makes hard-pressed office staff unnecessary.

But that's just the business context. Elsewhere, the role of digital technology is more pervasive and quite different in nature. It has become not so much an arm of the entertainment industry as eight prosthetic arms of an entertainments octopus. It gives people a means of filling not only their empty leisure hours but any spare minute.

And what does this have to do with California? Just this: that the development of the computer business to this point has been taken over by West Coast companies.

Apple, formerly called Apple Computer, has been the dominant influence. Microsoft, for a while, was a much larger and more influential company but it took its lead from Apple in certain important respects – Windows, for example. And Microsoft, be it noted, is based in the Pacific North-West, as is Amazon. Apple,

Facebook, Google, Twitter and many others are Californian.

These were people who brought an evangelical zeal to their business. The old-school East Coast computer salesmen sought primarily to make money; although they spoke about a business philosophy, what it boiled down to was to sell as much product as possible. With computers, the rich (who would primarily be the owners of businesses) would get richer. The West Coast newcomers were not averse to sales but set out also to change people's lives.

What qualified them for that role? Confidence, certainly, and abundant marketing skills. A number of young people have made fortunes teasing technology into products for which there was little justification beyond the assertion that they were 'cool'. And the world, like a gullible teenager, has accepted their definition of cool over and over again, bought their products and signed a blank cheque to cover the upgrades – the breathtakingly brazen aspect of the technology business has always been its insistence that something better is just around the corner.

Was there ever a time when the potential of technology was assessed in advance for its desirability and shelved if found unnecessary? Since the early days of the computer business, if something can be done somebody will do it. But more recently that construct has changed too. Now, if something can be imagined somebody will do it.

That might not matter so much if the imaginative people in question were a little less excitable. If, say, they had grown up in a world where Walt Disney's saccharine tales were only moderately successful and, then, only among the under-sevens; where the myths of the Wild West, the vigilante hero and the Road were regarded with a little less holy awe; where socialism was not a frightening, alien concept. In short, it would be less worrying if they brought some perspective to their work.

Instead, the next generation of 'consumers' faces a future of isolation and paranoia, in which the pinnacle of human achievement will be represented by virtual reality, artificial 'intelligence', computer-generated imagery and innumerable 'friends' whose liking must be asserted every 30 seconds to be convincing.

"What is plumbing but the prevention of treachery in closed systems?" asked Norman Mailer in *Of a Fire on the Moon*.[1] 'Cool' technology seeps through the cracks into ever more areas of life. As it does so, the discrepancy between the enthusiasm of its suppliers and the day-to-day reality experienced by the rest of us will become more important. Two current examples: driverless cars and the Internet of Things.

For a driverless car to be safe, its controlling intelligence would have to be reliable all the time. And that computer on your desk, the product of decades of improvement, operating in a stable, undemanding environment – is that 100% reliable all the time? Of course it isn't. From time to time it will do something inexplicable; it may even stop altogether, an event labelled decades ago with unexpected foresight as a 'crash'. From time to time you have to switch off and re-start to overcome an unknown and possibly minor fault that stops the rest of the machine from operating. That's going to be more than simply an inconvenience in a car.

Why, in any case, would you want a driverless care? Don't people enjoy driving? Possibly, but that isn't the point. Driverless cars bring three enormous advantages from the point of view of those running our lives: one, more vehicles will fit safely into the same amount of road space; two, the ruinous upgrade cycle that afflicts users of computers, software, mobiles and all other digital devices will be extended to cars; three, driverless cars are another step towards breaking us of our car habit altogether.

And the Internet of Things? This is the technology that brings hitherto independent machines into the orbit of networked digital control. From anywhere in the world you'll be able to switch things on at home, it is promised, so that the light, heat, ambience and dinner are all ready for your return.

Meanwhile owners of certain tumble-dryers are advised not to leave them on unattended if at all. Early reports suggested the Grenfell Tower fire started with a fridge-freezer. According to *Which?* in 2015, washing machines were the domestic appliance most likely to cause a fire. All this stuff that you're switching on

1 A book only partly about the contribution of computers to the Apollo 11 landing.

remotely, it might be setting fire to your home. Will that stop them selling it to you? Well, what do you think?

And in both cases, it almost goes without saying, the further down this road we go, the more vulnerable we become to hackers. As more aspects of daily life are pointlessly automated, the more anxious and uncomfortable we are apt to become. We will throw tantrums, having become infantilised by talking to our computer devices and pushing buttons on screens.

Signs of a backlash began to appear in 2017. Senior executives of the companies responsible for building social media platforms expressed reservations. Several of them, it transpired, would not want their children anywhere near the technology they'd created. Shades of Dr Frankenstein, who died childless after his monster strangled the doctor's bride, Elizabeth, on their wedding night.

Two factors make this re-appraisal irrelevant: first, those reporting it will rightly be ignored; second, it is too late anyway.

On the first point, the journalists writing about the perils of social media tend to be people who previously promoted them. They reveal themselves, unwittingly, as dangerously gullible. They are also, often, classic exemplars of the expression relating empty vessels to noise. Here, for example, in the *Guardian*, is a feature written by a man whose authority lies partly in the fact that he has issued 'about 140,000 tweets' in just over 10 years. That's enough for almost 40 novels. If we know nothing else about this individual, we know he's not averse to the sound of his own voice. In this characteristic he symbolises precisely what is wrong with social media: it provides a platform for self-important blowhards. In an earlier era such people would have held court in a thinly populated corner of a pub, or written, often, to their local newspapers.

But the possibility of silencing these biddable Jeremiahs has gone. Technology cannot be uninvented. Only the calamitous collapse of global electricity generation and distribution will put it back in its box. The gold is irreversibly become dim.

And what does any of this have to do with Chelsea? Nothing, really, apart from Chelsea's proximity to a museum that put on a show I found annoying in 2017. But it has plenty to do with football as part of the entertainment industry.

Eventually, football will be a game played purely to be broadcast by a variety of means to a worldwide audience. At the stadium, sound effects will compensate for the lack of noise coming from the corporate hospitality kiosks. The engagement of watchers around the world will be even more tenuous, but as long as they pay their monthly subscriptions and buy an occasional replica shirt nobody will worry.

One perverse characteristic of the Internet may yet spare us. A rising generation expects to stream or download content for free. The Internet itself has encouraged this cavalier attitude to theft. Threatening to undermine the provision of content, it is an unpromising model for economic success. And in an odd but defiantly symmetrical way, it is entirely consistent with the mood of Haight-Ashbury in the 1960s.

Chelsea 0 Oldham 1
Stamford Bridge, 30 October 1993

Cheltenham Town

Cheltenham Town are one of three English football clubs to be known as the Robins. They play in red, so there is little mystery about the nickname.

More intriguing, though, is that that the geographic locations of the three clubs form a triangle, almost isosceles, of which the sides are about 40 miles long. The other clubs are Swindon Town and Bristol City. That's not only a strange coincidence, it's a bit spooky, wouldn't you say?

Coincidentally I almost started my working life as a spook in Cheltenham. The town represents one of my life's great Sliding Door moments (although to be more accurate, most of them seem to have been Revolving Door moments).

Twitchy after a period of unemployment, I was keeping an eye on birds in two bushes in the spring of 1976. The one that became a bird in the hand led me to a short engagement as a computer programmer. The other bush, from which a tawnily camouflaged fowl flew off into someone else's grasp, was two-thirds of the way along a recruitment trail that led to Government Communications Headquarters (GCHQ) in Cheltenham.

I had passed through two interviews for GCHQ, the second of them in Cheltenham, but a firm job offer of any kind elsewhere was irresistible. Also to be considered was a short passage of fiction on my original application to the Civil Service; I had claimed to be able to speak Russian. Had this bluff ever been called it would have been interesting to see how far "Nu, vot aeroportye, Baris [Well, here we are at the airport, Boris]" would have got me. "Well, here we are at Cheltenham Spa railway station with a rejection slip, David."

I never regretted missing the opportunity to become a spook. On the other hand I didn't make much of the opportunity to become a programmer. The training I was given was enough for me to make some minor contributions to the Y2K bug before defecting for a life at a different kind of keyboard. I took a job in the IT trade press, as a journalist supposedly specialising in software. I knew only a little more about software than I did about Russian, but it turned out to be a meal-ticket valid for decades at the staff canteens of various branches of the media.

Looking around Cheltenham on a grey Saturday in January – this was one of many FA Cup 3rd round ties in this book – I reflected on how well I might have come to know the town. As a trainee programmer I knew the White Hart, Frimley, very well indeed, but I'm sure Cheltenham had a great deal more to offer. Parts of the town are very attractive indeed, whereas Frimley (and the building in which my working life began) features in a 1999 Phaidon publication called *Boring Postcards*.

Cheltenham, by contrast, has on its street name-boards Gardens, Parades, Terraces, a Promenade and a Royal Crescent. There are green routes available to pedestrians through the town. Its main shopping centre, the Regent Arcade, feels like a cathedral from some angles.

The Wilson, Cheltenham's art gallery and museum, is renamed and greatly expanded from when I was there. In a £6m refit the place acquired new galleries on four more floors, for temporary exhibitions, local specialities and an Arts & Crafts collection.

The name of the place demands an explanation. Edward Wilson was one of Captain Scott's companions in 1912. Born in Cheltenham in 1872 he specialised at first in natural sciences but eventually qualified as a doctor. Also an artist of some talent, he joined Scott's *Discovery* expedition (1901-04) as junior surgeon, zoologist and expedition artist.

By the time of the *Terra Nova* expedition in 1910 he was Scott's chief of scientific staff. Wilson was one of the five men to reach the South Pole in January 1912 and died with Scott and Henry Bowers about 11 miles short of the food depot that would have saved them. There's a fine statue of him, by Scott's widow Kathleen, on the Promenade in Cheltenham. The Cheltenham Art Gallery & Museum was named after him in 2013.

Other distinctions in the museum arise from Cheltenham's claim to be the country's most complete, intact Regency town, and from its Cotswolds archaeological collections. There is also a satellite museum to which music-lovers might be attracted, the Holst Birthplace Museum. This includes what is claimed to be 'the only Regency room open to the public in the town'.

At Whaddon Road, the only league football available to the public in Gloucestershire in those days, Oldham made what was becoming a familiar descent from spirited competitiveness into stumbling ineptitude. I believe this may have been the first ever meeting of the two clubs. I certainly hope never to see another. Had I worked for GCHQ, I suspect I would have waited for summer and gone to see Gloucestershire play at the Cheltenham Cricket Festival instead.

Cheltenham Town 2 Oldham 1
Whaddon Road, 6 January 2002

Colchester United

Another 'home' ground. I lived in Colchester from July 1975 to May the following year, being by turns an ice-cream man, an encyclopaedia salesman and, more extensively, unemployed.

The summers of 1975 and 76 are remembered for exceptionally hot weather – in 1976 there was alarm among louts nationally as pubs ran out of lager. But the intervening winter made a deeper impression on me. On the east coast, with poor employment prospects and anxiety over bills for food and heating, I remember it as severely cold. 'Severe' is close to the Russian word *syevyer*, meaning 'north', and must hence be related to 'Siberia', which is where the wind in Colchester also came from that winter. That tempered my feelings about Colchester specifically and the East of England in general for several years. In later life, able to switch on the second bar with abandon and to vary my diet beyond tinned mackerel and dried beans, I began to feel more warmly disposed towards the town.

I went to Layer Road, Colchester United's old home, only once, and witnessed an invasion of the field by Sheffield Wednesday's travelling supporters. Having stampeded down the field, they invaded the opposite end and disappeared. It seems they were simply trying to get to the main exit by the most direct route and saw a rather dull football match as no significant obstacle.

The Colchester manager in those days used to complain to the local paper that it was difficult to attract players, Colchester being seen as an end-of-the-line sort of town. This was an odd expression to use; anyone who has ever fallen asleep on a late train home from Liverpool Street will know that Colchester is far from the end of the line. With the town now falling inside the London commuter belt, perhaps recruitment has become easier for Colchester managers.

Closer to the beginning of the timeline, Colchester was briefly the most important town in the land. I almost wrote 'kingdom' but there was no king in the time before the Roman conquest. If the dominant Celtic tribe in the south of England, the Catuvellauni, built towns, they built Colchester (then called Camulodunon); if they didn't, they can be imagined milling and mustering in the area before sallying forth to demand tribute from their woad-painted fellows.

When the Romans invaded they headed more or less straight there. They gave Camulodunum a Latin ending and made it a provincial capital. If Boudicca had not burnt it down, might it have become the national capital? Probably not. The Romans rebuilt it and the town grew in importance into the second and third centuries; but it was overtaken in rank by many other settlements and eventually became a town third-rate footballers could not be attracted to.

Perhaps as a result, Colchester is a town with plenty of charm and individuality. Its character falls into step with you as you climb North Hill on the way from the railway station to the town centre; you can see it in the walls and windows, the roof-lines and railings.

Contrarily, as you ascend you are going deeper into the past. At the top of the hill, to the right, is the Balkerne Gate, built in the 1st century. This structure is worth a look. The Romans must have started work on it almost immediately, and that indicates a fundamental difference in the Roman Empire's view of Britain. Julius Caesar had led invasions in 55 and 54BC, but after slapping down the locals and taking hostages he withdrew, leaving not a single Roman soldier behind. When the armies of Claudius arrived in 43AD, they subdued the Britons, established a capital and started building.

The Balkerne Gate let traffic from London into Colchester. It may have been the first such fortified gate in the country; now, it's the biggest to survive and the best-preserved. With four gates it is unique in this country and unusual anywhere in the empire. A spectacular reconstruction of it in Alan Sorrell's *Roman Towns in Britain* shows that even then the Italians drove on the right.

The High Street runs east from here, past a small block or so of boutiques and piazzas down towards the historic centre of town, at least from a heritage point of view. Colchester Castle is the chief feature here. It squats sulkily at the entrance to Castle Park.

Rather military and featureless from the outside, it's the Roman equivalent of Aladdin's Cave inside. Its museum reflects the town's former primacy: there are magnificent collections of artefacts from the Stone Age through to the Romans. If you have time, or if you're particularly interested in the era, there's more to look at about four kilometres to the southeast at Gosbecks Archaeological Park. Also in that neck of the woods are the Lexden earthworks, an Iron Age hill-fort and burial site.

And while you're out that way Colchester has a surprisingly good zoo. Perhaps, on reflection, this might be where you'd choose to spend most of your free time if you're travelling *en famille*. They work hard at museums these days to appeal to younger visitors but you can't beat a good zoo, really, can you?

A little further on from the Castle, the Hollytree Museum offers glimpses of life in the town's more recent (1700 onwards) past. Look out especially for the chronometers and the tea fetish objects. The clocks, by the way, are something of a local *cause célèbre*; they used to have their own home in the town's Tymperleys Clock Museum, a victim of the passage of time.

Opposite the main gates of the park is Colchester's Natural History Museum. There should be enough here to keep you going for a while, but if the day is good save some time for a quick tour of the park. As you look out over the green slopes, try to picture Boudicca running amok.

Colchester also has history from the English Civil War period. Anecdotally, the building that now houses the Siege House bar and brasserie at the foot of East Hill is peppered with ordnance fired during battles for control of the approach to the castle.

And from a more reflective, pacific period, St Botolph's Priory demonstrates not only that Cornwall doesn't have a monopoly on implausibly named saints but also that nothing was ever wasted – the re-used Roman brickwork is one of the ruins' most distinctive features. There's another fine medieval religious building in better shape nearby at St John's Abbey Gate. Both, be it noted, were damaged during the Civil War.

All of that has aged rather better than the infrastructure

of my old life in Colchester. The Recreation, on the corner of Wimpole Road and Military Road? Converted into flats. The junk shops where I used to buy pre-loved books for 2p? Unable to sustain themselves once I'd taken my custom elsewhere. The Co-op, which provided the stamps that funded my sister's wedding present? Thriving, but in different guises and locations.

One final word about Colchester. The town has character but the new football stadium has none. Try not to spend too much time there. No-one will give it back to you, ever.

Colchester United 2 Oldham 2
Weston Homes Community Stadium, 30 August 2008

Coventry City

Football is fiercely tribal, but below a certain level you'll find fellow-feeling.

Supporters of underachieving clubs – and underachieving clubs aren't hard to find – will look on the occasional successes of similarly modest clubs with satisfaction and some admiration. In part their response is aspirational: if Barnsley, Bradford City, Oldham Athletic, Swindon Town et al can reach the Promised Land of the Premier League – and if Leicester City can conquer it – anyone can. But it's also partly sympathetic.

Conversely, those doomed for a certain term to follow struggling teams will take comfort in the misfortunes of others. "It could be worse," they will reflect on their own team's shortcomings. Until May 2018 the only exception to this, the only group of people to whom this form of schadenfreude was not available, were fans of Coventry City. For them it could hardly have been any worse.

Coventry dropped out of the Premier League in 2001 and their parachute didn't open until they had plunged into the fourth tier of English football.

Gravity took its toll in other ways. Their average attendance (at their long-time Highfield Road home) in the 2000/01 season was 20,535. Last year, in the palatial surroundings of the Ricoh Arena, it was 9,255.

In between times the Sky Blues have had a period in exile, playing 'home' games at Northampton Town. There, attendances fell further; 2,287 on average in 2013/14. More supporters followed Coventry away than 'at home'. Some boycotted home games altogether to express their disapproval at the move; others went to Northampton but watched half the game (ie the half they could see) from the hill overlooking the Sixfields Stadium.

The club has even visited rock-bottom sartorially. Its 1978 chocolate-brown away strip, reviled but revived briefly for a club anniversary in 2009, regularly appears in lists of the worst football strips ever. It has its own Facebook page.

However in May 2018 Coventry City won the League 2 play-off final at Wembley and gained promotion to League 1. A reported 37,000 Coventry fans cheered them on. The decline has apparently been arrested. Even in a fashion sense the club's reputation is being rehabilitated. The decision to play the final in a one-off striped shirt might have been mistaken for a money-making scheme, but the club had run out of shirts, having given away 30 boxes to a Syrian refugee camp in Iraq.

Will the sympathetic warmth extended to Coventry fans survive their success? I hope so, because of the warmth of the hospitality I received on my only visit to the Ricoh Arena.

That was to be expected to a certain extent since I was paying for a hospitality package. The leaking tub of my largesse was pushed out for my elderly dad, who could no longer cope with some aspects of live football. The Coventry City hospitality package gave us parking adjacent to the stadium, a slap-up lunch before the game (and before the arrival of the crowd), a lift to the appropriate suite and the option of watching the game from indoors.

Part of the package was the involvement of a Coventry favourite of yesteryear. Naturally, he was preaching almost entirely to the converted: when he asked if there were any foreigners in the room, mine was the only hand to go up. The jeering was good-natured, as though I suffered from some embarrassing minor ailment. He came over to talk to us afterwards. I had not at that time formulated my theory of the debt of gratitude owed by all football fans to Coventry City and was not therefore able to ask his views. Perhaps it was just as well; any goodwill might have quickly dissipated.

I undertook no sightseeing on that match-day visit. Later in the year, with spring in full sail, I went to the city to have a look round.

It's a singular place. There can't be many cities that ask as many questions about post-war reconstruction as Coventry does. Some people will consider the rebuilt medieval centres of cities like Nuremburg as extravagantly sentimental, while regretting at the other extreme the utilitarian concrete in places like Plymouth. If you're looking for a middle way perhaps Coventry Cathedral is a worthy attempt, but not everyone likes it and the attempt is not extended to the rest of the city.

The architect of the Cathedral, Basil Spence, apparently set out to create a container for pieces of art; the stained glass, contemporary statuary and the Graham Sutherland tapestry above the altar are in magnificent contrast to the plain lines and regular shapes of the exterior. The columns in particular, tapering towards the base, are breathtaking. Apparently they are not load-bearing and the original intention was to have them poised on spheres. On John Hutton's Great West Window, exuberant angels and rather austere saints mark the boundary between the new Cathedral and the old.

The Herbert Art Gallery & Museum is just across the square from the Cathedral. It's free, which isn't the least of its attractions; there's plenty to look at and – an important consideration for families – to do: interactive exhibits, Lego, dressing-up and an emphasis on keeping children happy. In the galleries you'll find it's particularly strong on 20th century British artists. The museum presents the history and development of Coventry, honouring such legendary figures as Lady Godiva but not shying away from less glamorous topics, like manufacturing industry.

While you're in this corner of Coventry, spare a little time for St Mary's Guildhall. This too is free and yet another of Mary Queen of Scots' places of detention.

If you were doing a Coventry tour before going to a match, the Coventry Transport Museum is on the way out of the city centre towards the Ricoh Arena. Alternatively, it's only a short detour to the Coventry Music Museum. If you came in by air there's the Midland Air Museum by Coventry Airport. Or you could just wander around the city, surprising yourself occasionally by encountering something really old amid the rather weary new stuff. Thank you, Coventry city.

Coventry City 2 Oldham 1
Ricoh Arena, 19 January 2013

Crawley Town

When I first started going to football matches, Crawley Town were playing in something called the Metropolitan League, which was a kind of second division to the Southern League. The quality of the competition at that level may be inferred from the early successes in cup and league of Tonbridge Reserves and St Neots & District.

Later, professional clubs entered their reserve or youth teams and the roll of honour is sprinkled with references to Chelsea 'A' and the like.

Crawley itself was not earmarked for a New Town makeover until 1947. It may not yet be regarded as finished: the Queen opened a key shopping development in 1958, but new 'neighbourhoods' continued to be built into the 21st century.

In other words, both town and football club are Johnny-come-latelies by Oldham Athletic standards. That doesn't mean, however, that they can expect to be put in their place by the much better-established club. Far from it.

For the trip to Crawley I had company. For reasons associated with a temporary displacement, I had been spending occasional nights in hotels, B&Bs and rooms attached to pubs in the north-west Hertfordshire area. In one such, a delightful B&B beside the Grand Union Canal, my room – clearly at other times the den or study of the man of the house – contained a book on the notable achievements of Joe Royle in the early 90s. At breakfast the following morning I mentioned this and discovered that I had stayed the night under the roof of another Oldham supporter.

We almost went to the Milton Keynes Dons 7-0 fiasco together but made firmer arrangements for Crawley. I picked him up and we drove round the M25 in leisurely fashion.

With another to consider, I was unable to follow my usual itinerary. Crawley may have several formal attractions – the Gatwick Museum of Left Luggage, perhaps, or the Gallery of 1960s Architecture. I wouldn't know. I didn't even look for an old town core and that did prove remiss. Knowing Hemel Hempstead quite well and having recently visited Stevenage, I knew that New Towns often had quite attractive old towns, however gruesome the new parts might be. But I didn't pay Crawley that respect because for once, I was going primarily to attend a football match.

That said, I may not have been the ideal partner for this kind of outing either: I drive at a very sedate pace; once parked I am reluctant to move the vehicle; and, for the return journey, I had to leave my friend to make his own arrangements because I had plans in Leatherhead on my way back. None of these would discourage an Oldham fan; minor inconvenience is a regular fact of life and almost unnoticeable alongside the disappointment of the game itself.

We arrived in what we took to be central Crawley in good time. With New Towns it can be difficult to be sure. We motored around for a while and eventually selected a car-park that served a large shopping mall. How did this become such a standard feature of New Town design? What happened to public gardens, elegant squares, civic institutions and extensive bus stands as indictors of the town centre?

Safely parked, we emerged through a multi-storey shopping mall to try to find (a) the street and (b) a pub. Looking at a map later, I find that Crawley has a High Street that is more or less central, with some parking; we found it on the day on foot, and visited what may have been the local Wetherspoon's. I thought this was for want of anything better, but I wonder now whether my companion was a beer-drinker who prized value-for-money. Either way, the day was going well.

He gamely went along with my suggestion that we might as well walk the rest of the way to the ground, rather than recover the car and have to find somewhere to park at the far end. Also, you get to see a bit more of Crawley that way, although if the truth be told there wasn't a great deal to look at.

The ground itself, with the suitably New Townish name of the Checkatrade Stadium, is perhaps a mile down the Brighton Road alongside a dual carriageway and not far from an M23 junction, as is also the modern way.

The Checkatrade Stadium has a substantial bar in which fans of both teams mingled happily. If anything, there may have been rather more Oldham fans – or perhaps the Oldham fans were more disposed to drink; perhaps Crawley is home to more Perrier Generation people.

The match itself offered up the usual measure of tedium. Neither team was especially proficient but Oldham were clearly less so than Crawley, who duly won quite comfortably. The away fans went off to a pub and I traipsed back into the town centre. I found the car-park without too much difficulty but the car eluded me. Twice I returned to the mall to retrace my steps and try to reverse-engineer my route. Eventually, anxiety at the car-park's closing time of 6pm growing, I worked it out and escaped.

Crawley Town 2 Oldham 0
Checkatrade Stadium, 6 April 2015

Crewe Alexandra

Crewe Crib Notes

Age 181 years
That's remarkably exact, not to say recent.
I'm dating it from the opening of the railway station. The town's been there since time immemorial.
That's remarkably inexact. Can you elaborate?
It appears as Creu in the Domesday Book, from an Old Welsh word meaning 'crossing'.
What's the Old Welsh for 'level crossing'?
This will only work if you ask sensible questions.
OK then; why 1837?
Because Crewe was a small collection of hovels before the coming of the railway, and might have remained so had the Nimbies of Winsford and Nantwich not objected so forcefully to the building of a station and locomotive works.
Appearance In 1837, a collection of hovels with a railway industry grafted on; now, a thriving municipality of about 75,000 and the former home of Conviviality, once of Bargain Booze fame.
That sounds worth a supermarket dash! How do I get there?
By car, M6 Junction 16. By train, direct connections from almost anywhere. Crewe lies at the junction of six railway routes, and 23 trains an hour pass through during the day, serving cities in England, Scotland and Wales.
Any blind spots?
Connections to Yorkshire and the East Midlands are not the best. Direct trains in that direction go no further than Derby. Crewe to Leeds, via Manchester, takes up to two hours to cover a distance of 61 miles.
And you're talking about cities – what if you live in remote and rural South Wales?
The 1.40pm from Clarbeston Road will get you there in five hours 44 minutes, direct, for £25.50. You might find a Bargain Booze

store more conveniently located, however.

Let's make a day of it. What else is there to do in Crewe?

Apart from change trains, you mean?

Is that what most people do there?

About half of them. In 2014-15, 2.7m people used Crewe station; 1.3m of them were classified as 'interchanges'.

That sounds like quite a crush in the Casey Jones.

Ah, you obviously had an unhappy experience with a British Rail burger in the 1970s. It's the Upper Crust now, or Hero's Bar, or the Pumpkin Café.

Even so, what's available off-site?

Crewe town centre is 10 minutes' walk to the north of the station, but if you turn left out of the station buildings you're on Nantwich Road, a busy street with plenty of coffee shops, restaurants, takeaways and bars.

And if your connection is delayed? What is there to look at in Crewe for an hour or so?

Crewe Heritage Centre, although paradoxically the intersection of six main railway lines makes it slightly difficult to find your way there from the railway station.

Isn't there a train?

There are trains aplenty on display, but none to deliver visitors from the station. Persist. It's not a long walk and it's an appropriately fine collection for a railway town. It certainly isn't just for railway buffs.

So I should leave my anorak at home, then?

Carry it with you. Tie the arms round your waist. You'll be uncomfortable without it.

Anywhere else?

Queens Park, recently spruced up after a Lottery Grant. It has a boating lake (a choice of conventional or spectacular bird/dragon-headed boats), a quite startling clock tower, bandstand, Boer War memorial and a café. The land was donated by a railway company, supposedly to stop a rival building a station on the site.

A commuter station serving north-west Crewe?

No, a station serving an entirely separate rail line or network. Rail-ways – or, at least, schemes for railways – proliferated in Victorian times. A period in the 1840s was known as Railway Mania or just The Mania.

The Mania sounds unsettling. Were capitalists of the period known as Maniacs? Thank goodness we know where we stand now.

Yes, no, and not entirely. With HS2, there has been some talk of a new Crewe Hub station.

Do say *All aboard! Change at Crewe for the Northern Powerhouse!*
Don't say *Oh Mr Porter, what can I do?*

Crewe Alexandra 3 Barnet 0
Gresty Road, 26 December 1991

Crystal Palace

In 1983 I was renting a cold-water flat above a branch of Barclays Bank, across the road from Streatham Common. Hot water had been advertised, but the flats were new conversions and imperfectly plumbed. The first time I ran a bath, water cascaded through the two flats beneath mine and flooded the banking hall.

Across the road was a pub called the Greyhound, such an unredeemed dive that I used it only to buy cigarettes when nowhere else was open. The rest of Greyhound Lane as it ran away towards Mitcham was lined by shops selling old office furniture and used white goods. Their stock overflowed on to the pavement, giving the impression of Brent Cross in the aftermath of a tsunami.

That was half a lifetime ago. The bank branch is now the Mere Scribbler, "Livelyhood's latest neighbourhood pub", and the Greyhound describes itself as "the most elegant bar to be found in South London". The shops, I imagine, sell exotic snacks and a thousand varieties of juice, all of them green.

I came to know the area well. My paid work that year was in the West End, from where I could make my way home to either of two inconvenient railway stations or by glacially slow bus. Both of the stations involved a walk and sometimes the bus too, if the road up through Brixton was particularly busy.

Unpaid work involved a project researching blue plaques. I was working on a very specific kind of London guide book. I intended it to appeal to tourists with particular interests: politics, the arts, music, social reform and so on. The book would usher them around a circuit of the houses in which men and women celebrated for their achievements in those fields had lived. At each home, the guide book would offer some details of the inspirational householder's life there before showing readers how to make their way to the next one.

This idea was in its very early stages in 1983. I began my research locally, by visiting the nearest blue plaques (Raymond Chandler in West Norwood, Will Hay in Norbury) and skulking outside hoping for a spark of inspiration, or for some contact from the spirit of the place. The spirit world declined to cooperate. But the plan crystallised into a series of guides for admirers of different categories of blue plaque holders. Only the first in the proposed series was completed – Poets – and of the 20 rough copies I produced for promotional purposes only four survive.

My plaque-related weekend outings took me before very long to the Horniman Museum and Gardens in Forest Hill. The Horniman has its own blue plaque and its own *genius loci*, which contributed nothing to my publishing project but which drew me back more than once as an ordinary visitor.

Tea-drinkers will recognise the name. This is the Horniman whose tea company generated one of those great Victorian fortunes, the disposal of which enabled the succeeding generation, Frederick John Horniman in this case, to add 'philanthropist' or 'public benefactor' to his epithet.

FJ Horniman visited distant lands, not all of them tea-growing, and with the aim of "bringing the world to Forest Hill" he set about 'collecting' objects and artefacts. As his interests became known, other travellers added their contributions. Eventually the collection occupied the entire house and the family moved next door. Known initially as the Surrey House Museum, it opened on Christmas Eve 1890.

In 1898 Horniman decided the building was inadequate and he had a new one constructed. At the same time, he made over to the people of London the museum, grounds and collections.

The scope of the collections is extraordinary and this Museum is unusually lively. Not many of the exhibits in the Animal Walk, aquarium and butterfly house are still long enough to gather dust. The Animal Walk is a thematic extension of the conventional natural history gallery with enclosures for various domesticated animals, including alpacas. The aquarium recreates different aquatic environments. The butterfly house is a very recent attraction in a carefully planted indoor tropical garden.

Also indoors is the unexpected pleasure of the Music Gallery. Horniman collected musical instruments, and here they are, all 1,300 of them, plus some on loan from other collections and museums. Interactive sound tables and the Hands-On Space let you listen to and make some music.

If you have time after the Horniman, you might take in one or two blue plaques as you make your way to Selhurst Park – Crystal Palace is the nearest football ground. En route, or not far from it, are:

- John Logie Baird, television pioneer, who lived at 3 Crescent Wood Road – handily placed for the Crystal Palace transmitter
- Leslie Howard, or Ashley in *Gone with the Wind*, at 45 Farquhar Road. This was a childhood address; Howard worked as a bank clerk, suffered shell-shock in WWI and took up acting in 1916
- Marie Stopes at 28 Cintra Park. Originally a palaeobotanist, she too lived in South London as a child. As a scientist and a pioneer in family planning she has plaques here and at the University of Manchester
- Emile Zola at Queens Hotel, 122 Church Road, in 1898-99. Persecuted for having championed Captain Alfred Dreyfus, Zola fled Paris in the clothes he stood up in. Although resident here only nine or 10 months, he wrote most of *Fécondité* and a short story called *Angeline*, enjoyed visits from both his wife and his mistress and developed his interest in photography. He told a journalist from *L'Aurore* he took pictures "of hotels, London pubs, as well as crippled bums in rags. I shot 300 pictures with a small 2.9x3.9cm camera that I hooked on the handlebar of my bicycle when I went for a ride"
- Sir Arthur Conan Doyle at 12 Tennison Road, 1891-94. This was the period when Conan Doyle began to make his name as a writer. He abandoned a potential medical career as an eye specialist to concentrate instead on the career of Sherlock Holmes. That was almost stillborn; Conan Doyle killed off Holmes in *The Final Problem*, written at Tennison Road, but resurrected him in response to a public outcry.

The match against West Bromwich was notable for a goal scored by Jeff Astle. In outline there was little remarkable about it: a firmly struck shot from a corner of the penalty area, rising into the opposite corner of the net. But we happened to be standing right in line with the ball's trajectory. When Astle hit it, we saw no movement of the ball until the net swelled to receive it.

And why 1969? That was a visit my dad and I made soon after the family had moved south; I can at least be sure who was playing that day. I've seen Oldham play at Selhurst Park since then, but I can't remember the opponents being Crystal Palace. Charlton Athletic and Wimbledon, yes, when they were homeless, but Palace? I'm not sure.

I never settled in Streatham and felt homeless myself for most of 1983. The following year I moved away. From the look of the developments at the top of Greyhound Lane, Streatham never looked back.

Crystal Palace 1 West Bromwich Albion 3
Selhurst Park, 20 September 1969

Derby County

This chapter is a cautionary tale in which a common saying or maxim introduces each episode. Fed like an ammunition belt into the word processor, they come out as a quick-fire demonstration of English folk wisdom.

The main theme is 'A stitch in time saves nine', because the Derby panel in my tapestry required two visits. On the first, a version of 'More haste, less speed' came into play. I made such good time on my way to Derby that I dallied over lunch. Eventually, I reached Derby with no time left to do anything but watch a football match.

That need not have been a problem. My oldest friend was from Derby and I could pick his brains. But the next adage, following on immediately, is the vital importance of 'striking while the iron's hot'. Before any brain-picking could take place, the Grim Reaper picked my old friend.

'If a job's worth doing, it's worth doing well'. I could still have given Derby the cursory treatment meted out to a number of other towns and cities in this guide. But two years later a journey north took me close to Derby; I decided to go and take a look at the place, and drink to my old friend in a Derby pub.

The fifth lesson, adapted for modern use, is that you should not believe everything you see on the Internet. Placing far too much faith in it, I planned my second visit to Derby carefully. Approaching from the southwest again I found a series of attractions that would steer me through the south of the city towards its thriving, beating heart.

Foremost among these suburban pleasure palaces was, apparently, Calke Abbey. According to the map put up by TripAdvisor, Calke Abbey was to be found in a district of Derby called Sunny Hill, on Stenson Road. And Stenson Road looked to be the second left off the A50 as it skirts the south of Derby.

Of course, it is nowhere near. The A50 is a dual-carriageway and the second left is a roundabout halfway to Nottingham.

Stenson Road has passed undetected underneath the road, miles back. Calke Abbey is, in any case, nowhere in this vicinity.

A miss is as good as a mile. Indicated by brown signs at the roundabout I chose when my faith in the A50 began to wane, Calke Abbey is perhaps 10km as the crow flies from Sunny Hill. It wasn't far, in fact, from where I'd had lunch on the previous visit.

Since I was heading that way I thought I might as well take a look. But the house closes from November through to the start of March, so I paid £3.80 for the park, the gardens and the shop. A fool and his money are easily parted. But there's good value in some of the promotional material you'll pick up.

The house is described with unusual candour by the National Trust. Its basic visitor guide is subtitled: "The un-stately home and country estate." The house sounds fascinating: "With peeling paintwork and overgrown courtyards, Calke Abbey tells the story of the dramatic decline of a country house estate. Calke's house and stables are little restored, abandoned areas vividly portraying a period in the 20th century when many country houses did not survive to tell their story."

You could probably spend a day there, although a bicycle might be necessary for the extensive grounds. Marked trails exceed 20km, including an 8km 'tramway' trail that follows the route of a 19th century horse-drawn tram across the estate. There are diverse habitats: a wetland area (with hide), a deer park, limeyards and woods. Dogs are welcome on a lead.

But the diversion to Calke Abbey threw out the rest of my itinerary, which needed Stenson Road as its starting point. Heading back into Derby I could not find the Sikh Heritage Centre at all and missed the Derby Arboretum at first. But the Royal Crown Derby Visitor Centre presented itself handily enough where I had slowed down for roadworks, and from there I was able to find my way back round the corner to the Arboretum.

I wonder if the locals call it the Derby Arby. Or would that sound too much like an unusually nasal band of cricket followers?

To be honest, it doesn't make as much of itself as it might. An arboretum sounds grand, and this was supposedly the first landscaped public park in England. At first, parking on Rose Hill, I thought I'd arrived at a playing field. Avenues of trees ran down either side of a football pitch. To the left, a large children's play area was deserted.

If at first you don't see the wood for the trees, you have to walk a little way to find the arboretum proper. One of the first signs you'll encounter of this being something special is the copy of a statue of a Florentine boar. The fountain is quite something too.

I remain unconvinced, though, by the identification of this plot as an arboretum. There are plenty of trees, certainly, but some indication of what they are might be helpful. In Berlin there's a park in which you become aware that the lamp standards have plates on them, and on reading them you find that you're in an open-air lamp-standard museum: they say things like 'Leipzig 1880s' or 'Wuppertal 1910'. Surely it isn't asking too much for an arboretum to identify its trees to interested would-be botanists?

There's no such problem at the Royal Crown Derby Visitor Centre. Here, in the museum and exhibition there's never any doubt what you're looking at, whether it's pottery, process, royal visitors or retail. 'Raised gilding' is the expression that will stay with me: the process by which you apply gold leaf in such a position that vigorous washing up will remove it almost immediately.

Also the Zeppelin mark: one night in 1916, the kilns were fired up and loaded and an air-raid caused the entire shift to take cover. When they emerged no-one was sure what state the contents of the kiln would be in – perfect, as it happened.

And on the staircase leading up to the museum there is a sensational decorative window demonstrating the translucent qualities of the medium. All this, of course, is in addition to the intricate beauty and variety of the ceramics on view.

The road into Derby from the Royal Crown Derby direction brings you naturally to the Intu centre and this could easily deceive you if you were apt to judge a book by its cover. It's like many another shopping gallery, with cinema and restaurants tacked on. If, however, you park and head north on foot into the Cathedral Quarter you're in a city of an entirely different character.

Is it a bit of pose for Derby to have a Cathedral Quarter? Perhaps, especially since it has only one other quarter – St Peter's – for balance. The other two quarters (eighths, actually, if the area within the ring road is intended) are not named.

On the other hand the Cathedral Quarter has cobbles, medieval street names (Wardwick, Iron Gate, Bold Lane etc) and it has Derby Cathedral.

The Cathedral has a quite fantastic interior, and the light, colours and decoration will remind you immediately of Royal Crown Derby. There's even raised gilding. The brochures will direct you to the tomb of Bess of Hardwick or the 20th century stained-glass windows designed by Ceri Richards; I'd suggest you stand in the middle of the nave and slowly turn through 360° and remember that you're in an English church.

The headstone of the painter Joseph Wright is also in the Cathedral, having been moved from his original resting place to make way for the inner ring road. There's a handsome memorial to Wright – an orrery – on Iron Gate, and in the Derby Museum & Art Gallery a Joseph Wright Gallery.

The Museum & Art Gallery contains examples of the three kinds of work Wright was best known for: portraits, landscapes and dramatically-lit scientific enterprises.

Upstairs there were two visiting exhibitions: the Derby surrealist Marion Adnams and, more difficult to categorise, Richard Long. Long's Cornish Slate Ellipse had pride of place, like an oval slate-brick patio. On the walls, mud-dipped dripped pictures from the river Avon near Bristol demonstrated that beauty is in the eye of the beholder.

Adnams' work was easier to get to grips with. About half the room held pictures of bare trees and animal skulls, with the other half dominated by her remarkable series of paper models of elegant ladies, painted and posed often in association with symbols of death.

Three further rooms in the Derby Museum & Art Gallery are worth looking at. For some reason there's a collection of mummies and grave objects. The letters are falling off one of the descriptive labels, leaving a mummy nameless and imperilling his or her chances of passing safely into eternity. Through another window a Victorian gallery is visible but inaccessible for safety reasons; and you have to go into the adjacent Derby Library to see it at all clearly from below.

And last but by no means least, Derby was as far south as Bonnie Prince Charlie reached in 1745. In a reproduction of the drawing room at Exeter House, the ill-fated prince considers his options and a recording enables him to think aloud.

Further up Friar Gate, beneath an elegant bridge that brought trains into the Great Northern Railways' Derby terminus, is the Pickford's House Museum. The rooms here are less historically dramatic than Bonnie Prince Charlie's study, but they illustrate life above and below stairs in the Georgian era in which the architect Joseph Pickford was active.

And again there are unexpected bonuses. On the top floor you'll find the Frank Bradley Collection of Toy Theatres, accompanied when I was there by a video promoting environmental awareness. On the middle floor, alongside a view of the garden, a rug framed on the wall reproduces in three dimensions the features of the self-same garden. A display of tea caddies rounds off the visit.

One of the main set-piece tourist attractions in Derby is the Silk Mill, but this was being refurbished when I was in the city and is not, I believe, due to re-open until 2020. I may be wrong: if it's open before then, try to see it. If it matches the rest of Derby's attractions in interest and variety it will closely resemble the spice of life.

As for the drink in a Derby pub, it needed company. No man is an island.

Derby County 0 Wolverhampton Wanderers 0
Pride Park, 16 February 2013

Doncaster Rovers

I set out in good time to give myself most of the day in Doncaster, a town I had never been to despite living only 22 miles away for three years. The fixture was an FA Cup replay and took place on a Tuesday evening. But I had made hardly any progress up the M1 when I found myself at risk of dozing off, so I parked at Newport Pagnell to rest my eyes.

My eyes required more than three hours' rest. You will have seen the signs at motorway service areas, warning you of the penalties if you abuse their free parking for too long. The idea of anyone voluntarily staying much more than half an hour at such a place had never crossed my mind. Now I know better. The limit is usually two hours, from which I conclude either that I was lucky to escape without a fine or that the signs are a bluff.

I can't remember what I'd been doing the night before. Whatever, it prevented me seeing much of Doncaster at all. Darkness was closing in when I reached the town, and by the time I'd parked and orientated myself Doncaster was shutting up for the evening.

I consoled myself with a glass of red in a Yates Wine Lodge, followed by a bag of chips on the way back to the car. Fortified, I made my way to the Keepmoat Stadium.

Doncaster gave me my first sighting of cheerleaders at an English football ground – the Vikettes, which I misheard on the PA as the Dykettes, no doubt with the moat theme in mind. Without intending any disrespect to the girls, I found it a dispiriting development: that nubile 'dancers' should be considered suitable entertainment for a stadium of football fans.

But then, half-time entertainment is and has always been variable in quality and interest. The television audience can pass the time listening to the views of the pundits. The actual audience, in the ground, often has to make its own entertainment.

By and large, half-time football-related diversions go down well or, at least, better than otherwise. Short matches played between groups of frantic children, many of them barely more than toddlers, are often unintentionally hilarious and the kids sometimes get a bigger hand than the footballers during the preceding 45 minutes. Penalty shoot-outs involving scouts and guides may lack the drama of a World Cup semi-final but you can't fault them for effort.

For adult volunteers a degree more difficulty is occasionally demanded: hitting the crossbar from a distant corner of the penalty area, for example. The reward at Barnsley for hitting the crossbar three times from three attempts in the 2016-17 season was... a season ticket for the following year.

Doncaster's Vikettes weren't the only dancing girls you might have seen at a football ground. At Bristol Rovers the Blue Flames are reported to have been "Simply awful, out of time, overawed and under-rehearsed"[1]. At Crystal Palace the Crystals claimed implausibly to be 'English football's only cheerleading squad' but at least they were of age. The Bolton Belles recently reformed after a period in the doldrums. On the other hand, Gully's Girls at Brighton led their last cheer in 2012. In addition to dancing, Gully's Girls are remembered among the Brighton faithful for fire-eating displays, which must have warmed the draughty Withdean Stadium a little.

Dancing isn't confined to cheerleaders. Grimsby Town fans have been entertained Bollywood-style at half-time by dancers from the Trishool Dance Academy of Leeds. This was colourful, dramatic and, to a degree, educational, but unfortunately confined to a distant corner of the ground.

An unintended source of half-time amusement is the habit of watering the pitch at the drop of a hat. The substitutes, rarely called upon in the first half, will get up to take some exercise at half-time; but if they're in the wrong place at the wrong time they'll need to be wrung out afterwards. Akin to this is Groundskeeper Willie's fastidious determination to keep the pitch looking like a carpet. To this end he (or she) will send out people with forks to repair divots. Their demoralised traipsing around the sward is an illustration of what the word 'desultory' means.

---

1 David Goldblatt's excellent *The Game of Our Lives: the Meaning and Making of English Football*.

Club mascots are another wearisome source of amusement. Originally, such mascots were real animals adopted and paraded by their clubs in the way that regiments of the British Army had their goats, wolfhounds, antelopes etc. Now the club mascots are Disneyfied Blobbies in a variety of cheerless guises, entertaining only when they transgress.

There have been punch-ups between mascots, invasions of the pitch, mooning and abuse. Sadly, such moments are rare; for the most part the mascots prowl the perimeter frightening children with their huge, gaping mouths and empty stares. This seems self-defeating: who, if not children, are they there for? Pointless and annoying, one thing is certain – the BBC will find mascots side-splittingly funny and will devote entire segments to their feeble antics.

The most famous mascot moment in English football was provided by a US visitor called Mackerel Jordan. Mackerel is one of a US group of mascots-for-hire called Zooperstars. Appearing for no obvious reason in the interval of an uninspiring game between Derby and Blackburn in 2016, the fish-headed mascot went through its routine of swallowing a kitman whole and regurgitating him without clothes.

Special and genuinely enjoyable events are rare. One such came at Manchester City's match against Liverpool in spring 2017; to promote the Open at Royal Birkdale that summer, Jose Maria Olazabal hit golf shots at a flag in the centre circle.

English football's official position appears to be that fans want only one thing at half-time: to shuffle for 15 minutes (or more) in a queue for a tepid cup of awful coffee and an over-priced pie. The idea that formal entertainment might be laid on for them appears to baffle most clubs.

At a fan consultation group meeting at Aston Villa in June 2017, one of the questions fans wanted answered was: "There is a lack of half-time entertainment. What is being done to re-introduce fan competitions?" The response from the club contained enough flannel to polish the chairman's limo for a lifetime. "Every aspect of the matchday experience, we are attempting to improve. We want to ensure that fans are not only entertained by the football but at everywhere they turn on a matchday. Halftime entertainment is something that is dependent on personal choice and is therefore difficult to please all parties. We will conduct some research to determine what people want to see and then look into reintroducing it if the desire is there."

Not everyone wants a half-time show. When a programme costs £3.50 you might want to squeeze out your money's worth by reading it cover to cover, including the chairman's notes and the adverts for the club's plumbing and heating partner (#FeelYourPassion). Some observers of English football see indifference to half-time entertainment as a positive quality that marks out true fans. "There's no stupid pre-game or half-time entertainment brought to you by sponsor x or sponsor y," says the FussballinLondon.de website. It isn't universally true, but we get the point.

The Doncaster match was also my first glimpse of a young Oldham player called Chris Taylor. Oldham since the mid-90s have had few stars. Teams with no stars occasionally win things: Greece and Denmark come to mind. Not Oldham, though; perhaps Taylor disqualified them by being a genuine star. Years later at the club's end-of-season dinner I was able to speak to him. "You've done enough for this club," I said. "You've fulfilled your side of the bargain. Now, for the sake of your career, you have to move on." He looked startled; unsolicited career advice from a clearly drunk stranger might not have been what he'd expected of the evening. But he moved soon afterwards to Millwall, which at that time meant going up a division. He later left Millwall to return to Lancashire with Blackburn Rovers. In 2017 he was back at Oldham, on loan and not making much impression. I'm not sure, then, whether my assessment or my advice was faulty. His timing, perhaps.

Doncaster Rovers 1 Oldham 2
Keepmoat Stadium, 27 November 2007

Everton

People who talk about 'the romance of the FA Cup' probably don't get out enough. Did Casanova seduce swooning signorinas by taking them to the early rounds of the Coppa Italia? Of course not.

Talk of romance is facile and clichéd. The FA Cup sometimes provides the satisfying sight of a top-flight team struggling to overcome plucky part-timers, and schadenfreude if they fail. For fans of would-be giant-killers, there's a day out and the merest brush of a contact with the circuits of the big-time. And that's it.

At Everton on the first Saturday in 2012, the minnows were non-league Tamworth. Their followers leaving Goodison Park after a predictable defeat would have encountered a line of taxis. If they were in any doubt, this would have brought home to them how bloated the big-time has become. Football fans, once the target of mocking chants ('Come in a taxi, you must have come in a taxi') now routinely go home in one.

I walked down to County Road and caught a bus back into the city centre. A taxi receipt can always be made to look like a legitimate business expense, but I had no business there in the first place.

Everton was one of my more eccentric outings. It came about by an accident just on the wrong side of foreseeable – which makes it carelessness, as if a gambler placed a bet without first ensuring that the horse had a normal complement of legs.

In the 3rd round of the FA Cup in the 2011-12 season, the luck of the draw pitted Oldham against Liverpool, at Liverpool. Anfield is among the most famous stadiums in the world and I had never been. I logged on eagerly to the National Rail Enquiries website, found irresistibly cheap tickets for Saturday 7 January and bought them.

The following day it occurred to me to wonder how many other Merseyside clubs might have been drawn at home. When I say 'how many' I mean Everton, really – Tranmere Rovers had been eliminated in the 1st round and New Brighton were last a power in the land in the 1920s. While I was checking I learnt that the Liverpool/Oldham game had been switched to Friday evening to avoid a clash with Everton/Tamworth on the Saturday. My rail tickets, still supremely good value, now applied to the wrong day and were non-transferable.

I thought about buying a single ticket for Friday, staying overnight and taking in both games. Unfortunately the price of rail travel on a Friday was mystifyingly high, as was the cost of a hotel room. Thrift, licking its wounds over the original ticket purchase, quailed at the prospect of good money being thrown after bad.

I considered simply cutting my losses and enjoying the 3rd round from the comfort of my settee. This familiar option had much to recommend it. But I had never been to Goodison Park either; I always enjoyed a train ride; and if I went to Everton I might learn whether someone truly pressed refreshing Mother Noblett mints into the grateful hands of supporters[1]. In the end, I made my decision contingent on the weather on the day, like an umpire's inspection.

A sunny morning was turning overcast as my train, packed with excited Tamworthies, arrived at Lime Street. St George's Hall, directly across the road from the station, looked like a good place to keep a lid on my own excitement.

St George's Hall is described by no less credible an authority than Visit Liverpool as "one of the finest neo-classical buildings in the world". That puts it in the same bracket as Somerset House, the Arc de Triomphe and the Capitol in Washington. When did a Liverpudlian knowingly undersell his or her city? Still, it's certainly one of the Seven Wonders of Merseyside. The tunnel-vaulted ceiling, the Minton tiled floor, the columns and arches are spectacular. In the Great Hall you could imagine a Busby Berkeley number being shot while next door, in the chilling reconstruction of the Criminal Court, Busby himself might be sentenced to be shot.

Just a few city blocks to the south are St James Gardens and

---

1 This is the famous Everton mint from which the club's nickname, the Toffees, derives. And the answer is No.

within them Liverpool Cathedral, the largest Anglican cathedral in the country. It's not only large but also relatively recent: its completion was marked by the Queen's visit in 1978 although they celebrated its centenary in 2004. Its predecessor, St Peter's in the city centre, was described by a later rector as "ugly and hideous". Halfway through the sentence he must have felt the need for more emphasis.

For a product of the 20th century it feels very traditional in style and atmosphere. You wouldn't say the same for Paddy's Wigwam, the Roman Catholic Metropolitan Cathedral at the northern end of Hope Street. This astonishing building, consecrated in 1967 and therefore older than its CofE equivalent half a mile away, is more modern in almost every respect except, perhaps, the inspiration of the architect and builders.

It opened at Whitsun, which in 1967 fell on 14 May. A little over two weeks later the Beatles presented to the world *Sgt Pepper's Lonely Hearts Club Band*. However shabby Liverpool was in those days (and in parts of the city it was difficult to believe that 20 years had passed since the end of the Second World War) the first light of a more confident day was filtering through the clouds. Sgt Pepper, no doubt coincidentally, was a significantly more spiritual album than any of its predecessors.

Sacred in purpose, the Cathedral provoked some profanity in the response of Liverpudlians. It was known not only as the Wigwam but also the Mersey Funnel. The interior, in which no seat is more than 25 metres from the altar, suggests a religion in which sinners might be swirled to Hell in a clockwise vortex in the northern hemisphere. The design is based on nothing more pretentious than a tent.

How different the Cathedral might have been had money been more readily available. Sir Edwin Lutyens prepared the first plan, envisaging a domed Romanesque church on a spectacular scale. For want of time and money that plan was discarded and a simpler suggestion by Frederick Gibberd adopted; the crypt alone survives from the Lutyens plan, in which it was to have been a vestry where 100 priests might robe themselves. It's 40 metres long. That idea might have come from the transition area in a triathlon.

Above, in Gibberd's sensational space, light filtered prismatically by stained glass flickers across the seating deployed in circles around the white marble altar. It is the largest Catholic place of worship in the country and arguably the most distinctive.

From the outside, with its tent-guy buttresses, its vertically exaggerated crown and its Rocky ceremonial steps, the Cathedral is magnificent. On a corner of the piazza a kick-about was in progress. It would have been a thoroughly Liverpudlian sight except that they were Tamworth fans.

There's a lot to enjoy about Liverpool: too much, really, for a few hours before kick-off. I can't imagine where else might you expect to see, within a few hundred yards of city streets, statues commemorating:

- William Huskisson, the first person ever to be killed by a train; Huskisson, incidentally, must have attended the opening of the Manchester to Liverpool railway believing it to be fancy dress – the statue depicts him as a Roman senator
- Queen Victoria, stern and stout beneath a dome on which Fame, appropriately, flourishes a long trumpet
- And as of 2017, a skinny Cilla Black.

But for statues of Liverpool's musical heroes, the Beatles at the Pier Head is the place to go. You'll also find Billy Fury at the Albert Dock to the south and the Titanic Memorial to the north.

The Albert Dock area could probably keep you occupied for days. I restricted myself to the Museum of Liverpool, hoping that way to cover most of the bases. Outside, within a few minutes' walk, you might narrow the focus on to maritime history, slavery, fine art, the Beatles and plenty besides; inside, this free Museum is vast and fascinating. Even the views from the windows are exhilarating. Can Everton playing Tamworth, or whoever the away team happens to be, be a better spectacle than watching this world go by? Persevere. With that sort of thinking, you'd never get to a football match at all.

Everton 2 Tamworth 0
Goodison Park, 7 January 2012

Exeter City

Any reservations about Exeter are mere quibbles. You might, for example, want to take with a pinch of salt the assertion of a *Guardian* travel guide in 2017: "Exeter is within easy reach of the rest of the UK." If the rest of the UK lived in Taunton that would certainly be true. But although it might be quite a journey, Exeter rewards the effort.

I see it on reflection as an image from a kaleidoscope – bright, colourful and ever-changing – though not done with mirrors. If I have a little difficulty getting Exeter into focus that may be partly because one of the big set-piece attractions, the Royal Albert Memorial Museum, was closed when I was there. (After a £24m refit it reopened at the end of 2011.) Also, I spent much of my time just wandering around, passively absorbing Exeter's variety. Any city with league football, a Decorated Gothic cathedral, Roman ruins and a waterfront has a lot going for it.

The Cathedral comes into focus sharply enough and may be allowed to blow its own trumpet: "Exeter Cathedral is one of the great cathedrals of England, and one of the finest examples of Gothic architecture anywhere." The west is the direction to approach from. Three ranks of carved figures stand across the entire width of the West Front. At ground level are angels; they support on the middle tier the kings of Judah; and above them are apostles, evangelists, prophets and images of the Virgin Mary and of God. Originally the entire assembly would have been in colour. It must have been an breathtaking sight.

Inside, the Cathedral fully lives up to the West Front's promise. The fan-vaulting, the stained glass, the Minstrels' Gallery, the memorials... Exeter Cathedral was built mainly between 1270 and 1340, which means that many of the people who worked on it could hardly have hoped to see it completed.

It is, then, an embodiment of skill, patience and faith. On the other hand, if the reputation for rapacity of Walter Stapledon, Bishop of Exeter from 1308-1326, was merited, many people of only moderate faith must also have made vital but involuntary contributions to the work.

If you're looking for some light holiday reading during your visit, try the medieval thrillers of the estimable Michael Jecks. *The Chapel of Bones* in particular has as its backdrop the construction site that was Exeter Cathedral in 1323 – it's worth boning up, you might say, if you had no shame.

There are appealing quirks in the Cathedral. Its ribbed columns are often likened to trees; the 60 Green Men among the carvings presumably feel right at home. It's an oddly ambiguous motif to repeat so often in a house of God.

Jack in the Green becomes Jack of the Clocks at the nearby St Mary Steps Church, where an automated step-jack strikes the hour. This spectacular mechanism is known as Matthew the Miller. In a plinth above the clock sits Matthew, flanked by his sons. They wield pikes with which they strike quarter hours; on the hour, Matthew leans forward and a larger bell tolls.

This is a rare survivor of a number of remarkable clocks in the city. There was apparently one at St Petrock's with chimes that played psalms. In the Cathedral, an earth-centred astronomical clock is said to have been the inspiration for *Hickory Dickory Dock*. And the Exeter Civic Society teasingly refers to the "Famous illuminated clock at St John's" without saying what made it Famous. The explanation may simply lie in the Society's weakness for random capital letters; elsewhere it records the destruction of St Edmund's in the 1970s "by Vandals".

The local tourist information office proposes themed walks and underground tunnels. I went instead to a football match. But later, I compensated for that descent into the underground tunnels of low culture by visiting the campus of the University of Exeter to see a play.

The Northcott Theatre was putting on *The Ministry of Fear*, a dark Graham Greene novel turned into an opaque play. Someone had decided the production would benefit from musical accompaniment. The first half proceeded to the sawing of a bow across what might have been a one-stringed instrument.

I sensed the interval would be much too short for me to drink enough to fortify myself against any more of that. There were two predictions I could confidently make about the second half: first, that it would be longer than 45 minutes and second, that Oldham centre-back Sean Gregan would not turn up unexpectedly in the penalty area to save the day with a late equaliser. I left at the intermission.

The walk back into the city centre down Pennsylvania Road made me feel very old. Along the way, there were the sounds of students settling in for a Saturday night – the early stages of parties filtered through windows. I was abroad in a lively, attractive city with nowhere to go, and I wasn't even able to sit through a complete play. I returned to the hotel, ordered a room-service burger, made two surprisingly expensive phone calls and watched *Match of the Day*.

The Sunday dawned warm and bright. In the castle grounds sprightly daffodils danced. William the Conqueror is said to have chosen the site, known as Rougemont for the red volcanic rock on which it stands. Now privately owned, the castle earns its keep as a venue for weddings, parties and other events.

I strolled through Northernhay Gardens and Rougemont Gardens and, after a coffee and a glance at the paper, made my way via the area known as Friernhay towards the river.

Or, to be more exact, the waterfront. It was the Exeter Ship Canal, built in 1566, that enabled Exeter to maintain a port on its doorstep. Before then the River Exe had been navigable as far as the city, but local nobles effectively cut it off by building weirs to power their mills. Ships docked at Topsham until the canal was built.

Now, the area below Exeter's South Gate is called the Quayside and it's a fine place to pass a Sunday morning. Two watercourses, a marina, waterside bars and restaurants... It's perfect for watching the world go by, or for striding out and using the footbridges to complete a circuit.

Parts of Exeter are undeniably plain. That's largely because the city was bombed on a score of occasions during World War II. Exeter was the first target in what became known as the Baedeker

Raids, from the declared German intention "to bomb every building in Britain with three stars in the *Baedeker Guide*". Bath, Canterbury, Norwich and York were also targets.

A pity, then, that one of my other abiding but small-minded memories of Exeter is the exorbitant fee my hotel levied for domestic phone calls. In response to an emailed complaint, the hotel chain put me on a mailing list and continues to this day to keep me informed of their latest offers and promotions.

Will I name them? The jury's out.

Exeter City 1 Oldham 1
St James Park, 6 March 2010

Fleetwood Town

This is an entry for which, regrettably, I can offer no supporting evidence. I know I was there, and that it was a night match, and that Macclesfield wore all blue, and you will have to take my word for it. If I were to offer anecdotal support – the unforgettable detail that the Fleetwood forward line contained players called Haddock and Fish – you'd think I was making it up.

The reason for this failure of memory is twofold. First, we are going back almost 50 years. Second, it was a Northern Premier League (NPL) fixture and therefore not covered by the Internet's multiple head-to-head archive sites.

An archive website has supplied the date of the match; from my own resources I would have been guessing at the month, although the year is easier.

The NPL was founded in 1968. Fleetwood (not Town in those days) entered the new league from the Lancashire Combination (along with Morecambe, who have also done quite well for themselves). Macclesfield's fellow graduates from the Cheshire County League were even more distinguished: Wigan Athletic, tenants of the Premier League not so long ago, were playing at this level in 1968.

This match took place in the inaugural NPL season, and I would have been prompted to make the trip, presumably, because Macclesfield were top of the league at the time. They were to be champions of the NPL for its first two seasons. Why did they not win promotion? Because there was nowhere to be promoted to.

The Football League closed shop was still in operation. At the foot of the old Fourth Division Bradford Park Avenue, Grimsby Town, Newport County and York City all applied successfully for re-election in 1969. It was not until 1972 that Barrow became the first club to drop down into the NPL from Division 4, to be replaced by Hereford United.

Astute geographers will notice that Hereford is not in the north of England. The NPL expanded to accommodate Barrow, while Hereford's promotion from the Southern League must have put noses out of joint not only in Macclesfield but also at Chelmsford City, who actually won the Southern League that year. Crucially neither Chelmsford nor Macclesfield had heroically beaten Newcastle United in a televised FA Cup tie in the recent past.

Despite the match being on a Monday evening in late March, I cycled to Fleetwood from our home in Ansdell. Unlike the jaunt to Wycombe Wanderers 43 years later, distance was no object in those days, nor temperature, nor ambient light.

It would have been 14 or 15 miles from Ansdell to Fleetwood, probably a little over an hour if the usual Fylde coast gale had been blowing. My bicycle was equipped with dynamo lights: a small generator picked up power from contact with a tyre. This arrangement would hardly be permitted now. The lights were feeble at the best of times and completely dark when the bike was stationary. To compensate, cyclists in those days gave themselves a better chance of hearing the approach of the car that would kill them by not wearing a helmet. This applied to motorcyclists as well. Car drivers entered into the spirit of the thing by driving much smaller vehicles, many of which were incapable of speeds higher than 45mph.

Fleetwood's floodlights, which were barely stronger than my bicycle lamps, made the Macclesfield strip the remaining detail of which I am certain. Wearing relatively dark colours, lurking Silkmen were hardly visible at the far end of the pitch. At half-time, when it became possible to upgrade to the stand at no extra cost, I was able to move to a position closer to the halfway line and see what was happening at both ends.

I must have been an odd, unsociable teenager. To spend upwards of two hours pedalling through the storm on a March night to go to a non-league football match in which I was interested in neither of the teams... As solitary vices go, it seems relatively harmless but odd nonetheless.

Fleetwood 1 Macclesfield Town 2
Highbury Stadium, 24 March 1969

Forest Green Rovers

Approaching Nailsworth from the M5 through Dursley was an almost mystical experience. The wooded slopes of a Cotswold outlier filled the windscreen, rising towards a summit lost in low cloud. In the grey afternoon of a gloomy day, it might have been a land where intrepid, lantern-jawed explorers would find dinosaurs, or ferocious savages protecting hidden treasure.

Nailsworth isn't quite that colourful but it doesn't disappoint either. It clings tidily to the hillsides above and around the confluence of two small rivers or streams. The population in the 2011 census was 5,794, so my arrival added about 0.02%. A full house at Forest Green Rovers would almost double it – the ground holds 5,141. This surely makes Nailsworth the smallest place to host a league football club by a wide margin.

Being small, Nailsworth obliges you to look closely for points of interest on an intimate scale. Could you beguile away half a day here? Yes, especially if you are of a reflective disposition or enjoy pre-loved, upcycled and re-purposed interiors shops. But if you aren't, and without taking a very long lunch?

Yes, again. Nailsworth has impressive and touching pieces of public sculpture and street furniture. Across the road from the Britannia, in the intriguingly-named Cossack Square, is a waist-high bevelled white plinth with a memorial to 'Short and Bright lives'. The weathered bronze piece could be a dove, or hands releasing a dove, or petals. By artist Kim Francis, who now lives in the Cotswolds, it might make you think of Dürer.

Alongside this lovely object are two benches, each with a commemorative panel. Neither suggests short lives but they too are moving, in their own way and in juxtaposition to the sculpture. One specifies the length of the lives: 81 and 91 years respectively.

Similarly poignant and unusual in its site (on a gatepost most of the way up the hill to the football ground) you'll find a small oval plaque. It remembers Private Wallace Creed, killed in March 1918 and commemorated on the Pozières Memorial in France.

The town has a more conventional war memorial – though not entirely conventional, being also a Grade II listed clocktower. The designer was architect Peter Falconer, son of the Arts & Crafts architect Thomas Falconer. He gave it a square footprint and it tapers slightly towards the top, where cylindrical pillars support a slightly overhanging square cap. It includes two 18th century bells and a clock by Gillett & Johnston.

Just across the road from here is the Nailsworth fountain, a piece of Victorian Gothic celebrating the philanthropy of one William Smith. Restored in 2009, it was first put up in 1862 in the memory of local solicitor Smith, who made it his business to give Nailsworth a reliable supply of clean drinking water.

Why would the two streams not have been up to the job? A number of buildings around Nailsworth call to mind mills in their shape and character. The local website Nailsworth.com gamely tries to drum up interest in a kind of Mill Heritage Trail, but it seems that most of the buildings are either in residential use, derelict or gone. It's a pity. If nothing else, the site's careful documentation of these mills suggests what extraordinary diversity there has been in Nailsworth's industrial past, from walking sticks to divans, from fine broadloom cloth to engineering.

Of much more recent vintage, on the west side of the street called Old Market, you will find two golden pillar-boxes. The rower Pete Reed OBE was born in Seattle but brought up in Nailsworth. He won gold medals in the Men's Four at Beijing in 2008 and London 2012, and in the Men's Eight at Rio. The local paper announced breathlessly: "Pete has the world's largest recorded lung capacity of 11.68 litres, almost twice the normal average." The 'normal average'... don't you just love a journalist who thinks more words will automatically sound more impressive?

Pete may have built up his lung-power by walking repeatedly from the town centre to the football ground. It's 15 minutes and consistently, challengingly uphill. Apparently Forest Green's home is only 3 metres off being the highest league ground in the country and it feels like it.

That may not be the case for very much longer, though. The

club has plans for a new stadium beside Junction 13 of the M5, on the other side of Stroud. Forest Green Rovers don't do things by halves; they already promote veganism at the New Lawn, and the Eco Park planned for the club's future will be entirely of wood to a design by Zaha Hadid.

While all this is going on, Forest Green Rovers intend to be rising through the league. They aim to be in the Championship within five years. That would put some pressure on Nailsworth's resources. The landlord of the Britannia said league status had not made much difference to the numbers coming through his doors on match days: perhaps 20 or so more than before, he said, adding that many above that would oblige him to put on more staff. When Leeds United or Aston Villa come to town some temporary local employment may be generated.

Nailsworth has two other pubs that do food, plus a winebar; seven restaurants (two Indian, an Italian, a Mediterranean, a Modern British, a seafood specialist and the intriguing Wild Garlic bistro and rooms) and two Chinese takeaways; two hotels; two coffee shops; and three supermarkets.

That's only in its central area: Nailsworth sprawls along the Stroud road and out to the west, so there may be dispersed nuclei I didn't find.

By the way, simply wandering around is fun, because of the hills. There are innumerable steeply sloping passageways and flights of steps and odd little promontories of land. One of the connecting paths is called Arnold's Lane – admirers of the early Pink Floyd will regret the apostrophe 's'. As for Cossack Square, no support can be found for the legend that prisoners from the Crimean War were detained there.

When FGR move to Junction 13, Slimbridge wetland wildlife reserve will be a more obvious distraction and the sophistication of metropolitan Stroud is just down the road. Even so, it will still be worth going to have a look at this pleasant little town.

Forest Green Rovers 2 Newport County 0
The New Lawn, 29 August 2017

Fulham

Craven Cottage is possibly the most attractive football stadium in the country.

Its location, with the Thames on one long side and with playing fields and parkland to the south, would make an estate agent salivate. From its quaint pavilion in one corner, you might expect David Gower to come on as a substitute. The gable detail on the roof of the Johnny Haynes Stand could be a tiara. Another gable proclaims to people approaching the ground that it is 'The Fulham Football Club'. That definite article is a classy touch and helps to put Chelsea in its place – Stamford Bridge is also in Fulham.

Yes, there are small consolations to seeing your team take a serious drubbing at Fulham. It's a fine place to go to watch a football match. Besides, in 1976 the drubbing would not have been unexpected: Oldham Athletic were punching above their weight in the Second Division. Nothing much was expected of them, and they delivered.

Later, in their First Division and Premier League days, a better team played better football but against much better opponents and the result was occasionally the same. And the connection between those afternoons and a cold day by the Thames in 1976 is that a superstar was on the field.

George Best wore the number 7 shirt for Fulham that day. To add that Bobby Moore played in Fulham's defence and was hardly noticeable demonstrates the power of the George Best factor. The crowd was swollen, appropriately enough, by large numbers of Manchester United fans – their game at Queens Park Rangers was called off. The decision to go ahead at Craven Cottage must have been marginal: half the pitch looked frosty and players had trouble with their footing all afternoon. Oldham wore orange but the ball wore its usual white.

Best, in my recollection of the game, was a barrel-chested veteran who controlled the game from the midfield, exerting himself to a minimum but conducting his orchestra with every silken touch. In fact, as YouTube's seven minutes from an ITV round-up show indicates, he still looked in good shape and could be seen helping out in defence as well as sparking attacks from all over the field.

His contribution to the exquisite third goal was one to drool over: Best won the ball by selling an outrageous dummy close to the touchline, about the half-way mark, and slid a pass along the line to the winger whose hanging cross was nodded in by the onrushing striker.

Best's goal, Fulham's fourth, was also a thing of beauty. He chipped the goalkeeper from about 20 yards out – the goalkeeper was only a couple of yards off his line, but the ball sailed over his head and clipped the underside of the bar before settling in the back of the net. The goalkeeper slipped on the frosty goal area trying to get back; could Best have anticipated on that? Of course he could.

Another 5-0 defeat, then, and another case of consolation being easy to find. Aside from the atmosphere of Craven Cottage and the presence of George Best, I also fixed my car's heater.

I had driven to the match in the first car I owned, a Morris 1000 bought for £120 from a gentleman called Pharoah. The car had a number of eccentricities. On a very cold December day, its refusal to transfer heat from the engine to the passengers was notably inconvenient.

All the external paraphernalia was there, clearly visible, but it did not work. Meanwhile, under the bonnet, the engine reached such impressive temperatures that on Lakeland hills it needed frequent rests to cool down. But no means seemed to exist of sharing the heat from the engine with the interior of the car. On winter days and nights, if a car journey was necessary, we used to set out with hot-water bottles.

On that particular afternoon I had forgotten the hot-water bottle and was resigned to chilly discomfort. After a comfort break somewhere en route, I dropped a lit cigarette into the footwell of the passenger side. Searching for it beneath the passenger seat I noticed a dangling wire at the back of the drum-shaped moulding that suggested a fan housing. Encouraged, I got out and opened the passenger-side door – it was already as cold inside as it was out – to be able to view the assembly from below and, sure enough, there was a lug on to which the terminal on the wire slid. I made the connection, closed the door, got back into the driver's seat and started the engine.

After a brief grinding noise something began to whirr that had not been whirring before. Clouds of dust billowed from vents below the windscreen. The desiccated corpses of insects that last roamed the earth in the 1950s were spat out. They were followed by gusts of tepid air. The temperature in the car began to rise perceptibly, the engine not having cooled down much during my stop. I drove on in unwonted comfort, congratulating myself warmly.

Fulham 5 Oldham 0
Craven Cottage, 4 December 1976

Gillingham

At first sight Gillingham looked so unprepossessing that I turned round and caught the train back to Rochester, to spend half a day there instead. Not for the first time in this so-called tour of the homes of 92 league clubs, I can scarcely claim to have visited Gillingham at all.

Rochester, on the other hand, is a self-consciously endearing place. It makes the most of the heritage it has and, equally, makes up for the deficiency where it hasn't. Romans? Check. Charles Dickens? Check. Olde England? Check.

Was Rochester as pleasant as I recall, or does it owe most of its appeal to the fact that it was not Gillingham? Not having given Gillingham a fair crack of the whip I can't be sure. But in the ward of Rochester Castle the question seemed hardly to matter.

I like a castle that has trees in the grounds. It gives the impression that in times of danger not only would the peasants and their herds be offered shelter, but also the local vegetation. The pigs would continue to have roots to snuffle around and the caterers of the liege lord might find truffles to grace his table.

On the subject of pigs, there is a lovely story from the distant past of this castle. When King John besieged a gaggle of barons holed up there in 1215, he had mines dug underneath the walls and fired them using the fat from 40 pigs. This dramatic assault was not decisive but the garrison eventually surrendered two months later, on the point of starvation. The besiegers, one imagines, had plenty of pork in their diet.

The area around the keep has been a public park since the 19th century. Dickens used the castle ruins in *The Mystery of Edwin Drood* and *The Pickwick Papers*, and his ghost is said to haunt the moat on Christmas Eve. Where it goes the rest of the year must remain a matter for conjecture. Dry-shod, the ghost of a White Lady frequents the ruins at other times.

In fact Dickens grew up in Chatham, not Rochester, and spent his declining years a little further away again in Gads Hill.

But Rochester has no intention of allowing its association with the author to slip its mythical moorings. On the High Street is the garden chalet in which, ahead of his time by over a century, Dickens did his writing. Not far away is the bricks-and-mortar model for Satis House from which Miss Havisham never emerged after her near-marriage experience.

The Cathedral is another bonus. It is very ancient – perhaps the second-oldest cathedral in England – and it costs nothing to enter and look round, although they ask for donations and you may pay to view the manuscripts that apparently pre-date Magna Carta.

In Gillingham itself, you'll find the Royal Engineers Museum, the Strand Leisure Park and the *Medway Queen* paddle steamer, one of the 'small boats' of Dunkirk. Another time, perhaps.

Gillingham 2 Oldham 1
Priestfield Stadium, 9 September 1999

Grimsby Town

Grimsby needs to work on its time-keeping if its to make the most of any tourism potential.

The Town Hall, with its much-vaunted Time Trap Museum to amuse the kids, is closed on Saturday and Sunday. Grimsby Minster, known for its stained glass, two pipe organs and outstanding cakes, is open every day but Saturday. For a while I thought I was going to have to go shopping (look at Abbeygate for chic boutiques) or spend several more hours than I'd planned in a pub.

Happily the Grimsby Fishing Heritage Centre is open on Saturdays throughout the year. Even better, it's very good. The promising impression Grimsby will have made on you since you left the train at Grimsby Town, dissipating in the closed faces of some of your tourist targets, will be restored.

While we're on this subject, Grimsby Town is not the best station for Grimsby Town FC. The football club is technically in neighbouring Cleethorpes and the nearest railway station to its Blundell Park ground is called New Clee. I hope that's clear. If you disembark at Grimsby Town you leave yourself either a bus ride or a brisk 40-minute walk to get to the stadium.

On the plus side, at Grimsby Town you immediately encounter a distinctive Grimsby sight: a kind of parquet pavement in 50 shades of grey stone, roadway and pavement alike, indicating a shared space on which it is as well, despite appearances, to take care. In the sun it's a fine sight, and it also serves to identify the central area: if you walk back to the main railway station from the football ground you'll know when you're getting close.

The Fishing Heritage Centre is a short walk north of the main shopping areas, overlooking an arm of the docks on which board-sailors practice. From a distance, they look like a poster for *The Magnificent Seven* gliding along the water towards you.

Back to the Fishing Heritage Centre. In 2017 it was £6 for adults, £2 for a child and under-fives went free. The ticket also covered a guided tour of the *Ross Tiger*, an old trawler drawn up alongside. The museum guides you through the lives and the processes of trawling and the *Ross Tiger* shows you something of the conditions trawlermen lived in.

The museum begins with a formal museum-style explanation of the history of navigation and exploration; so far, so predictable. But the style of presentation changes abruptly when you are guided through a door on the top floor into what proves to be the first of a series of tableaus – reconstructions of all aspects of life on and around Grimsby docks.

The first is the backyard of a trawlerman's home, with vocal sound-effects; from there you pass to the fish dock and then on to the vessel, as it were, with stage sets representing the radio room and the bridge.

There's a figuratively chilling interlude with a display devoted to apprentices: short of labour, the industry 'recruited' from the workhouses and orphanages of other Midland towns and cities, where the boys had usually never even seen the sea.

The sequence of sets then moves on to a recreation of a fish deck, dark and encrusted in ice, followed with a dramatic change in temperature by the boiler room. Through the galley and the crewmen's quarters, you emerge eventually on to the fish dock of the home port where unloading and payments are explained and demonstrated.

Finally, the story moves on to land, with a 1950s fish and chip shop to indicate where the catch ended up, and a pub of similar era to show the crewmen, off-duty but smartly turned out in suits, collars and ties. By now you are on the ground floor, having circled the interior of the building who knows how many times.

Because the displays are so well done it seems like quibbling to find fault. But why, when you've put so much care into putting such a museum together, would you skimp to save a few quid on decent proof-reading? The information boards are clear and informative, as you would hope, but they are not error-free and whoever produced them didn't know how to coax a proper apostrophe out of his or her computer. That hideous wedge that inferior software inserts is not an acceptable element of typography.

That said, it's a fine and unusual museum and the appeal to people of all ages is clear. There are screens throughout for kids to use, plus other examples of interactivity, plus explanations of quaint old terms like 'shilling'.

The tableaus obviously work well on youthful imaginations. In the recreation of the pub I stood at the bar and made a few notes. Alongside me, mannequins representing a dour barmaid, a standing drinker and two men (one of whom bore a startling resemblance to a young Christopher Walken) at a table populated the bar. Around us, a recording projected memories of the bar (the Freeman Arms) and the circumstances of life in those times, when Freeman Street had 50 pubs and a dozen pawn shops. Into this harmless setting came two small boys running ahead of their parents; when I moved, one of them took fright and ran shrieking back to his mother. "Ey, ma, one of 'em's alive in 'ere!"

If you're tempted, by the way, to look at Freeman Street now – it is on the way to the football ground – don't bother. A long straight road running inland from the docks, Freeman Street looked well past its best. Most of the commercial properties were shuttered and boarded up on a Saturday afternoon. A kiosk that may once have added a touch of Parisian gaiety to a street corner was so heavily fortified that it could as easily have been a Belfast police station during the troubles.

But you mustn't leave the Fishing Heritage Centre just yet. On the first floor, on the way to the beginning of the 'tour', there's a permanent exhibition of ceramics and paintings and a temporary exhibition of photography, called (when I visited) 'Steaming Home'. By Ash Gollings, these were pictures of trawlermen alongside fragments of their memories of the life. The recollections were as striking as the faces and the tattoos, but the most extraordinary aspect was the degree of nostalgia many of these men expressed for what must have been an awful working life.

One in particular, a deckhand called John Bee, waxed lyrical about the Aurora Borealis. "What we saw... nowadays people would pay thousands of pounds to see. Y'know the Northern Lights? We used to get that. A free display all night, while we was gutting. And it just used to warm your heart..." And at last, a true apostrophe.

If you have time, overshoot the football ground, cross the railway line and walk along the front into Cleethorpes. If you want fish and chips, the locals recommend Steel's in Cleethorpes. And at the match itself, try to get a seat high up in the main stand; if the game is dull, you can watch the shipping moving up and down the Humber.

I was at Grimsby the day after England struggled to break down plucky Malta. Grimsby against Crewe was like watching Barcelona by comparison.

Grimsby Town 1 Crewe Alexandra 0
Blundell Park, 2 September 2017

Huddersfield Town

I'd looked forward to seeing Huddersfield for years, after maligning it in a careless outburst of prejudice.

I had organised a New Year break in Rome. My partner, from the New World and uncertain what the Romans had ever done for Arizona, was strangely unenthusiastic. I noticed this and commented on it: "Anyone would think I'd booked us into..." and my mind flicked laboriously through its cellular grey card-index for an example of somewhere unglamourous and non-eternal. The name it came up with was Huddersfield. She knew nothing of Huddersfield either, but then, neither did I.

Is Huddersfield less attractive than Rome? Probably. On the other hand I doubt we'd have had to suffer such a tiny hotel room in Huddersfield. Swings and roundabouts...

It's a fine town, as it happens. And if you arrive by train you'll notice that its railway station is much more impressive than Termini.

You emerge from the station into St George's Square, where the wide-open spaces are almost Arizonan. It feels as though a medieval fair ought to be taking place there; instead, a statue of Harold Wilson is the unflamboyant centrepiece; nearby, on a bench, a local indigent who might have been the cat-lady from *The Simpsons* mutters to herself.

Turning to look back at the station, you'll be startled to find that you've disembarked at a building that closely resembles Buckingham Palace or, (without a dome), the National Gallery. Around you are other notable reminders of the wool trade's Golden Fleece days: in the George Hotel a small museum recalls the formation there of the Rugby League in 1895; the Tite Buildings, once a wool warehouse, have been converted into student accommodation of distinction.

Walking through the town, I found in Market Place a Remembrance Day ceremony reaching its two-minutes silence. All Saturday morning activity ceased and most of the passers-by paused. In the parish church of St Peter a coffee morning was in progress and book sales spilled out on to the pavement. I turned right into Cross Church Street, which gives you a fine view of the tower of St Paul's and, over its shoulder so to speak, the Victoria Tower on the distant Castle Hill.

Alternatively you could leave Market Place by Market Walk, known locally as Wappy Nick. Central Huddersfield has some very colourful street names: the Beast Market is at least explicable if anachronistic, but where Wappy Nick and Primitive Street come from is anyone's guess.

Outside the Library & Art Gallery sit two statues representing Literature and Art. In a basket at their feet are what may be large chess pieces, but outdoor chess is a seasonal game and November is out of season. In the library is the visitor information desk; upstairs is the town's art gallery.

In the gallery you come fairly quickly to some of the stars of the show: Epstein, Moore and Sickert. There is humour through-out. Notes alongside the bust of Einstein by Epstein refer to 'some-what dishevelled charisma'; a letter-writer to the local newspaper proposed that Henry Moore's *Falling Warrior* be renamed *Hud-dersfield Rate-Payer*; and the merits of the Sickert are beyond my competence to evaluate but he must have been one of the most popular artists of his day – around the walls, the number of pieces by people who were 'friends of Sickert' is striking.

And you're never far from Lowry country. The gallery has two and they are displayed in a corner, so that you can admire both by simply swivelling your head. I'm not a fan – it's another aspect of Northern heritage I can't get to grips with, along with tripe, fish-ing and whippets. But Lowry liked Huddersfield. "I used to visit all the industrial towns and stop a couple of nights in each," he said. "Huddersfield in particular I'd go back to." Friedrich Engels was another admirer: "Huddersfield is the handsomest by far of all the factory towns of Yorkshire and Lancashire."

Elsewhere on the walls, dozens of big names are represented. The Bloomsbury Group is prominent (and Roger Fry is damned with the faintest of praise, being "never regarded as the greatest of painters"); there's constructivist art in some variety and carvings in wood, plaster and marble; Einstein crops up again in a large painting by Chris Gollon inspired by Bob Dylan's *Desolation Row*; and in an anti-chamber the work of local artists is promoted.

In a separate gallery across the hall, Amy-Jane Blackhall has the place to herself with her Flourish Award-winning *Everyone is a Moon*. This is a large abacus-styled structure in which the phases of the moon, depicted in hand-made glass spheres, stand in for whatever the spheres on an abacus represent. Notices ask you not to touch – presumably the space-time continuum might be disturbed if a moon goes out of kilter.

The Tolson Museum, about a mile down the main road out of Huddersfield towards Wakefield, offers similar variety and occasional humour. On the day of my visit there was a special event on 'Muslim Roots in the British Army', organised by young people from the Huddersfield Pakistani Community Alliance. On such a day the Tolson Half Pig, a kind of exploded view of a pig, might have been quietly put into a cupboard: but it was there, skeletal on one side and complete on the other, resplendent in its glass case in the tea-room. In another cabinet, a lepidoptery exhibit was shamelessly anachronistic: a circle, almost a chaplet formed by dozens of pinned butterflies (perhaps fritillaries), was surrounded in the manner of a clock-face by mirrored red admirals at the points of the hours.

Upstairs, where the history of Huddersfield is presented, I went the wrong way round and got the impression of rather haphazard arrangement until I realised my error.

Even so, it was highly entertaining. In the distant corner of one room was a Cabinet of Curiosities, which contained among other things the collections of flints and shoe buckles of a Mr Frances Buckley. His drawings of where the flints were found were so meticulous that the War Office employed him to depict battlefield positions in World War I. No explanation for the buckles was offered, beyond the coincidence of his surname.

On a nearby wall was Huddersfield's star fossil, an ancient shark-like fish with implausible dentition. The *Edestus newtoni*'s lower jaw accommodated something like a circular saw, if the scientists are to be believed. Did it prey on telegraph poles? What happened when it bit its tongue?

Huddersfield's industrial past was celebrated in occasionally gory detail. The section on the cloth trade noted that some Luddites were hanged and dissected. The role of stale urine in the scouring of cloth was hard to ignore. The fancy trade, in which colours and patterns were woven or knitted into cloth, seemed an uncharacteristically frivolous activity for a Yorkshire town. And the origin of the word 'spinster' – an unmarried daughter put to work spinning to earn her keep – was an etymological bonus. Throughout, in this section, there were plenty of machines, models and mannequins to admire.

Downstairs the Tolson has another speciality – a transport museum. One of the outstanding names here is David Brown, perhaps best known now for tractors but at one time the DB in the Aston Martin DB series cars.

I walked down to the John Smith's Stadium from the Tolson, taking the woodland path known as Kilner Bank. Alternatively you might go further in towards the town centre and follow either the line of the Huddersfield Broad Canal or the River Colne. Either way, it's a pleasant approach to a fine stadium.

> **Huddersfield Town 1 West Bromwich Albion 0**
> *John Smith's Stadium, 4 November 2017*

Hull City

If you missed your chance to go to the European City of Culture 2017, don't worry: you can make the journey to Hull and back at any time.

Some of the special events will have moved on, but the city and most of its people will still be there. The railway station will still be called Hull Paragon. Hull will still be the home of the boiled sweet. And its public conveniences will still look as if the Tsar is expected at any moment.

Hull has a self-confidence that is easy to like. The woman who engaged me in conversation over dinner on the Saturday evening wasn't inclined to be self-deprecating. She was interested in economic matters and held firm views, which she wasn't slow to express. It grieved her to be staying at a hotel on a Friday but she had the builders in and couldn't abide the dust. She looked in at home at intervals during the day, not to make them a cup of team but to keep them on their toes with random spot-checks.

Thin-faced and florid as though from the cold wind sweeping off the North Sea, she pecked vigorously at a plate of chili con carne and sipped a small glass of cider. It was not a meal she took seriously. Learning that I had ordered the full English breakfast for the following morning she was almost scornful. "I get a lovely breakfast at' train station for £4.95, wi' a mug o' tea," she declared. "That does me all day." In the event she was right; it was not so much that the Campanile's breakfast was in any way inadequate, but that you would have paid £8.75 not to have to listen to the radio station it regaled its guests with on a Saturday morning.

At dinner, a television shuffled images silently in a corner. "Can we 'ave't rugby league on?" my fellow diner enquired of the waitress. "It'd be better than this rubbish." The waitress ignored her and we finished our meals as we started them, to the accompaniment of what may have been *Now That's What I Call Music #273*.

I was dining early in order to be at the Hull Truck Theatre in good time for the 7.30pm start of *Richard III*. It would be unfair to include Shakespeare among the things that made me laugh in Hull. He was not a northerner and, according to the programme, he went out of his way to make disobliging remarks about them. The examples quoted there were unconvincing... But that's *Richard III*, isn't it? Shakespeare's determination to blacken the name of the Tudors' arch-enemy turns Richard into one of his least convincing leading men.

What's left is the humour, reinforced by the company's presentation of the Bard with a northern voice. That worked particularly well in short bursts: for example, Richard on learning that Richmond means to claim the crown, demands: "Is't chair empty?"

The Northern Broadsides company's other quirks were equally effective. Drumming was a constant background feature until the eve of the Battle of Bosworth, when it moved centre-stage and where the actor playing Richard (Mat Fraser) revealed himself as an outstanding drummer. Fraser, by the way, has thalidomide-induced Phocomelia. Richard is often represented as a hunchback – not here.

As the battle loomed, the rear walls of the theatre slid apart to reveal enough extras to suggest armies, in billowing dry ice, and with a bracing chill of night air. It made for a thrilling climax.

Had it been daylight, the delivery bay of the neighbouring St Stephen's shopping mall would have been revealed. Shopping seems to be one of Hull's several peculiarities. The main shopping streets are quite dull and contain a high proportion of boarded-up properties. Behind them a maze of service roads, car-park accesses and simple cobbled lanes can send you round in circles. But at intervals throughout the city there are lavish malls like St Stephens, and elegant if somewhat tired old-fashioned arcades.

The contrast between the grand public buildings and the shabby post-war space-fillers is equally marked, and echoed again in the juxtaposition of elegant parks and weed-ridden ancient wasteland.

The public buildings include some of the most interesting public conveniences you'll ever have seen, but don't depend on them all to be open. The ones at the base of King William III's gilded equestrian statue look as though the botanical gardens have a branch office there.

It's an odd city. The shops confirm this. You'll find curious speciality shops, catering for the fans of fantasy fiction, conjuring, fancy dress, but I didn't pass many generic charity shops and the only second-hand books I saw were in the Hull People's Memorial Exhibition Centre, where exhibits of Hull at War help to raise funds for veterans' charities.

The streets also have an unfinished air. Hull is full of orange plastic barriers to keep people away from incomplete renovations. You might easily walk past the Beverley Gate site, mistaking it for roadworks, where one of the original gates to Edward I's King's Town upon Hull has been found.

None of this, be it noted, depends on Hull being a European City of Culture. You could go there any time and enjoy all this and more. Much more, as it turns out: the Museum Quarter, the waterfront, the Ferens Gallery and, projecting out on to the River Humber like an unexploded cod, the Deep, a remarkable collection of aquatic environments.

The City of Culture made a difference, of course. The cascade of poppies known as the Weeping Window, from the installation at the Tower of London in 2014, was at the Maritime Museum for the spring of 2017. The railway station (Paragon is perhaps the second-best railway station name in the world after Auckland Britomart), probably doesn't always look so colourful, with its market, its WWI soldiers and its replica of Amy Johnson's aeroplane.

The Ferens Gallery offered the first look at the results of Spencer Tunick's 2016 'Sea of Hull' project, in which thousands of people stripped off, were painted blue as if in woad and allowed themselves to be photographed en masse in Hull and environs.

Also at the Ferens for that summer, Ron Mueck's extraordinary sculptures were a rare attraction. These were human figures of an extraordinarily lifelike quality. People gasped as they entered the first room, overlooked by a giant figure of a young girl leaning against the wall and confronted by what looked like the mask of a sleeping man on an even greater scale. But not all the exhibits were out-size. The figures on a much smaller scale, as for example a naked couple sleeping in the spoons position, were if anything more disturbing because they looked plausibly like pets and you half expected to see them breathe or twitch.

The Ferens is free and has some surprising items to show. A Rembrandt, for example, recalls the story that Rembrandt spent some time in Hull, supposedly fleeing bailiffs after he went bankrupt in 1661. There's also a sketch by him and another large canvas by Franz Hals. I could go on, and am seriously tempted to: don't miss the Bridget Riley, in which the geometric shapes eventually make the frame seem like a rhombus; or the Lucien Freuds, part (with Mueck and Tunick) of a show called, simply, 'Skin'; or the Francis Bacon. But perhaps the Ferens' greatest treat is the pile of longshore-drifted beach-combed detritus that will be the first thing you see as you come in from the street.

One specific 2017 attraction was Fountain17 on Humber Street, across the A63 from the city centre but definitely worth attempting the crossing. Fountain17 was inspired by a coincidence of anniversaries: the centenary of Marcel Duchamp's Fountain, a men's urinal rotated through 90° to suggest a drinking fountain, and the 200th of Armitage Shanks. The locals knew it as The Toilet Gallery.

The exhibition was not large but it was colourful and provocative. Exhibits fell into three broad categories: urinals in their usual aspect, decorated to a high degree; sanitary ware rotated to suggest something else, plus being highly decorated; and others, which category included models, diagrams, images and, throughout, abstractions. My favourite was a digitally altered version of a famous photograph: a conventionally-dressed Duchamp playing chess with a prodigiously voluptuous naked woman, and a phantasmogoric Hull skyline replacing the bland interior of the original. The programme notes concluded: "The composite is an ironic take on the arts commissioning process, celebrity 'cultcha' and shameless borrowing."

I was told that Fountain17 may tour after 2017, presumably under a different name. Alternatively the exhibits may be sold off for charity – the exhibition in Hull was free to visit, but proceeds from the sale of the £5 programme supported a bowel cancer charity.

I lacked the time to do justice to the Museum Quarter. At least four institutions are signposted in what is actually more of a Museums Quadrangle, and I managed brisk (ie under an hour) tours of only two. If the lighting were better the Streetlife Museum might be said to highlight transport and retailing in Hull. It does a good job of relating progress in various sectors to life in Hull – the Bicycles Gallery is particularly comprehensive – and 21st century technology is applied to enhance your visit. You can take a carriage ride, for example, or use video games to recreate aspects of the streetlife of the past.

Darkness falls early in the Hull & East Riding Museum too. I got no further than the Iron Age and cannot therefore comment on such later episodes as the Enlightenment, but the early galleries represent times when fire had only recently been stolen from the gods, and men were sparing with it. Perhaps the use of high levels of artificial light would have been inappropriate. Certainly I left with a very positive impression, without even have got as far as the Dark Ages.

The Wilberforce Museum, honouring the Hull MP William Wilberforce, remained unexplored as did the *Arctic Corsair*'s role in the Cod Wars. The point about Hull's global reach was made, however.

It was reinforced in the Maritime Museum. Anyone who appreciates fine modelling will love the Maritime Museum: scale models of ships punctuate all the galleries and many of them are exquisite. The basic division within the museum is between Hull and its Fishing Fleet and Hull and Whaling. You will increase your vocabulary in either.

The penultimate stop on my tour of the European City of Culture was Holy Trinity Church, not a cathedral – the city has none – but the largest parish church in England. Just inside the north transept's door I was greeted by a lady seated beside a poster and a table on which publicity material lay.

"Are you here for the exhibition?" she asked.

"No, I'm here for the largest parish church in Christendom," I replied. "The exhibition will be a bonus."

She looked very doubtful, but not at my assessment of the appeal of the exhibition, as it transpired. No, the whole of the church to my right was cordoned and curtained off and sounds of work came from the other side. In what remained – about half the ground area of the record-breaking building – one quarter was available for worship and a third was occupied by the café and gift stands.

I headed for the chancel and sat for a moment. Robert 'Mousey' Thompson, the furniture maker who carved a mouse into all his work, was a Yorkshireman and released seven mice in Holy Trinity. Unable to see one from where I sat, I was too discouraged to search the accessible parts of the church. Instead, almost automatically, I turned to look at Shirley Goodsell's paintings of Hull.

This was one of the redeeming features of the City of Culture: what renovation took away with the one hand, community gave back with the other. Wandering around the back of the altar, past where the lectern was stored (did you know that lecterns are often in the form of eagles because eagles are said to be able to look into the sun, and the Bible enables Christians to look directly at the word of God?) I found myself in the café. The soup of the day was minestrone, and not bad.

Back through St Stephens, out along Londesborough Street and across the triangle of rough ground left within an intersection of railways, the walkway led me finally to the KCom Stadium, home of Hull City Tigers. The Tigers needed a win to help them stay in the Premier League; Sunderland were condemned by a defeat a week earlier to relegation to the Championship.

I already had a ticket. I'd parked near the stadium early in the day and walked back into the city to look round, but not before buying a ticket. My first effort was thwarted when I found myself in the Hull Rugby League club's shop by mistake. Next door, at the right counter, the young man said he would gladly sell me a ticket but it would cost £5 less from the machine in yet another room. I duly tackled the machine (or, at least, one of the two of four that were working). Eventually it yielded a flimsy scrap of printed paper which looked no more impressive than a receipt for a coffee in Starbucks. The man at the next machine had reached a similar stage in the transaction. "Is that it?" he asked me, incredulous.

"Yes," I said, "I think it must be. The machine has finished its cycle, anyway, and I expect that barcode is the critical thing."

He looked unconvinced. "No wonder nobody comes," he said.

A tense, difficult game for the home side ended badly, and there were scuffles on the way back to the Walton Street car-park. Sunderland fans may have been involved. Towards the end of the game they had been chanting: "Two-nil, to the Championship." Their humour will be tested if they go down again and find themselves playing at Oldham.

Hull City 0 Sunderland 2
KCom Stadium, 7 May 2017

Ipswich Town

Most of my virtues are negative: I don't drink to excess, I'm no spendthrift, I'm respectful to the point of timidity around women. I think of Ipswich in a similar light. It has never done me any harm and, looking back, I feel a tepid facsimile of affection for it.

The first lack of impact Ipswich made on my life was in my earliest postgraduate days, when I was penniless in Colchester and looking for work. I attended a job interview with a magazine in Ipswich. The magazine was something to do with farming and the job concerned the drumming up of advertising business. I didn't make a success of the interview.

In retrospect that was a blessing. Had I become a successful ad salesman on a farming title, how different my life would have been, how different the people with whom I would have come into contact.

Without dramatic retraining I would not have met L at work and subsequently married her. The supine role of Ipswich in my affairs made little impact on her at first, but in 1991 we spent two happy hours there.

Towards the end of April in 1991, Oldham Athletic were handily placed in what was then known as the Barclays League Division Two – now the Championship, the second tier of English football. Oldham were second in the table with four games left to play. They were 11 points ahead of the team in third place, and another point would guarantee them promotion to the top flight.

The last time Oldham had played at that level, Bonar Law was Prime Minister and his Cabinet included a Secretary of State for the Colonies. As the Ipswich manager John Lyall said in his programme notes on the day Oldham came to Portman Road, "they are now on the threshold of a long, long awaited return to the First Division".

Lyall went on to welcome "everyone from Oldham here tonight". There was no reason to doubt his sincerity or the warmth of the welcome he extended, but 'tonight' was an odd touch – this was a 3pm kick-off and barring the Apocalypse darkness would not fall until after 8pm.

The time of the kick-off fitted conveniently with a morning departure from north London for a proposed walking weekend in East Anglia. As the route inevitably passed through Ipswich, it would have been perverse not to break the journey for 90 minutes or so, for lunch, say.

In fact L saw through the ruse as soon as we passed our first Ipswich pub. It was a bright, sunny day and the drinkers had overflowed on to the pavement. Although they were wearing blue shirts and might have been home supporters, the sponsor's name (Bovis) revealed them to be from Oldham, a fact I couldn't help but comment on.

We stopped for a light lunch and made our way to Portman Road. Out of belated consideration for L, I bought us seats in a family enclosure: Block D, Row J, Seats 30 and 31, £8.50 each. The seats were at the right end of the ground for a perfect view of Oldham's Ian Marshall scoring the winning goal. The family enclosure was exactly the right place to share the excitement of young fans watching their team win promotion to the top flight of English football for the first time in living memory. One of us would not have missed it for the world, and the other was able to use it as leverage for many a week to come.

Ipswich left its benign impassivity over our mood for the rest of the weekend. For months, in fact for years, I was able to accept adversity on any scale with greater philosophy than before. Faced with some setback or difficulty, I would reflect: "Still, Latics are in the First Division." It started that weekend and was immediately helpful.

We drove from Ipswich along the A12 to a village called Walberswick, had a truly fine dinner and spent a celebratory night in a pub/hotel there. On the following day we set out for the walk the weekend had initially promised.

Suffolk is a county of flat fields and drainage ditches. We found ourselves at one point on the wrong side of such a ditch; the going was not easy on the ploughed field on our side, while on the other side of the ditch there was a clear path on flat, short, well-trodden grass.

The ditch looked jumpable. It was shallow – the surface of the water was perhaps two feet below the level of the field – and not especially broad. The run-up, across chunky clods of earth, was tricky but the landing area looked flat and welcoming.

Taking care to keep the cigarettes and matches out of harm's way – we were both smokers in those days – I went first and cleared the hazard with feet to spare. L followed; but her approach lacked confidence. Her jump was more vertical than horizontal and she came down in the middle of the ditch. I hauled her out to the accompaniment of some plain language. Her feet were soaked, as were her shorts to mid-thigh level, and frantic splashing left its mark elsewhere.

Fortunately I didn't actually say: "Still, Latics are in the First Division." Instead we lit cigarettes, calmed ourselves and devised a plan to enable us to continue the walk.

As on the previous day, the weather was bright and warm. L took off her trainers, socks and shorts and wrapped my jacket around her waist, tied with the arms. Barefoot, she walked on and I followed at a safe distance, whirling items of clothing around my head to speed the drying process.

The shorts were almost wearable by the time we reached the margins of the field. The trainers took longer, but they too dried out propped in the sun in a pub beer garden. Of course she looked like a bag-lady on vacation, but she wasn't to know that. And I can still see her dropping into the ditch, as though in slow-motion, in exactly the way that the ball dropped in the Ipswich penalty area and Ian Marshall was first to it.

Ipswich Town 1 Oldham 2
Portman Road, 27 April 1991

Leeds United

I had arranged to meet a friend at the Billy Bremner statue outside Elland Road at 2pm. Because I was late there was no opportunity to examine the statue then; but after the match I took a proper look at it.

And like the player himself, it surely is a piece of work. It depicts the combative midfielder with arms aloft, acclaiming the crowd. Originally in bronze, his kit has subsequently been painted the white of Leeds United. This ill-advised improvement makes it look as though the Leeds legend has blacked-up. The oddly gilded dreadlocked hair doesn't help. All things considered, it is one of the strangest statues you'll find outside a football ground. Unlike Michael Jackson, now removed from Fulham, it is at least a statue of a footballer.

Further along the concourse in front of the East Stand is a statue of Don Revie. This too is odd but in a Madame Tussauds kind of way. At the level of the upper body it seems life-size; from the chest down it is exaggerated in the vertical plane, as though Don is on short stilts that make him 8ft tall. Nor does it look much like him, but a shortfall in the facial resemblance department is the least of Leeds United's problems where statues are concerned.

The reason I was late, I should say, is that the 52 bus from Vicar Lane in the city centre comes no closer to the ground on a match day than the better part of a mile away. It would have been as quick to walk but the weather was capricious: bright sunlight one minute, snow the next, all accompanied by a brisk northerly wind. Also, Elland Road and some of the city's southern suburbs are amputated from Leeds city centre by the M621 motorway, which might easily discourage a pedestrian unfamiliar with the area.

It was a complicated visit. My first destination was a student hall of residence off Headingley Lane, to take a niece to lunch. This turned into a morning coffee and a late veggie breakfast at the Original Oak, before she made her excuses and left to take lunch with company her own age. I drove back through the city, parked near the football ground and caught a bus back in to see the sights.

It was quickly clear that Leeds has much more to offer than I had allowed time for. So I strolled around the centre, where there was plenty going on.

Outside the Town Hall a political rally was just breaking up. There were local elections in the UK in May 2016; in some places the traditional May Day rally was held on 30 April; but the leaflet pressed upon me by an earnest outrider urged me to vote Remain in the UK/EU referendum scheduled for June.

Meanwhile down a pedestrianised offshoot of the Headrow (an odd name for a main street, suggestive again of an exotic hairstyle probably involving beads) a music festival was in its early stages. It crossed my mind that this might have been where my niece was headed, so I resisted the temptation to go and have a look.

Instead I wandered more or less at random through Leeds city centre. On the Headrow itself is Leeds Art Gallery, closed until the end of 2017 for repairs to the roof. If I wanted to see the gems of Leeds' collection – Bacon, Spencer, Canova and others – I was in the wrong place anyway, because they were all on loan elsewhere at the time. The Henry Moore Institute, more or less adjacent, was open, and there are also pieces of sculpture and art around the city. Yorkshire Sculpture Park is not far away near Wakefield.

If you walk down toward the station, Leeds' statuary redeems itself on City Square with a particularly impressive Joseph Priestley. This pioneer is best remembered as the discoverer of oxygen or, as he knew it, 'dephlogisticated air'. Priestley was also a theologian who helped found Unitarianism in England; his ministry was at Leeds' Mill Hill Chapel.

The university area has a number of galleries. If Leeds' past as the focal point of the wool industry interests you, the Ulita Archive of International Textiles is the place to go. The Stanley & Audrey Burton Gallery, in the university's Parkinson Building, displays pieces from the university's own collection and puts on regular temporary exhibitions. There's also a gallery at Leeds College of Art, whose former students include Moore, Damien Hirst and Barbara Hepworth.

What else did I miss? The Royal Armories, most obviously, and the Leeds City Museum. The locals also speak highly of the shopping, especially the Victoria Quarter arcades. Kirkgate Market is where Marks & Spencer started. And if you're there early in the season, the unmistakable Corn Exchange hosts the Leeds Rum Festival in late September.

Lonely Planet named Leeds among its Top 10 European Destinations in summer 2017. It is surely worth a second, longer visit. Whether its football team need detain you a second time is an open question.

When I was there they lost ineptly to a team already relegated. It rather took the gloss off my friend's pleasure in showing me Elland Road. It's easier and more generous to remember the Leeds United of my youth, when they were briefly (spring 1972) the best team in the world. Now, sadly, they aren't even the best team in Yorkshire.

Leeds United 1 Charlton Athletic 2
Elland Road, 30 April 2016

Leicester City

Leicester illustrates a depressing truth about the shallowness of the modern era. The past becomes foreshortened. When 15 minutes of fame are achieved, centuries of modest accomplishment can be discarded. Leicester, you might say, is a dipstick in the sump of the celebrity culture.

The city colludes in this forgetfulness. Its very name is self-effacing. The 'cester' suffix indicates strong Roman credentials and some towns would have milked that down the centuries. Not Leicester. Even the pronunciation of its name conceals the Latin element (except among puzzled Americans: 'Lie-Sestuh'). The 'c' is silent and any echo of marching legions shuffles into the nearest fosse.

It could have been worse: in the neighbouring county of Northamptonshire, athwart Roman Watling Street, there's a town that sounds as if it's called Toaster. Perhaps that's where Pop-up Heritage belongs, but it applies to Leicester too. From the layers of cultural accretion going back beyond the Roman invasion, the first things about Leicester that will pop into most of our heads date from this side of August 2012.

That was when the bones of the infamous Richard III were famously discovered in the car-park of a social services office. Social services! After the Princes in the Tower episode, Richard of York was hardly a man to be left alone anywhere near a Child Protection department. The discovery and the circumstances of it were startling, but the commonplace nature of the site added a touch of pathos.

Together they put the city on the map (literally, as new editions of the Leicester town plan provided directions to the Richard III Visitor Centre). But just three short years later, an even more exotic feather sprouted in the city's cap: its football team won the Premier League title.

Hitherto the exclusive preserve of English football's Big Four (the composition of which changes periodically but which never in a million years would have been expected to include Leicester City) this astonishing achievement gained Leicester global fame and affection.

Dwarfed by those events, distinctions for which Leicester might otherwise be known have shrunk and receded even further into the distance. Some may be no great loss: could the founder of the city really have been the original of King Lear?

But others provide context. As recently as the 1950s Leicester was a byword for prosperity and inclusivity. A world-leading centre of production of first hosiery, then footwear, knitwear and accompanying engineering, Leicester's booming industries employed large proportions of women, and family incomes were correspondingly high. The city's unemployment figures in 1946, in a population of 263,000, showed no women at all registered as unemployed and just 100 men.

More recently, Leicester has become possibly Britain's most lively, ethnically-diverse city. It's a former winner and regular pace-setter in the Curry Capital of Britain competition. Its two-week Diwali festival and Belgrave Mela are arguably the largest in the UK. The indoor market, once the largest in Europe, could still lay claim to being the most colourful.

Leicester's other distinctions are more particular. It is home to the National Space Centre, for example. Why Leicester? Woomera, South Australia, where Britain's first independent entrant in the Space Race underwent trials, might be a more logical choice. But it's easier for most of the nation to get here than to Woomera. Also, according to *Australian Geographic* magazine, Woomera makes $1/8$th of South Australia a No-Go Zone: "A place of secret military testing, nuclear explosions and a heck of a lot of sheep."

Originally the Blue Streak rocket tested at Woomera was intended as a ballistic missile. But Britain's scientists in the 1950s and 60s were less skilled than North Korea's are now, and the rocket was pensioned off to a non-military project called the European Launcher Development Organisation. Blue Streak proved unsuitable in that role too. British children in the 1960s thought of Woomera as an elaborate fireworks display.

The real reason for the National Space Centre being in Leicester has more to do with the University of Leicester running a particularly energetic Space Research Centre. Touchingly, it has a surviving Blue Streak: there's also a Soyuz spacecraft from the Russian space programme, a Thor rocket from the US nuclear arsenal, control centres for real operations, a planetarium and, in the Rocket Tower, one of the country's most distinctive buildings.

The New Walk Museum & Gallery, by contrast, has dinosaurs and mummies. What more could you ask for? An earthquake simulation? Yes, that too. And in the gallery, Picasso ceramics and German Expressionists among many others. New Walk itself is an attractive path leading out of the city centre towards the railway station.

In 2013, when I went, the city and its football club were still in the second division. The resting place of Crookback Dick was disputed between Leicester and York, and Claudio Ranieri was just another of the victims of Chelsea's hunger for the Champions League trophy. He too was known mainly for his nickname: the Tinkerman.

If you park in the area known as West End, you're not far from the football ground and your walk towards the city puts the River Soar on your right. Bede Park and Castle Gardens make up for the built environment in this part of Leicester, and the bridges that take the carriageways of the A47 into the city are startlingly attractive.

At the base of the eastbound carriageway is Richard III Road, and a plaque on the bridge notes that this Victorian structure replaces an earlier bridge over which Richard III crossed with his army on the way to Bosworth in 1458. There, as physics students who made only the most basic progress with the visible light spectrum will recall, he Gave Battle In Vain. A second plaque relates the legend that on the return journey, his lifeless body by now slung over the horse, Richard's head was "dashed and broken" by contact with a stone his spur had dislodged earlier.

The Victorians decorated the bridge with white and red roses, like the ferryman in *The Outlaw Josey Wales*, who adapts his patriotic singing to suit his customers – *Dixie* or *The Battle Hymn of the Republic.*

On the east bank a large stone records the tradition that the defeated king's body was thrown into the Soar. "Near this spot," it suggests hesitantly, "lie the remains of Richard III, the last of the Plantagenets 1485". The bridge, known as Bow Bridge, is now part of the official Richard III Trail.

There are many historic buildings and sites within a stones' throw: Leicester Castle (little more than a mound), the Prince Rupert Gate, High Cross and Guildhall, and the Jewry Wall Museum.

Haunting Prince Rupert's Gateway is the legend of Black Agnes, the 'black' describing her deeds and not her face, which was blue. What shade of blue? The legend is silent on this detail, but if her face were the electric blue of a mandril's, what colour might Black Agnes' backside have been? There could have been a dash of bright red: she had iron claws and a preference for the flesh of children, whose pelts she would hang around her no doubt expansive waist. Black Agnes skulked in the shadows of the Prince Rupert Gate after dark.

The Jewry Wall itself is authentic Roman brickwork, part of a bath house originally. It overlooks a grassed area where the foundations of other walls run, and opposite stands the Jewry Wall Museum. This is another aspect of Leicester's heritage that is seriously overshadowed by recent events. Without Richard III and Claudio, it would be a much better-known jewel in the city's crown: the Roman frescos, medieval stained-glass panels, a 1st century sculpture and other Roman treasures bely the undistinguished accommodation, which might be mistaken for a 1960s polytechnic.

That's another characteristic of Leicester: it has some marvellous buildings and fragments, and almost all are compromised by calamitous neighbours. The Haymarket Memorial Clocktower is a case in point. Adorning the hub of the city's shopping streets, its Victorian Gothic stone carvings celebrate four of the city's most historically prominent citizens, notably the medieval cryptodemocrat Simon de Montfort. Behind it, in three decks of battleship grey and glass, is a building surmounted by a parapet of what look to be gigantic trifle fingers.

As for the famous car-park, that is suitably understated. But the Cathedral not far away is splendid. In 2013, the late king was commemorated only by a plaque in the floor recording his burial in the Church of the Grey Friars. The monument has been updated since then, as has Leicester's entire image.

Leicester City 2 Huddersfield Town 1
King Power Stadium, 19 October 2013

Lincoln City

It's not quite the Aurora Borealis, but something magical happens in Lincoln Cathedral on a bright, sharp December afternoon.

The low winter sun streams in through the windows of the south transept and projects stained-glass colours on to the opposite wall of the nave. Grey masonry becomes lilac, pink, and cowslip yellow. Austere waves of moulding acquire crisply contrasting lines and deep shadows. Illuminated like a manuscript, the recesses along the north wall take on the gentle aqua tints that children's colouring books – 'Just add water' – used to have. The dramatic wooden stations of the cross, the *Forest Stations* by William Fairbank, glow and shimmer in fields of gold.

This will happen on any sunny afternoon between November and February, I suppose. But I was in Lincoln for just half a day and perhaps once only. It was as if the Northern Lights had drifted south and put on a show, just for my benefit.

The Cathedral itself was quiet. Fantasising over the light, I went through what I could remember of the Amazing Blondel's 1971 album *Fantasia Lindum* in my head. Lindum was the Roman name of Lincoln. The Amazing Blondel performed in an era before videos, when coloured lights were the most elaborate embellishment you could expect at a concert.

If the sun isn't shining Lincoln Cathedral still has plenty to offer: so many different styles, of worship as much as of architecture. From Romanesque to modern, not many intervening periods are overlooked. Over the left-hand door of the Norman west front of the Cathedral there's some early-Church weirdness: writhing carved figures warn those of us found wanting on the Day of Judgement what we can expect.

The Cathedral's monuments include the shrine of St Hugh and the tombs of Eleanor of Castile, wife of Edward I, and Katherine Swynford, third wife of John of Gaunt. In the Treasury you'll find treasures going back to the early Christian era and, if your timing is good, a lovely volunteer whose knowledge of the extent of the See of Lincoln is humbling. There's a display of William Morris stained glass and an imposing statue of the Virgin Mary.

You could easily spend quite a lot of time in Lincoln Cathedral. You could equally easily spend quite a lot of money. It was £6.40 to get in, late in 2017, and collecting boxes for the Repair Fund, the Music Fund, the Fabric Fund and the Flower Fund punctuate your circuit of the building. Then, of course, there's the shop.

Around the corner you might spend a further £6.10 on the medieval Bishops Palace, which is said to be valued by National Trust members for its peace. Perhaps the price puts people off. French autoroutes used to be quiet for the same reason.

Through the market and across the way is Lincoln Castle, where tickets to the three attractions – Wall Walk, Victorian Prison and Magna Carta Gallery – are £13.40. The Magna Carta not being on display, I confined myself to the Wall Walk for £6. The full circumference is about a third of a mile, with comprehensive information boards along the way telling of battles, a siege, public executions and burials and the general bloody history of the city. Mostly, though, the walk is for the views: eastward to the Cathedral, south over the city and, no less dramatic, westward to Cottam power station.

Being free, the Museum of Lincolnshire Life is undeniably good value. Laid out around a central courtyard with a children's play area, it's a series of galleries (stables?) in which cameos of life are presented. The right-hand side is domestic, mainly, and the left commercial. At the top are larger spaces for transport, industry and agriculture, dominated by machinery and vehicles.

Some of the highlights are military. The Royal Lincolnshire Regimental Galleries have a particularly effective recreation of trench warfare. And not far away you'll find a World War I tank.

The Lincoln engineering firm of William Foster & Co was responsible for the first military tanks. Their prototype, called Little Willie, went from design to trials in just 45 days; its successor, Big Willie, took 141 days and changed the nature of warfare. They first went into action at the Battle of the Somme in September 1916.

The tank on display is appropriately mud-coloured and is

called Daphne. Its armaments mark it out as a 'female' tank. As for the name, a tag relates that from July 1917 tanks were named according to their battalion letter. Not all sounded as friendly as Daphne: A was for Aggressive, B for Bellicose and G for Germicide, for example. But Daphne, understandably dirty and decayed and generally difficult to recognise when found in a breaker's yard, was originally thought to be an F for Flirt.

These vehicles and their fearsome successors came to be called 'tanks' by accident. When HG Wells wrote about tanks in 1903, neither the word nor the military vehicle existed and Wells called them 'land iron-clads'. Thirteen years on, in Lincoln, the early machines were referred to obliquely to keep their purpose a secret. The Lincoln prototypes were called 'water carriers' and were supposedly destined for service in Mesopotamia; workers referred to them as 'water tanks' and, later, simply 'tanks'.

The rest of the Museum of Lincolnshire Life (identified on some signposts as 'Moll' – don't be misled) provides a solid supporting cast for Daphne, a genuine star. Even the small upstairs section, which feels like something of an afterthought, is worth a few minutes of your time. The Gatehouse Gallery was empty on the day I visited, and the display entitled 'Village Green' seemed half-hearted. But the Victorian schoolroom was good and a room devoted to nonconformism in Lincoln, especially John Wesley's brand, was informative. Apparently Wesley commented in 1761: "I find the work of God increases on every side; but particularly in Lincolnshire." Wesley was born about 25 miles north of Lincoln.

And the Hossack Collection was extraordinary. Ron Hossack seems to have been a man of infinite curiosity who never threw anything away. His collection, donated to the county, includes jet jewellery, a midget Bible and a stuffed lizard among many other truly odd things.

On a warmer day in Lincoln, you might head for the Brayford Pool area in the lower part of town, or Lincoln Arboretum, a short distance east of the city centre. If you were looking for art there are galleries at the magnificent Usher Gallery (part of the Collection Museum, which also houses archaeology), St Martins and Harding

House. Or you might just wander around, enjoying the feel of the place.

The football club left me with mixed feelings. The people I spoke to could not have been more pleasant. On the other hand, it was the most one-eyed, aggressive and annoying crowd I've sat in for a long time.

When a Lincoln player went down under a challenge, the cry of "Off, off, off!" arose automatically from the stands, directed at the Accrington tackler; when an Accrington player went down, it was "Cheat, cheat, cheat!" That was above the almost continuous monotone thudding of a drum and, at home-team corners, an air-raid siren – this is Bomber County, after all.

Lincoln City 2 Accrington Stanley 0
Sincil Bank, 16 December 2017

Liverpool

For my visit to Anfield I assumed a disguise. To spare the feelings of the people sitting near me I passed myself off as a Watford fan. Fortunately, they knew even less about Watford than I did and the deception was a success.

It was necessary for convoluted reasons. As on my previous attempt to watch Oldham play an FA Cup tie at Liverpool (see Everton, above) my preparations were half-baked. Where two years earlier I had equipped myself with a rail ticket for the wrong day, on this occasion I had no match ticket at all. I therefore ignored the many attractions available on Liverpool's redeveloped waterfront and its character-rich city centre and headed straight for the football ground to see whether I would be able to get in.

My oversight was a calculated gamble. This was the third time in four years Liverpool had drawn Oldham Athletic in an early round of the FA Cup. Although the visiting supporters' allocation was snapped up within hours of tickets going on sale, I reasoned that the home fans might be a tad jaded with low-level third tier opposition. I envisaged Anfield half-empty, echoing to the strains of *Jingle Bells*: "Oh what fun it is to see Athletic win away..."

As the day approached my confidence in this unlikely scenario began to ebb. Taking into account the legendary loyalty and fanaticism of the Liverpool support, plus the initiative of Everton two years earlier (when the appeal of low-grade opposition was enhanced by a mightily attractive reduction in the ticket price), I reflected that entry into Liverpool's third cathedral might not be the straightforward matter I had expected.

From Lime Street, then, I headed for the bus stop and hence to Anfield. It was a grey, damp morning, approaching midday. Although kick-off was still three hours distant a good number of people were milling in the stadium precincts. Some, I discovered when I found myself in the wrong queue at the ticket office, were there to collect tickets for future home games. No-one was there to buy a ticket for that afternoon's home game for none was left. There had been a run on Oldham Athletic tickets. The cupboard was bare. The lure of the Latics was irresistible to Liverpudlians.

I stood on Walton Breck Road and considered my options. Behind me, one of the great theatres of world football loomed, inaccessible. Across the road a pub called the Park was already thronging with supporters enjoying the magic of the Cup. Along the road trundled buses that would take me back, bereft, to the railway station.

On an impulse I found a steward and explained to him my dilemma, though not in its entirety. It seemed unnecessary to identify myself as a supporter of Oldham Athletic. Instead I invented a business appointment in the city the following day (the cup-tie took place on a Sunday) and an urge to see a football match at Anfield to make the most of the visit to Liverpool. The steward told me that seats would become available from time to time, usually through season-ticket holders not able to use them. He told me to return at 1.30pm to see if he'd found anything for me.

That gave me about 90 minutes to kill, coincidentally the length of a football match. In most towns a pub would be the answer. But the Park looked unappetising and in any case this was Anfield. It would have a museum.

As indeed it did, and the museum was doing brisk business among the younger supporters. If JK Rowling is to be congratulated on persuading a generation to read books, perhaps the likes of Liverpool FC can take credit for encouraging youngsters to visit museums. It is more likely, of course, that the Anfield Museum is a very special once-only attraction, but who knows? A pair of Kevin Keegan's boots may strike a particular chord that will resonate imperceptibly until, in Bloomsbury one day, the tuning-fork spirit is drawn into the British Museum to admire some Egyptian coiled sewn sandals from the Middle Kingdom.

Football boots were a feature of my interest in the museum mainly because I was hoping for some understanding of the cult of the Anfield Boot Room. None came. Perhaps such revelations are granted only to the truly devout. Mysteries abound in a club of the size and history of Liverpool. Supporters of lesser clubs – most of the rest of the Football League, then – cannot expect to understand the simple importance of heritage. 'This is Anfield', indeed.

I completed another circuit of the stadium and returned to my steward a little in advance of 1.30pm. He recognised me, which was encouraging, but had no ticket for me, which was not. "Come back at 2.15pm," he said, casting me out into the hinterland of Liverpool 4.

I set off south along Oakfield Road with no purpose beyond killing time. Time proved typically determined to cling to life. At the junction of Belmont Road and West Derby Road I turned right, then right again at Boundary Lane, and so back to the stadium. It was a dispiriting walk through increasingly steady drizzle. But at the south-western corner of Anfield my steward introduced me to a season-ticket holder whose son was unable to use his ticket, and the seat was mine if I wanted it. And so I watched a game at Anfield through the kindness of Scousers.

Actually my benefactor was from St Helens, though originally Liverpudlian. He would accept no money beyond the face value of the seat and I saw none change hands between him and the steward. I believe both acted from motives of simple philanthropy, and I immediately felt guilty to be deceiving them. If I was, of course.

Oldham contained Liverpool moderately well and came very close to scoring a spectacular goal. Had it gone in, people might still talk of a Petrasso Turn. But I was not called on to restrain myself and, as a Watford fan, I was able to applaud good football when called upon to do so. I drew the line, however, at singing *You'll Never Walk Alone*. Not after half a day spent traipsing lonely as a cloud through one of Liverpool's less lovely suburbs.

Liverpool 2 Oldham 0
Anfield, 5 January 2014

Luton Town

It's so obvious that gravity varies from one day to the next that it's hardly worth arguing about. Getting out of bed is so much more difficult on some mornings. The explanation can only be that gravity has increased overnight, like barometric pressure, and it makes you feel heavier and less mobile.

As with gravity, so with time. There are places where time passes more quickly or, to put it in a more worrying way, where you age more quickly. In one case I can't escape the way nominative determinism comes into play. I used to spend a seventh of my life every week in the vicinity of Old Street. This was where typesetters and compositors gathered. If they did so for protection – safety in numbers – it hasn't worked. Desktop publishing has wiped them out. But for a time they bestrode the publishing world like leaden-footed Colossi. My days in Old Street began very early and usually with a hangover, and they proceeded at the leisurely pace set by the typesetters. There was always something to read to pass the time, but it was usually a back copy of *Drapers Record*. I remember also a magazine for GPs, in which a pictorial quiz headed something like 'Name that Disease' was a regular and distressing feature.

There's nothing in Luton's name to put it in such company. But it too makes me feel old. I should qualify that. From certain points of view, I am old. Whose points of view? First, my own: when my grandparents were the age I am now, they were old; and only two of the four made it to this age. Second, my nieces' and nephews': although I am neither decrepit nor the wearer of elasticated slacks, I know that from their perspective I belong to an era almost as distant as the Victorians were from me when I was their age.

To return, however, to Luton, which I probably won't except to go through the airport. It's perverse, too, that I should associate Luton exclusively with the negative aspects of air travel rather than the positive – the exotic destinations and, in the case of Whizz Air, the exotic colour of the aircraft.

Luton also happens to be associated with significant events in my life. I gave up smoking there in 2004, sustaining myself through a 1-1 draw between Luton and Oldham with a pack of Wrigley's Extra. It's easy enough to explain how that would age you. When you stop smoking you accept that a significant source of enjoyment is closed to you forever. No occasion, you sadly acknowledge, will be enhanced by a cigarette again, ever. Previous attempts to stop have shown you that a single cigarette leads inevitably to a pack of 20 and a resumption of the daily addiction. A decision that may add years to your life withdraws a small portion of its zest. If you don't feel like that about it you shouldn't have been smoking in the first place.

But the memory of Luton that ages me most is the company I was keeping there 23 years earlier in 1981. My friend and colleague Sean died 18 years ago at the age of 53. He drank and smoked and was an unlikely candidate for three score years and ten, but 53 is harsh. As you outlive your friends, time takes abrupt leaps forward. Parts of your own life can no longer be independently corroborated, leaving gaps whose emptiness gradually seeps into your own memory.

Then there was F. She was 25, vibrant, blond and full of life. In *The Idiot*, Dostoevsky describes such a woman through the words of another character, Lebedev. "'She was a colourful woman,' said Lebedev, who had gone rather pale." In F's company you glimpsed life at a higher level of intensity. It was a mistake to hope to gain access on other than an intermittent basis but equally impossible not to try. The idea that such a creature was attached to me seems incredible in retrospect.

It takes an effort of will to recognise yourself across such a chasm of time. Regarded from a distance, youth is a psychedelic mirage. Everything that mattered is exaggerated and everything seemed to matter so much more. It's as if colours were brighter, noises louder, emotions more fragile and everything else just a little bit... more.

Think of a band you loved when you were young. Find them on YouTube playing something you have reason to remember. It won't make you feel any younger but it should remind you of some of the compensations of having been young once – just the sheer excitement.

As F, Sean and I approached the visiting supporters' end a steward said: "Three, eh… that makes 13 of you." He didn't exaggerate. We had an end to ourselves and congregated shyly behind the goal.

The importance of the fixture was simple. As the end of the season approached, Luton were pressing for promotion from the Second Division and had beaten Chelsea the previous week. Oldham faced relegation. Unaccountably, with five minutes left Oldham led 1-2. After 85 minutes of almost unbroken chanting "You're going to get your fuckin' 'eads kicked in" in our direction (and with so few fuckin' 'eads, not in our general direction but individually, at each one of us) the Luton fans invaded the pitch.

The uncomplicated layout of a football pitch gave them only one direction to take. The three sides, two long and one short, funnelled them towards us. Our position looked very vulnerable. Sean, who liked a ruck, wanted to stay and see what happened. I wanted to get us away. Did I mention that F was blond, lovely and therefore distinctive? It seemed unlikely that if we stayed until the end we would be able to filter into the crowd and file away unnoticed. I had my way and we reached my car unscathed. We passed into Luton's Saturday evening hinterland for dinner.

Behind us, Oldham held their lead and both teams remained in the same division for another year. Ahead of us, to complete a day of prodigies, snow fell in Bedfordshire on a night in late April, settled on the M1 and made lane discipline something of a lottery. Fortunately there was hardly any traffic. It was all a very long time ago.

Luton Town 1 Oldham 2
Kenilworth Road, 25 April 1981

Macclesfield Town

There may well have been a Venetian trader called Marco Polo in the 13th century. But the Marco Polo who became famous for exploring the Silk Road was, in fact, a young lad from Cheshire whose main contribution to the world of commerce, before he headed east, was to establish professional dog-walking as a legitimate business activity.

His name was Mark, recorded by history as Marco via Marcus because they used Latin names for official documents in the 13th century.

As for Polo, not everyone had a surname. When a man acquired one it often came from his occupation – Smith, for example, or King – and nobody regarded dog-walking as a man's job so Mark's was a compromise and included a mishearing. 'Of Bollin' became 'O'Bolo' and subsequently 'Polo' when Mark was looking for a sponsor.

The name of one client's dog, we happen to know, was Sam. It survives in the name of one of the most famous Asian cities still associated with the Marco Polo legend. Pausing overnight on the long journey through central Asia, Mark daubed a three-board box-panel at a camp-site: 'Sam, Mark and' on the top board, 'Eeyore the pack' and 'animal woz ere' on the lower two. No sooner had they moved on than a windstorm buried the two lower panels, and when the dust retreated the letters had been erased. Subsequent travellers assumed the place was called Samarkand.

Macclesfield wasn't much in those days. Let's just say that many a muckle hadn't yet made a Maccle. The field lay in readiness, but the settlement was little more than a small group of hovels close to a ford across the River Bollin. And that's how it all started.

Mark of Bollin never set out to visit Kublai Khan, discover the Silk Road and bring untold riches back to Europe. Far from it: he was walking Sam one morning and it crossed his mind to discover the source of the River Bollin. Perhaps he was inspired by one of the odd feats of endurance people embarked upon in those days.

One Macclesfield man walked to London in just under 50 days, and another walked backwards to Buxton, twice.

The source of the Bollin, to Mark's surprise, was barely three hours' gentle stroll away. The adventure was an anticlimax. Sam was hardly exercised either. So they pressed on a little way until they reached another stream's catchment area. They found a spring that ran away southward and decided on a whim to follow it. The stream proved to be the source of the River Dove, which flows into the Trent, which finds its way eventually to the Humber. By the time they reached Hull the nature of the quest had changed. Adventure had become a daily requirement, like caffeine (which Walter Raleigh, trying to stay awake long hours to invent the 3-speed bicycle, had not yet discovered).

Besides, peasants were not supposed to wander off willy-nilly in medieval England. Mark and Sam had been absent for almost a fortnight. One of them was going to have some explaining to do if he went back. If, on the other hand, they did not return, it would be assumed that bears had eaten them and all would be well. Some of the more superstitious villagers would go to the edge of the woods and perform a small ceremony to placate the bears, of which there were none.

Weighing it all up, and trading on Sam's potential as a ratter, Mark found a ship that would take them to Europe. In the Low Countries they set off to find the source of the River Zwin. They continued to wander o'er hill and dale in the direction of the rising sun until there were no more hills to wander o'er.

As for the story of Marco Polo in a Genoese prison dictating his memoirs to a fellow inmate, there is some truth in it. He was jailed on his return to Europe for impersonating a Venetian trader, and the fellow inmate was not taking dictation but translating. As Wikipedia wisely concludes: "Some have viewed the book with scepticism." How could they not?

Because Marco never returned to the banks of the Bollin, none of this necessarily has anything at all to do with the growth of the silk industry there. But it may help to explain why there is no mention of him in Macclesfield's justifiable pride in the part the town has played. The Silk Museum and, next door, Paradise Mill, are silent on the subject of Marco Polo, the prodigal son.

The Silk Museum has more to say about the product and what was done with it. Some of its arrangement of processes, samples and collections may feel a little haphazard at times, but overall it is very impressive. As a museum it is informative; but the silk turns it into a gallery and many of the exhibits are simply gorgeous. The Macclesfield School of Art may have been as important to the silk industry here for the impetus it gave to design.

There's plenty of the finished product on show, whether it be small – buttons, cards, handkerchiefs etc – or large, as in bolts of fabric, banners or fashion. My favourite turns the functional wartime use of escape maps printed on silk into a triumph over postwar austerity, by making skirts and blouses out of the maps.

There are pictures in silk too. But the Silk Museum has a conventional gallery space and when I was there the artist celebrated was Charles Tunnicliffe, born in Macclesfield in 1901. Tunnicliffe, best known for his depictions of birds, will be remembered by generations of children for his work in Ladybird books, Brooke Bond cards and many, many books, including *Tarka the Otter*.

You'll find more paintings at the Old Sunday School Heritage Centre. Pride of place belongs to Joseph Wright of Derby, who produced three portraits of Macclesfield worthies. In other respects the Old Sunday School is a surprisingly amusing place. There isn't much about Sunday School but plenty about Macclesfield. The basement takes you into another world, where pious women were bricked up in cells and the More Useful Knowledge Society tried to strike a blow for reason.

And Victorian enterprise is celebrated in its most bare-faced manifestation. Marianne Brocklehurst, the daughter of a prominent silk manufacturer, visited Egypt in 1873. "We liked the idea of smuggling on a large scale under the noses of the Pasha's guards," she wrote in her account of the journey. She bought a mummy, discreetly, but when she opened the sarcophagus to look for grave goods she found none. So she buried the mummy and shipped the sarcophagus home.

Her collection is usually displayed in West Park Museum, a building probably best seen in a sepia tint. It's a little way out of the town centre along the Prestbury Road. Because it was closed when I went to have a look, I was denied the chance to admire Macc Panda, a stuffed Giant Panda donated to the collection by one Captain Henry Brocklehurst after he shot it in China in 1835. If we ever need to butter up the Chinese, we could offer to return some of their looted treasures.

But in the Old Sunday School a collection of Marianne's Egyptian artefacts, drawings and diary entries was ample compensation. The Old Sunday School also has a fine café where gruel is not available.

Macclesfield Town 3 Barrow 1
Moss Rose, 10 March 2018

Manchester City

The house I was born in has a Manchester postcode; I feel I owe the city some sort of loyalty. On the other hand, I'm a supporter of Oldham Athletic. During their Premier League days they were occasionally referred to as 'the third Manchester team', and that was as close as I ever came to identifying with Manchester to any great extent.

My childhood memories of Manchester are of a dark, shabby place where you might easily have thought the war was still going on. In some places it has hardly changed. For example, many people will arrive in Manchester at Piccadilly Station. So let's consider the view from platform 14. Down below is the frontage of Mayfield Station, promising Locomotive Trains to Wilmslow. That could be quaintly retro: Wilmslow is one of the posher commuter towns in Cheshire; but Mayfield, by contrast, is a ruin. Passenger trains last ran there in 1960 and the building was closed in 1986. Nothing obvious has been done with or to it in the years since. A bomb-site would be an improvement. Mayfield Station is on Fairfield Street, named neither because it is fair nor a field.

Mayfield was also the name of the bar on the balcony at Manchester Piccadilly. If you ordered a glass of wine there, they were apt to bring you a large one and a bill for almost £10. You wouldn't put up with that sort of behaviour in your local, would you? The bar is now called The Mill and more has changed than the name.

I was walking along the towpath of the Rochdale Canal, through the cavernous sector between Oxford Road and Deansgate, when it occurred to me that the fault lay not in any Mancunian attitude to civic housework but in my own sense of perspective. As a timid child, alarmed no doubt by the big city's noise, bustle and trolley-buses, I looked back only as far as the Second World War; Manchester asks you to look back to the Industrial Revolution.

On the south side of Whitworth Street, through an arch beneath the line westward from Piccadilly, there is a sort of courtyard paved to look like decking. To the right, Starbucks; to the left, beyond a low and recent coniferous hedge, an ancient brick wall topped with coils of barbed wire protects a four-storey industrial relic (the Hotspur Press, previously Medlock Mill), complete with chimney.

Framing this stark contrast on both sides, enormous modern apartment blocks rise to more than twice the height of Medlock Mill's chimney. One has monochrome panels, the other a selection from the cream-yellow-green section of the Pantone chart. It looks as though a race of giants, having overwhelmed and enslaved the resident population, chose to live where they could keep a close eye on the natives toiling in their dark, satanic mill.

(In February 2018 the *Manchester Evening News* reported plans to redevelop the old building. One below-the-line correspondent commented: "Bulldoze it and build something attractive. The way people carry on on here, you would think it was Durham Cathedral.")

If Manchester streets were rendered as flats on a stage set, the main colour would be the vermilion brickwork, tinted with moss or faded with exposure, blackened with age in places. The curves of railway arches intersect with the vertical straight lines of Victorian buildings all over the city. And grafted on to this are the modern blocks that dominate the skyline.

Projects like the Town Hall refurbishment are a complication. Shrouded for a non-invasive facelift that is due to be completed by 2024, it won't be looking its best for another six years. But elsewhere you'll see things that have needed attention since 1924, or possibly earlier, so six years isn't an extravagant wait.

Past, present and future can be seen – intimated, in the case of the future – cheek by jowl all over the city. The attitude to 'heritage' oftens seems informal. Many structures are ravaged by time but they invariably contribute character. The waterways are perhaps the most interesting and attractive points of development: Salford Quays, obviously, but also Castlefield.

In some places that informality offers a sense of continuity and in others the moral is less clear. On the south side of Liverpool Road, for example, the Roman origins of Manchester are exhibited in a small park. In a far corner there's evidence of rough sleeping in a cluster of tents; this is not somewhere you'd find Siteseeker icons.

Across the road is the Museum of Science & Industry. It's surprising they didn't add '& Space', because this must have the largest floor area of any museum outside London. (Also Major Tim Peake's spacesuit was on display, like some sort of hunch-shouldered inflatable.) With two vast warehouses, two halls and a railway station, it can be quite intimidating.

My first impression was that it lacked cohesion: here's a re-entry module, and here's an area devoted to the cotton trade, and over here are some robots... But the thing to do is to leave the first building, the Great Western Warehouse, until last. By then, you will have realised that the museum is not nearly as overwhelming as you might have feared.

In the second 1800 Warehouse, for example, two of the three floors appear to be for administrative use and the exhibition on the remaining level is reassuringly compact and sensibly organised. The station building houses a large ticket office and a large waiting room and has the air of an airport terminal from which all flights have been cancelled. It is, nonetheless, the oldest inter-city (Manchester to Liverpool) railway station in the world, and on the platform some of the oldest deckchairs in the world are deployed. A small exhibition dealing with recycling completes this section of the tour.

The Power Hall contains power units, mainly locomotives and industrial engines. Across the way in the Air & Space Hall some of the *pièces de résistance* are drawn up – aeroplanes from the triplane era to the jet age.

The National Museum of Football also felt big and, at first, disorientating. But there's plenty to enjoy, including some table games guaranteed to generate nostalgia – the section has its own kiosk for doling out old coins to feed the machines.

The Museum also avoids elitism, by and large; obviously, many of the set-piece attractions like the Hall of Fame are populated mainly by players from big-name clubs, but the achievements of lesser lights are celebrated too. Bury's record score in an FA Cup

Final is an example. An exhibition of Stanley Chow's work was a highlight when I was there. You could easily spend hours, and it is free.

The only Oldham player I found in the Hall of Fame was Denis Irwin, for his achievements with Manchester United and the Republic of Ireland; and an exhibit featuring Oldham specifically, called 'Where Did They Finish the Season', was broken or, as they put it, 'injured and receiving treatment'.

Often rewarding for reasons of simple pleasures – it's good to see the statue of Michael Jackson in a football context again – the Museum has only one serious flaw: how can the café attached to such a place not offer Pukka Pies?

Manchester Art Gallery has more Hall of Fame entrants. If your enjoyment of Lowry has been piqued by occasional sightings at other galleries around the north of England, this is the place for you. In Manchester they show Lowry alongside Adolphe Valette, his tutor. I'd say Valette was a better painter than a tutor and that the juxtaposition does neither any favours.

Upstairs, the Pre-Raphaelites are probably the main attraction. The notorious *Hylas and the Nymphs* is here, and you can't help but notice that whatever else people might say about the nymphs, their eyes are straight out of Midwich. Another picture in which the eyes have it is FR Pickersgill's *Samson Betrayed*; a magnificently naked Delilah, a furtive man with clippers and a bystander are all clearly terrified lest the slumbering giant wakes up before his power is drained.

While you're here, don't pass up the opportunity to look at the moveable feasts on the second floor. Apart from anything else these are quite different display spaces; light, high-ceilinged and somehow more relaxing.

If I found Manchester museums and galleries large and diffuse, the People's History Museum was certainly a corrective. It is cohesive and knows exactly what it wants to show you. The first thing you'll see is a display devoted to the Peterloo Massacre, and then it's straight into slavery, the Chartists, the Levellers, Tom Paine, Women's Rights and more. Its handsomely printed plan with colour-coded areas and suggested visitor routes isn't always easy to follow on the ground, but by the time you reach the rather small Time Off section at the end (football and music, but less on the opium of the masses) you will have begun to look at museums in a new light anyway. Conventional museums celebrate the product; the People's History Museum respects the process.

Anthony Burgess, who was born in Manchester, said: "At the time of my birth, Manchester was a great city, Cottonopolis, the mother of liberalism and the cradle of the entire industrial system." The historian AJP Taylor wrote: "Manchester has everything but good looks... the only place in England which escapes our characteristic vice of snobbery."

Manchester City 0 West Bromwich Albion 2
Maine Road, 30 December 1967

Manchester United

Old Trafford describes itself grandiosely as 'The Theatre of Dreams' and it surely is a theatre, which naturally begs questions about dreams and, particularly, the ability of football to make them come true.

Sweet dreams and nothing else are implied here. But the theatre managers, the impresarios and the players must know better. It would be a hollow theatre that guaranteed pleasant dreams, and they'd have to be pretty shallow. Holding tight to such dreams would be like praying for something trivial – you really can't expect God to have nothing better to do. At the Theatre of Dreams, then, something must be at stake. Sleep, the real theatre of dreams, presents an occasional nightmare.

A theatre that repeatedly put on bad dreams or, unpredictably, nightmares would specialise in short-run productions. It would take steps against those eventualities. Through professionalism, training and faith in the process it would hope to reduce the risk.

I gave my sister and her husband (a Manchester United supporter) a Matchday VIP Experience as a way of saying 'thank you' for a very considerable favour. They did the driving to cover the 200 miles to Manchester, quite a considerable favour in itself. Perhaps I need to find a less demanding way to say 'thank you' for that...

The Matchday VIP Experience was theatrical from the start. Our tickets were for the Red Café Pre-Match package. Three hours before kick-off, we parked within 100 metres of the stadium. At the entrance to the Sir Alex Ferguson Stand we were politely patted down and any bags checked. Within, we ascended to the Red Café.

There, the production was in full swing. Centre-stage, a bar from which we took a glass of Prosecco, with extras in red uniforms sweeping to and fro like Virgin Atlantic stewardesses. Around the margins, canteen tables and chairs or benches at which more extras sat in the guise of diners. The décor was predominantly red, the lighting dim but punctuated by bright spots. People who were neither diners nor hostesses moved apparently at random into and out of our way: a small film crew, as though a celebrity was arriving; gaggles of thickset men in suits; people taking photographs of other people posing beside a trophy that may or may not have been a prop. The colour, the lighting and the context suggested Hell's Kitchen. This is Scene 1, the Parlour of the Red Devils.

We were shown to our seats at a table on a slight platform close to one of the more restful margins of the room. Glass revealed a pasty Manchester skyline; on other sides the walls were decorated either with pictures of players in triumphant poses, team slogans in huge letters or large screens playing highlights from recent victories.

Lunch was not served immediately. There would, in any case, have been no room for it on the table where it would have competed for space with quizzes, guess-the-result contests, forms similar to the football pools, menus and a good deal of cutlery and glassware. On our chairs, red and emblazoned across the back with the name of a player, were small goodie-bags that contained a match-day programme and a branded travel-plug.

Expecting little from the menu – a triple burger had been mentioned on the website – we were surprised to find cordon bleu options: an Asiatic starter, or lentil and chickpea soup, steak, roasted coley, a vegetarian option called Munchkin Pumpkin; dessert or cheese board; and a wine list. Only my sister took an alcoholic drink; we may have placed the lowest drinks order in the room. Well, the website had promised a lively atmosphere.

The food, it turned out, wasn't spectacularly good and our hostess not especially attentive, but the atmosphere made up for it. A former player was part of the package and Russell Beardsmore arrived at our table. He turned out to be a delightful man. When I confessed to being an Oldham fan he affected deafness. "Who? Who?" I took his picture with my brother-in-law, upon whose brow he had accidentally gobbed in his eagerness to be heard above the hubbub. It was a kind of benediction.

Close to three hours passed agreeably. Many people, it transpired, were there as a birthday treat and they were invited into the body of the kirk to be applauded and pictured alongside Russell. Eventually the PA packed up and this entertainment was cut short. We submitted our competition entries and bought a £10 raffle ticket for charity. And at around 5.15pm we made our way to the seats.

This was the second or entre-acte of the theatrical experience – the Second to Seventh Upper Circles. From the loud vibrancy of the Red Café we passed through a series of quiet and resolutely grey stairwells and staircases. Having shared the Café with a crowd we now had the innards of the stadium almost to ourselves. The flights of steps seemed endless. Our tickets were for seats in Block N3408, hinting at the possibility of at least 47,712 blocks of seats (the 14th letter of the alphabet multiplied by 3408). Eventually we emerged on to a kind of plateau: a broad, enclosed internal terrace with refreshments along one side and access to the auditorium through the other. And so we finally passed into the theatre itself, with the stage spread out before us like a brightly-lit and carefully-brushed card table, and the audience of 75,000 in place, in anticipation.

The sharpness of the colours – predominantly green in the gingham pattern the mowers achieve, but also red and the parti-coloured messages of the club's commercial partners – under the lights gives the scene a degree of artificiality. This impression is heightened by the distance between our vantage point under the roof of the stand, on a level with the top of the Sir Bobby Charlton Stand opposite, and the pitch itself. It is a stage prepared for the willing suspension of disbelief.

When the actors arrive and the play begins it is, at first, just like a football match. Worse, it goes badly for the home favourites: Newcastle look spry and take a lead for which they are good value.

But this is the Theatre of Dreams and Manchester United have at least two players capable of shaping a football match in their sleep. The Frenchman Paul Pogba and the Spaniard Juan Mata begin to tease opponents with feints as though with a toreador's cape and it is apparent that the Newcastle defenders are at full stretch. The left back in particular is completely bemused by Pogba's sleight of foot on the left-hand side of the Newcastle penalty area. Once the defender is beaten, the move seems to unfold in slow-motion. Time is not an issue. Pogba has the leisure to pick out a colleague in front of the goal and lob the ball to him to knock into the net.

Disputes over what function a dream might normally perform are irrelevant in this theatre. They have no role in assimilating the events of the day; nor are they produced by random brain activity; there may be some attraction in the Jungian idea of a dream as a message from the beyond, or at least from beyond the conscious mind, but what sort of message, exactly? The possibility of an ideal, perfect form of football?

Perhaps. A good dream slips away as the dreamer wakes, and although you may try to go back to sleep and find your way into it again, such dreams are elusive. A recurrent bad dream will make you fretful about going to sleep in the first place. In both cases, belief in the possibility is the vital factor.

Halfway up the West Stand, decorating a balcony, is a large sign saying 'MUFC The Religion'. To a previous generation of United fans, Lou Macari was God. Is it coincidence that the most faithful football fans will attend once a week, and perhaps more often at Easter and around Christmas?

Events on the pitch may genuinely have a religious dimension. Sympathetic magic is being invoked. Pogba baffling defenders is an image from a cave painting and it stays in the mind. Onlookers, having seen it depicted, will believe the image is a prediction of future events at least as much as a record of past. Under the right circumstances, with appropriate preparations, it will happen again, they believe, against new opponents.

Many football fans will go to watch their team week after week hoping to see them avoid defeat or, worse, humiliation. But supporters of elite clubs will take their seats expecting to see their team win, and why not? They know (although their evidence is mystical) that such a result may be conjured from strength of will and fidelity to dreams.

Manchester United 4 Newcastle United 1
Old Trafford, 18 November 2017

Mansfield Town

It's easy to explain the popularity of the expression 'back in the day'. Vague but hazily nostalgic, implying a better time in which we were all much younger, it spares the speaker the trouble of recalling the precise date in question or looking it up.

Since everyone now uses the expression, eventually nobody will bother to remember or find out any notable date. There will simply be 'the day'. "In the beginning was the Day."

Sticking 'So' on the front of every sentence is equally reprehensible. From the speaker's point of view it has two tawdry attractions: one, it provides an extra millisecond of unearned time to think; and two, it conveys the sense of logical reasoning, as when 'so' is used to introduce "a clause of purpose or result"[1].

So, back in the day, it was impossible to complete a car journey of any distance without encountering town centres. Often you encountered the same one repeatedly. The driver – usually your dad – would be inexperienced behind the wheel, inadequately assisted by navigational aids (your mother with the road atlas) and easily deceived by a one-way system. It took a very long time to drive anywhere, back in the day.

But we were happy, playing 'I Spy', sucking Everton mints and annoying our siblings. If all else failed, there was always a sing-song.

The 'day', in that instance, refers to the era before bypasses and motorways. It ended, to all intents and purposes, in late 1958 when the M6 opened to take traffic around Preston. The floodgates didn't open immediately but the number of motorways, ring-roads and bypasses grew from that point.

I'm not sure Mansfield was ever on the way to anywhere in the bottlenecked way that places like Queensferry (not so much the Gateway to North Wales, more the Puissance) and Bridgewater (ditto the West Country) once were. But if you drive around Mansfield you will miss a sensational viaduct. Along the eastern side of the

---

1 *Fowler's Modern English Usage.*

town centre a series of spectacular arches carries the railway (here known lyrically as the Robin Hood Line) away towards Worksop. You can't look at it without relocating Worksop in your imagination as a place where you might find a Castle in the Air or a Rainbow's End.

The Robin Hood Line, by the way, is not entirely poetic licence. Mansfield was originally a woodland town surrounded by Sherwood Forest.

Is the railway viaduct the most interesting feature of Mansfield town centre? It isn't a particularly lovely urban environment. But you probably won't be going to Mansfield to admire the architecture and the civil engineering. You're probably going to an FA Cup 1st round tie.

If you get there early enough, begin at the Mansfield Museum. To reach it from the railway station you'll walk through the town centre and can come to your own conclusion on its loveliness. The Museum, which is free, feels in some ways like an extension of the walk and indeed you'll find there a booklet proposing Mansfield's Heritage Trail, on which Mansfield Museum is the first stop.

It's a fine example of a local museum. Many of the exhibits were collections donated by local people, including the widow of painter, antiquarian and historian Albert Sorby Buxton. Buxton's watercolours recall the townscape back in the day. (Another great advantage of the expression is that it can be applied shiftily to any era.) Trained at the Slade and head of Mansfield School of Art in the late 19th century, Buxton painted buildings and views that are long gone (and in at least one case had gone before he sat down to paint it) but they have charm and interest.

Also on permanent display is a series of exhibits entitled Made in Mansfield. These recall the people and companies that thrived in the town: the Metal Box Company, Barrs Soft Drinks, Mansfield Brewery and the Shoe Co. Local involvement in mining, quarrying and engineering are also celebrated.

I picked up the Heritage Trail book but didn't have time to follow it. Instead I went back to the bus station and took the bus that stops at the gates of Newstead Abbey, the home of Lord Byron.

From the gates, you should be aware, there is a walk of over a mile to the Abbey itself. Benches are not provided. You may enliven the walk in your mind's eye by picturing yourself following in Byron's footsteps: perhaps he too walked this way, squiring a Mansfield floozy home on foot when the brougham was in for a service.

But it seems unlikely. The more you read of Byron's troubled life and times as you make your way round the premises, the more improbable a fatally attractive womaniser he seems. The idea that he ever limped along his drive from the bus-stop seems fanciful in the extreme.

In contrast to the later image of a man of action, Byron was as apt to be fighting the flab as fighting the enemies of Greece. He associated thinness with mental clarity and creativity. Ahead of his time as a student, at university he followed a diet of biscuits and soda water; prone to binge, he would wash a super-sized meal down with magnesia. He smoked cigars to ward off hunger pangs.

Byron's height as an adult was 5ft 8ins and his odd eating habits brought his weight down from 13st 12lbs to 9st at one point. Constantly on his guard against corpulence, he also had to live with a deformed foot. He took exercise with the same moderation he applied to his diet: none. Remarkably, he became a strong sportsman and, as a swimmer, might have been known as Flipper to his friends had he lived 180 years later. He also helped the weight-loss along by wearing layers of woollen clothes to promote sweating. Mad, bad and fragrant to know...

How much time Lord Byron spent at Newstead is open to question. The Abbey says he lived there "at various times" between the autumns of 1808 (when he was 20) and 1814. Also between those years he:

- Undertook the Grand Tour, an expedition cut short by the Napoleonic Wars
- Crossed Portugal and Spain by land and then crossed the Mediterranean to Greece
- Moved on to Smyrna and Constantinople where he famously swam the Hellespont

- Became a celebrity on his return to London with the publication of *Childe Harold's Pilgrimage*
- May have had affairs with (among others) a 14-year-old Italian boy, a 12-year-old Greek girl, Lady Caroline Lamb and his half-sister Augusta Leigh.

Stately homes are usually interesting for the décor, the furnishings or the architecture. Newstead Abbey is good to look at and some of the rooms are memorable, but it's the former lord of the manor, his strange character and activities, that will stay in your mind as you make your way back down his curving, wooded and interminable drive.

Newstead Abbey took up more time than I had budgeted for. I had then to decide between the mining museum at Pleasley Colliery and the FA Cup tie at Mansfield Town. Two hours later, having made a bad decision, I had a dire goalless draw and acid reflux from an exceptionally poor burger to show for it.

Mansfield Town 0 Oldham 0
Field Mill, 7 November 2015

Middlesbrough

Middlesbrough is a town of many charms and it dispenses them liberally like items from a bracelet; or perhaps more like beads from a rosary, as though it were anxious to be loved.

Its generosity begins at the railway station. At platform level Middlesbrough Station is a modest halt: two tracks and two platforms to match the two-car runabouts that scurry through on their way either to Saltburn or to Darlington. Those trains are called Class 142 Pacers, and it would be no surprise to learn that there are 141 superior classes of rail coach.

If Middlesbrough felt slighted in its civic dignity it would be justified. For a town of about 150,000 people to have a station no bigger than that of, say, Cheddington (pop 1,754) and to be served by far less impressive trains must be galling, to say the least. But Cheddington and most other railway stations in this country have one of two means of passing from the outside world through the ticket office to the platforms: either anonymous, ill-favoured or malodorous passages or a box-like footbridge. Middlesbrough has catacombs converted into a gallery space, plus echoes of an abandoned monastery.

In the passageway below, the arches are built from huge blocks. Just seven raise the piers above head height and another eight form the shallow arch that spans a gap of about 10ft. They lead you through to a well-lit gallery on the walls of which notable Teesiders are commemorated in ingenious and attractive form.

The walls are tiled and decorated at intervals by large postage stamp-style linocut and drypoint pictures. The faces these stamps bear are of local people who have made refugees and asylum-seekers welcome. This is so unexpected and uplifting that you can't help but emerge from Middlesbrough railway station feeling much better than when the UK's 142nd-best rolling stock delivered you into it.

Most of the station's exterior was shrouded in scaffold cladding in February 2018. Just enough was exposed to give the clear impression that the railway station was built in a disused abbey. Apparently a Mr William Peachey was responsible for its Gothic frontage in 1877. Perhaps he had recently visited nearby Rievaulx.

South of the station, Middlesbrough unfurls itself like a tapestry with flecks of gold thread. They aren't always obvious: perhaps you need to see them from the right angle for the reflection to catch your eye.

For example, the name of Ayresome Gardens might ring a bell; Middlesbrough played at Ayresome Park for almost 100 years. The Gardens' millennium arch at first appears impressive more for the fact that somebody took the trouble than for any great artistic merit. It might be a cross between an ice-hockey goal and a supermarket trolley. A lot of wisteria would help. But its depiction of what the people of Teeside did in 2000 is wonderful: plaques designed by local schoolchildren indicate musical instruments, sport... so far, so good... and shopping... and, illustrated by a picture of a submarine, water travel.

Turning away, pondering the capacity of great art to make you think, your eye may be caught by a lump of metal in the grass. Is it? Might it be? Yes, it's a small pumpkin. And over there, is that an avocado? Middlesbrough is a town in which you can stub your toe on art. These are sculptor Andrew McKeown's 'world fruit', a collection of cast-iron fruits and vegetables.

There's another reminder of Ayresome Park in Albert Park across the road from the Gardens. Albert Park, by the way, is another repository of rare treats. Almost everything – trees, benches, niches, a sundial etc – has an explanatory sign attached.

A bust of pioneering ironmaster Henry Bolckow monitors foot traffic through the Park at ground level, in a stone cabinet and protected by a sturdy grill, almost inviting children to poke Bolckow through the bars with a stick. The face and the style of the bust suggest Socrates. Perhaps Henry wasn't available for a sitting on the crucial day.

Again, you will move on lost in thought... until the statue on a nearby grassy knoll invites you to wander over to see who it is.

Brian Clough, with his boots slung over his shoulder, is making his way to Ayresome Park. It's very touching. There are statues of Middlesbrough greats at the Riverside Stadium, but Cloughie in a public park is different. And he's heading casually for the ghost of a stadium where he was phenomenally successful. In 222 league games for Boro, he scored 204 goals.

Beyond Brian Clough, casually littering the grass as though left by a retreating glacier, are fragments known as the crystallisation sculpture. These angular blocks are again the decorative work of Andrew McKeown.

If you've arrived at Albert Park from the direction of Ayresome Gardens you can't help but pass the Dorman Museum. Here Middlesbrough is at its gracious generous best.

The Dorman is free and informal. Downstairs there are spaces devoted to Middlesbrough themes: the Tees, industry, churches, natural history, interrupted briefly by a room full of stuffed birds and, presumably, blown eggs. One oddity: local museums often celebrate local industries; the Dorman celebrates individual shops and businesses.

Upstairs a Hans Memling triptych casually decorates a landing. Nearby is the largest collection of Linthorpe Art Pottery on public display anywhere in the world.

Next door to that is a room devoted to the career of versatile designer Dr Christopher Dresser, a man whose mind's eye clearly could not behold any household object without imagining a dramatic improvement. Ceramics, metalwork, furniture, textiles, glass... Dresser was a man of panoramic influence (over the Arts & Crafts movement, over Anglo-Japanese style, for example) and some of his designs became enduring classics – Clutha glass, the Hera peacock etc.

On the other side of the building there's a cosmology gallery, Earth in Space, that seems quite generic by comparison. But this is where you'll find the dinosaur, so let's not knock it.

Also on this floor are rooms devoted to 20th Century Woman, appropriate to the suffrage centenary, and an odd little room called Four Corners, which seems to be where they put things that don't necessarily fit anywhere else. And the *pièce de résistance* is the H2O gallery, "a discovery gallery for children based on the theme of water".

I thought I was witnessing an assisted suicide as I crossed the threshold of the H2O room. On the left, set into the floor, is a composite large-screen pond. Schools of silvery fish glitter and swim hither and thither. The people in front of me by the water included, in a wheelchair, an elderly person whom they heedlessly wheeled into the pond. Ripples spread across the screen and there was some shrieking, but the wheelchair was consumed not. The water in the screens reacts realistically to a foot in the same way.

The pond sets the bar very high, and the rest of H2O does well trying to live up to it. The models, the games, the interactivity and the representation of the Tees are all good fun.

The Dorman's café also attracts good reviews but I was on an unforgiving schedule. There was still Mima, the Middlesbrough Institute of Modern Art, to take in on my way to the Riverside.

In the event Mima occupied less time than I'd expected because much of it was closed for filming. On the upper floor was an exhibition apparently marking the 10th anniversary of the building's opening. The arrangement of the exhibits, we were told, challenged the 'white box' layouts of conventional galleries. What that meant in practice was that some of the art was too high up the wall to see properly, particularly with the light bouncing off it. Still, the Bridget Rileys were visible and Grayson Perry's urn was at ground level. A modest Lowry was of St Hilda's, in Middlesbrough, prompting the thought that the artist may have turned them out like postcards. Mima, like the Dorman, is free and its catering attracts praise.

Linthorpe Road, where the food of many nations might be found and shops sell lentils by the sack, leads back towards the station. There are Gallicly eccentric but not incorrect spellings – the Kilimandjaro restaurant, and a bistrot; the flattened dome of the Crown – more a bridge, dentally – is a landmark if you lose your way.

Victorian Middlesbrough drapes itself around the railway

station like a shawl concealing piano legs. Exchange Square is the focus of the 'Historic Quarter' in which eighths and sixteenths are gradually being restored. The home of the Kalinka nightclub prompts memories of the Alhambra; the Zetland Buildings line the north side of the square like a smile revealing sparkling implants.

Opposite, the ramp of the A66 recalls days of less enlightened urban planners. The square itself is quiet and sterile; a statue of the ironmaster Bolckow broods over it from a more conventional level than in Albert Park.

The plan is apparently to link the Historic Quarter to the Boho development, reconnecting Middlesbrough to the river. Boho is in its infancy.

A fence shields you from the wasteland on the way to the old docks and the football ground. A panel on it declares that this will soon be the coolest place in Middlesbrough. The casual invitation to incredulity is breathtaking. The person responsible for the text, one imagines, returns home after a day at the keyboard and relaxes with Andy Williams on the stereogram and a Baileys in his hand. His misapprehension over the years of what constitutes cool will encompass menthol cigarettes, double denim and Howard from the old Halifax ads.

Still, a wall bearing Ian Horne's *Ironopolis* poem, and a lonely building with 'Ciao' above the door are steps in the right direction. The direction, that is, of the award-winning Middlesbrough College building (modelled, apparently, on the hull of a ship), the Riverside Stadium and the Temenos 'butterfly net' sculpture. They knew Anish Kapoor on Teeside long before London 2012. Access to the football ground seems to have been modelled on his Orbit Tower in the Olympic Park.

Temenos, by the way, is Greek for a piece of ground next to a temple – sacred ground, in other words. Flanking the approach to the main entrance of the stadium stand two more giants, Wilf Mannion and George Hardwick, guarding the gates.

The area north of the railway station might become known as the Quarter that Time Forgot. Through the Albert Bridge, Cleveland Street heads for the Tees and quickly leaves Middlesbrough's groundplan behind it. The town opens out into green spaces, some landscaped, others less so. This is where the original settlement grew up, but nature from a more distant past seems to be re-asserting itself. Street names hint at a thriving history: Commercial Street and Vulcan Street, for example. But the land looks as though a meteor struck the earth some time ago and wiped out the giants that bestrode this riverbank.

You can imagine a tour guide, perhaps with waxed moustaches, ushering you towards the Tees Transporter Bridge. "Move along there, please. Nothing to see here." Nor is there, much, although if you cross the road and wander through one of the more landscaped areas you'll find the plaque indicating where the altar of St Hilda's stood. This was the spiritual centre of the original settlement. Temenos hints at what has happened to spirituality since then.

Middlesbrough 2 Reading 0
Riverside Stadium, 10 February 2018

Millwall

This visit in 1990 was my second to the Den. Why would anyone other than a Millwall supporter go there more than once? Millwall's reputation was not at its most forbidding in 1990 but that's the thing about reputations, isn't it? From a reputation we infer behaviour that doesn't come and go according to the calendar. Reputation blends into prejudice and before long it's impossible to say where the truth lies.

Football hooliganism, according to the received wisdom (except perhaps among fans of Millwall), was invented by Millwall fans in the 1960s. Its heyday, if that's the right word, might have come and gone by 1990, but there had in recent times been some unpleasantness at an FA Cup quarter-final tie against Luton in 1985, when 81 people were injured, 31 of them members of the police force. On examination that may have been a case of dogs and bad names: of the 31 people arrested, many identified themselves as supporters not of Millwall but of West Ham and Chelsea. But in 1988 41 authentic Millwall fans were arrested at Highbury on the occasion of another FA Cup defeat.

Another related topic on which the received wisdom is fairly confident is that however sanitised and 'family-friendly' the game might seem now, hooliganism never went away completely.

I can't really confirm or deny that. In almost 60 years of going to football matches I have never witnessed hooliganism on any substantial scale. I've seen invasions of the pitch and running scuffles between small groups; I've felt the air of menace young men in numbers can project. But "the old ultraviolence", as in Anthony Burgess' *A Clockwork Orange*, has passed me by – at which I touch wood nervously.

I would agree, though, that the possibility of violence persists. Some football fans seem to be a hair's breadth away from incandescent rage much of the time. That's during the match, at any rate. How they release the build-up of tension I cannot imagine.

Taking all that and Millwall's reputation into account, you

would think that any sane travelling supporter would make the trip to southeast London once, to be able to say he or she had been to Millwall, congratulate him or herself quietly on getting out unscathed and cross it off the list.

That's probably what I would have done, but some time after my first visit to the Den I became friendly with a graphic designer who, with me, was roped into a publishing project that never actually came to anything. While that was failing to happen, he (as a Millwall fan) talked me into going to a match with him.

We met in a pub on New Cross Road, where he and his group of mates congregated before a home game. For me, from leafy Highbury, it was the pub from the land that gentrification forgot. The group of mates took well enough to having to entertain an outsider. But could I rely on their discretion? And if I couldn't, how tolerant would the other inhabitants of the pub be? It was 40 minutes suffused by anxiety. In theory, it's no bad thing to spend a little time outside your comfort zone; but the haircuts, the footwear, the reputation and the presence around the corner of the chillingly-named Cold Blow Lane combined to make me so nervous that it was impossible to take any enjoyment from the occasion.

The same thing would have applied to the match itself, had it not been clear from quite an early stage that it was going to be a 0-0 draw. You can sometimes tell, can't you? Some goalless draws are exciting, dynamic affairs; others are so dreary the teams could play for a fortnight and not score.

The possibility that I might have to suppress excitement if Oldham scored, or simulate it in the case of a Millwall goal, receded as the match wore on. With about 10 minutes left the Millwall fans, of whom I had been so nervous all afternoon, began to sing to the tune of *Guantanamera*, "Home in a minute, we're going home in a minute." It was perfect. Now I don't feel the need to go again and can look back with something like affection.

Millwall 0 Oldham 0
The Den, 29 December 1990

Milton Keynes Dons

The wanderings of the Milton Keynes Dons are positively Biblical alongside the homebody inertia of most football clubs. Aside from the growing band with shiny new stadiums on the ring road, most have not moved since their earliest days.

The club that became the Dons, originally Wimbledon, left Plough Lane in 1991, had a long ground-share arrangement with Crystal Palace, flirted with a move to Dublin and fetched up in Milton Keynes in 2004.

That wasn't quite the end of the restlessness. In 2007 the club moved again and might justifiably have changed its name. The closest mainline railway station to its latest home, Stadium:mk, is Bletchley. As the name of a football club, Bletchley Park would have had something of a ring to it, or even better the studious-sounding Bletchley Park Dons.

It's difficult to know how much to say about Bletchley Park itself without issuing a spoiler alert. The atmosphere of the wartime establishment is recreated so carefully and with such ingenuity that it would be a pity to dilute the effect, however slightly, by describing too precisely what a visitor can expect. Lighting, props and the deployment of several more or less advanced technologies will surprise you as you make your way around the site. Some may make the hairs on the back of your neck stand up.

On entry, you'll be given a leaflet of suggested itineraries – two hours, four hours, all-day – and suggestions of where to start. It's helpful up to a point, but the layout of Bletchley Park may leave you wondering whether there's a code you will need to crack to make any sense of the place. Numbered Huts and lettered Blocks are dispersed around the Park apparently at random. Don't worry: whether you saunter around as the mood takes you, or work your way through methodically, you're sure to be entertained and intrigued. Think of the Park (BP, as they refer to it) as a series of exhibitions, demonstrations and interactive exercises, with short walks between them to absorb and take stock.

The figure of Alan Turing (and, inevitably since the film, of Benedict Cumberbatch) looms large over BP. According to the *The Imitation Game*, Turing brought genius and sheer bloody-mindedness to bear on cracking the Hun's codes. His contribution, historical and dramatic, is commemorated around BP in various places but most notably (and, apparently, of greatest appeal to visitors) in a recreation of a set from the film.

This kind of window-dressing of history used to strike me as a particularly American form of deception, necessitated by their lack of authentic history. At the Alamo in San Antonio, for example, pride of place among the museum's exhibits used to go not to Davy Crockett's coon-skin hat but to the facsimile worn by John Wayne in the 1960 film. (The display case may have been updated after the 2004 remake.)

But time moves on and tastes change; the meanest TV soap opera provides tours, tea-towels and an experience, and it would be nothing short of negligent of BP not to make the most of an Oscar-winning film. It's odd, though, isn't it? When you could be standing in the very space occupied by Turing having a brainwave 70-odd years ago, you choose instead to look at a space similar to the one occupied by Benedict Cumberbatch quite recently.

Bletchley Park as a tourist destination concentrates on the interception, decryption and translation of enemy signals. But there are other, peripheral, small museums: the National Radio Centre, a Pigeons at War room and the splendidly modest Holley-Cornelius Toy & Memorabilia Collection.

You may come away from Bletchley Park wondering how you would have held up in those times, under those circumstances. Much of the work, especially that undertaken by Wrens, was clearly arduous. Some of it, however, had an intellectual challenge that looks to the Sudoku generation like fun. As for the dispatch riders, "riding in all weathers, through the day and night", people would pay to do that kind of thing now.

Two simple faults need attention:

- Adjacent to Bletchley Park is the National Museum of Computing, about 100 metres from the cluster of codebreakers' huts. But fencing and a gate bar the way; to get to the Museum, which is a separate establishment, you need to go back to the main entrance and up a service road – a distance of perhaps 500 metres in all.

- The catering. Hut 4's cafeteria is fine but the food may be a further aspect of the recreation of wartime deprivation. If the pasta dish I had was representative, it would be only fair to charge wartime prices too. (On reflection I suppose fascist pasta would not have been on any British menus between 1939-45.)

On the subject of price, the cost of entry in 2015 was £15. The ticket served as an annual pass, an empty gesture as far as most visiting fans will be concerned but who knows, they might be lured back. They might even want to look at Milton Keynes as well.

The journey from Bletchley Park to Stadium:mk was baffling in the daylight and almost impossible after dark. I attempted it on foot; having arrived by train, there seemed no reason not to. On the map it looked hardly any distance at all.

In a way I suppose it exposed me to the authentic Milton Keynes experience. I negotiated roundabouts, bus stands, underpasses, dual carriageways and vast expanses of superstore car-parks. Eventually, when the stadium loomed on the northwestern horizon, glimpsed at last from a corner of an Asda car-park, it was possible to head confidently towards it. Before that point navigation had been a question of faith in a general sense of direction through the sequence of paths along which no-one, surely, was ever intended to walk.

The reverse journey, in the dark, with no stadium to guide me and with the misery of a 7-0 drubbing fresh in the memory, was a profoundly depressing experience. It would not have surprised me if I'd encountered zombies along the way.

On the subject of the 7-0 drubbing, three things stand out. First, it happened to be the second Saturday in succession on which I had watched an unusually emphatic home win; the previous week I had been at Birmingham City's 6-1 success over Reading. I wondered if my presence might be somehow talismanic, if I might hire myself out to clubs in need of a morale-boosting substantial home victory. Second, building a hotel along one side of a stadium seemed inspired, especially for people who booked their rooms unawares. Third, and crucially, the seats at Stadium:mk were the most comfortable I have ever known at a football ground.

Milton Keynes Dons 7 Oldham 0
Stadium:mk, 20 December 2014

Morecambe

A journey by train through the heart of the country on a fine summer's day... At Milton Keynes Central, the station announcer has caught the mood. The tone of his messages is inconsistent but verges on chummy.

First, there's a friendly reminder to people understandably baffled by the number of cards that tumble out of an automatic ticket machine. "Users of ticket-vending machines should be sure to pick up all their tickets – a return portion has just been handed in to the ticket office," he declares. Then, marginally less friendly but helpful in the long run, a note to opportunist travellers: "The next train at this platform is the 08.38 Virgin Trains service to Liverpool Lime Street, calling at Stafford and Runcorn. Please note that tickets marked London Midland are not valid for travel on this service." But to sweeten the pill, he has a jocular response to the threat of terrorism: "If you see an unattended bag or suspicious behaviour, report it to a member of staff or text British Transport Police: remember 'See it, Say it, Sort it!'"

Contrasting with this readiness to treat the travelling public as morons, the station managers align themselves all the way up the West Coast route with tertiary education. At Stafford, the place-name shares space on the station boards with the University of Wolverhampton; we pass through so quickly that no-one could possibly read whatever the University of Wolverhampton has to say for itself. But at Crewe, notices for Manchester Metropolitan University Cheshire Campus plainly announce it as "the University for World-Class Professionals". What? In the era of fake news it seems a little precious to take exception to this claim. But where does exaggeration tip over into outright lying? And is this the explanation for the current scorn for the opinions of experts: have people already begun to disregard all forms of communication?

The train is going eventually to Holyhead and a young lad in an Ireland shirt is behaving himself in the quiet coach. Outside the window there are further glimpses into the lives of others: actual dog walkers and implied show-jumpers. History, too, in the traces of ridge and furrow, distant church spires, canals and farms. It is vibrantly colourful: golden crops, vivid green copses, colonies of rosebay willowherb offering a living definition of magenta (named inexplicably after a French military victory). Pylons march towards shimmering horizons.

Such views may not be available for very much longer. Trains in future will pass between high fences serving as baffles to shield encroaching new houses from the noise. Either that or they will go through tunnels. As long as the signal for our phones is reliable...

The train "arrives into Crewe". The eccentric use of prepositions is a theme of the trip: enticing ultimate destinations is another. Having been on a train headed eventually for the Emerald Isle, I change on to one going to Glasgow. Tomorrow, destinations will include Manchester Airport and London.

For now, though, I am arriving into Preston (the University of Central Lancashire) and on only as far as Lancaster. There, with more justification, the merits of the University of Lancaster are proclaimed. The weather has changed: the sky is overcast and a chilly wind sweeps across the platforms. The station announcer greets us and directs to Platform 5 those heading for "the sunny seaside resort of Morecambe". On the footbridge, as on the Ponte Vecchio in bygone days, commerce is setting out its stall – a pie vendor displays his wares on a trestle table. Further up the line, Kendal Mint Cake? Morecambe FC, by the way, is famous for its high-quality pies.

On the approach to Morecambe the amount of pebble-dashery grows significantly. But at the station the first sound is a discordant siren belonging to the emergency services. Can this be how they collect unpaid library fines on the mean streets of Morecambe? No, it's an ambulance, and as the wailing dies away the clamour of gulls replaces it as more suitable seaside soundtrack.

Silent seabirds decorate the roundabout in front of the station: a sculpted pair of gannets is engaged in some necking atop a chunk of millstone grit.

They introduce one of Morecambe's several appealing features.

Public sculpture, as often as not featuring seabirds, is common all over the town. When you come upon the cockerel outside the retail park it's quite a shock to find other kinds of fowl included in the programme. Elsewhere there are cormorants on Marine Road (the prom), creatures that might be guillemots outside Frankie & Benny's, a dove (with lines from the *Book of Genesis)* in front of the old station building and all manner of birds on the bollards in Morrisons car-park.

As you wander through the town towards the front, and the hotel you've booked into, more of the town's artistic public face announces itself. Gable ends are often adorned with paintings of Morecambe folk engaged in typical activities.

Perhaps this is a deliberate policy to divert attention from the shabbier aspects of the town. Certainly Morecambe is a town that rewards looking above street level, largely because so much of the street level prospect is ill-kempt, uninspiring or simply boarded-up. The centre especially is not a thing of beauty. There are some impressive or even spectacular buildings, notably the most enormous primary school I ever saw. On the other hand there are many indifferent buildings. Morecambe has an Art Deco Trail, of which the most conspicuous example is the Midland Hotel but even that isn't a particularly encouraging start: it's Art Deco with Nuremberg Rally influences.

Perhaps it's just the weather. Along Marine Road, in fine drizzle, the town has an out-of-season air. People – holidaymakers – are few and none is wearing a kiss-me-quick hat, eating candy floss or dragging along a reluctant child. At the pavement, where it costs nothing to park, hardly anybody is parking; across the road in the pay-and-display car-parks vast acreages are unoccupied.

The first child I encounter is not a holidaymaker but the son of the proprietor in a second-hand bookshop that would be a credit to Hay-on-Wye. The child is dressed as Denis the Menace and he is reading a comic. He may be a prop of some kind. The bookshop extends inland and, it transpires, to either side, in very narrow, claustrophobic spurs, like a maze where the false turning is almost immediately apparent. The walls, brought closer together by shelves on which books are often two deep, make these passages single-track lanes without passing places. Often you are so close to the spines that reading the titles is difficult.

The businesses along the sea front are an odd mixture. Further down from the bookshop you'll find the usual penny arcades, tea shops, chippies and burger bars but also a discount furniture store and a B&M, both of them in Art Deco buildings. As the number of boarded-up premises (many of them restaurants) increases, the idea that any tenant is welcome grows. A medical supplies company rounds off the collection of odd-balls.

At the Globe Arena I was introduced to the oddities of pre-season friendlies. In the absence of a programme the teams were read out over the PA. Some players were introduced simply as 'Trial-list' – most of the Morecambe defence, in fact – and they remained anonymous because none of the shirts bore names. The Blackburn fans were treating it like any other fixture; as the evening wore on several familiar chants were rolled out. "Who the fucking hell are you?", obviously, but more unkindly: "What's it like to see a crowd?"

At half-time I wandered over to ask a steward about the prospect of watching the second half from the other side of the ground. "Nil," he said. "You can't go out and come back in on the same ticket. You used to be able to but they changed the rules. Once you're out, you're out."

Back at the hotel my sleep was interrupted first by sounds of partying, at 3.30am, and then by a downpour. Perhaps the second doused the first.

The partying was indistinct until a male voice, not unhappily, declared clearly: "Be off with you, we don't want your sort here." This was followed by female giggling and a muffled reply. "No, go away," male voice said, sternly. More giggling, at which point rain began to fall. Water pattered on the panes, gurgled along the guttering and dribbled into the drains. The gulls, never wholly silent all night, resumed after the rain at 4am.

The following morning was dry and clear and disclosed the glory that Morecambe has to offer. Along the sea-front, across the bay, the Lake District dominates the horizon. The town's promotional literature quotes Bill Bryson to the effect that Morecambe Bay "may be the most beautiful bay in Britain". Bryson can only have qualified it because he had not seen all the others and felt a need to be scrupulously fair. There are occasions, though, when nothing but a categorical declaration will do full justice to the bay in question.

The view from Marine Road, past the statue of local lad Eric Bartholomew, aka Morecambe, past the north-facing beach and its attendant mud-flats with oyster catchers, curlews and sundry other waders, and finally across water (the thought of which makes you catch your breath, as though it were lapping at your midriff), all of this is merely a prelude to the peaks and fells in the glittering distance. It sets the town at your back in a quite different light.

On the promenade the town council has put up a cute metallic arc of craggy stage flats to show you what you're looking at. In the foreground, somewhere called Cark; to the right and a little higher, Hawkshead Moor; in the far distance, Helvellyn; and all the others, some familiar (Coniston Old Man) and others not (except, perhaps, to followers of Wainwright – Pike O'Stickle, for example). And of course there is the traditional seaside telescope. Ignore it, enjoy the view and breath that fresh air.

Morecambe 1 Blackburn Rovers 2
Globe Arena, 21 July 2017

Newcastle United

You have to take your stovepipe hat off to those Victorian railway engineers. They weren't going to let anything stand in the way of progress. In Newcastle, faced with the ancient castle that gave the city its name, they simply ploughed straight through it to drive their line on towards Edinburgh.

The bridge – really an elevated causeway – through the castle grounds is an elegant stone structure and, by the standards of Newcastle bridges, unspectacular. In the right light its masonry almost blends with the famous keep. You could imagine medieval carters setting up repair shops under its arches, where hot hacks would be re-sprayed. But to bisect an ancient monument... At Berkhamsted Castle, in Hertfordshire, the line built by Robert Stephenson skirts part of a moat and is deemed close to vandalism by the townsfolk; in Newcastle, the railway runs at second-floor level where it occupies most of the space between the keep and the only other remaining building, the Black Gate.

It isn't entirely fair to present this as an example of cavalier Victorian destructiveness. By the beginning of the 19th century the Black Gate was a slum. Other buildings in the area were pulled down to make way for civic improvement (and railway building); the Black Gate might easily have become one of them. Instead, thanks largely to the 19th century Corporation and the Society of Antiquaries, it survives as part of Newcastle's informal heritage trail.

It's a trail with many stopping points. Newcastle scores highly on two important counts: many of its set-piece attractions are intended specifically for young families; and almost all of them are free, asking only for donations.

The Discovery Centre, to the west of the city centre, ticks both boxes. On a Saturday morning it is alive with children and their parents. Attractive exhibitions with titles like Newcastle Story and Story of the Tyne share floors with Play Tyne, a play area for under-sevens, and the Play & Invent space. There are fantastic models of sections of the city and river, of fishing quays and shipyards and of many engines and vessels. With a Challenger Tank on the forecourt and the world's first steam turbine-powered steamship *Turbinia* dominating the ground floor, the museum isn't short of life-sized replicas or the real thing either.

The Newcastle Story is particularly good on life in the city through the ages and has an extensive 20th century section. But the Stuart period holds a treat: an illustration of a Newcastle Coat, which was a barrel with holes for arms and legs, to be worn around town by drunkards. The exhibition is notably low on sentimentality: there are, for example, pictures of blind-back houses – terraces with no windows at the back and therefore no view of the spoil tip to the rear of the living quarters.

The Discovery Museum spares a separate display for the *RMS Mauretania*, the most famous ship ever built on the Tyne. The *Mauretania* was the biggest ship in the world when she was launched in 1906 and the fastest until 1929.

If you walk from the Discovery to the Great North Museum, you can take in a section of the city's West Wall, with inset Chinese garden; a memorial to the Gallowgate Lead Works; the arch into Chinatown; and without too great a diversion, the column on which stands a statue of the 2nd Earl Grey, prime minister and tea champion in the 1830s. If you want to sample the view from the top, after just 164 steps it can be yours.

Turn left up Northumberland Street and you're on to a pedestrianised city precinct with fairground rides and up to three buskers, one of whom – a sign of the times – is a rapper. At the top, across a couple of intersections, is the Hancock, now known as the Great North Museum.

This is another real family attraction. A dramatically posed and lit skeleton of a Tyrannosaurus Rex sets the tone. But the main thing about the Hancock is its variety. Through the opening natural history gallery, you're into a superb Hadrian's Wall exhibition with a scale model of the entire length of the wall running down the centre of the hall. Around the periphery, finds from the area are interspersed with images of people telling their stories of the time.

Slender murals of landscapes run all around the walls as if you were out there, walking beside the Wall.

Are museums based on the collections of individuals bound to seem quirky? On the Hancock's first floor the contrasts are marked; across the width of the building there are successively rooms devoted to World Cultures, Natural Northumbria and Ancient Greeks. Within this, of the many individual items worth mentioning, here are just two: a samurai in full kit, demonstrating where the inspiration for a Star Wars stormtrooper came from (apart from the horns); and a frankly aroused lyre-plucker on a Greek vase.

Still for the most part free, the Laing Art Gallery charges for special exhibitions. In January 2018 it was the war artist Paul Nash, and *The Menin Road* alone was worth the £7.50. Even so, for free you get some fine British oil paintings, watercolours, glass and silver. And don't overlook the hallway into the café: it has a Henry Moore *Seated Woman*, a tea-pot collection and a metalwork representing fronds on a sea-bed which you are invited to touch. I thought the artist missed a trick: a mild electric shock would have made a point.

The route from here to the Black Gate takes you past Newcastle Cathedral; St Mary's Roman Catholic Cathedral is further west, not far from the railway station. They are an interesting contrast, if you have time. St Mary's is very quiet and dark, with something soft and sepulchral about its atmosphere; St Nicholas' is brighter, sharper and more lively.

Then beyond the castle you're on to the Quayside. To the right, the Jacobean Bessie Surtees House was closed, it being Saturday. Open or shut, Bessie's story is a romantic one; she eloped with the man who would become Lord Chancellor, and the timber-framed window through which she defenestrated is there to be admired.

To the left is the Newcastle Quayside, passing underneath the famous Tyne Bridge and leading to the Gateshead Millennium Bridge across which you can walk to Sage Gateshead and the Baltic Centre for Contemporary Art.

Just before you reach the footbridge you'll pass the Wesley Memorial Fountain, marking the spot where John Wesley first preached on Tyneside in 1742. His text was the verse from Isaiah that ends: "The chastisement of our peace was upon him and with his stripes we are healed."

Even from here it's less than 30 minutes' walk to the football ground; Newcastle is a very walkable city. Its streets are hardly a gridiron, though, and fortunately St James' Park is another of the features to be highlighted on the tourist signposts.

At the top of the East Stand at St James' Park I experienced for the first time the passing of a large flag above the heads of the crowd, along the line of the stand. Three rows from the back, I was close to the flag's hem as it swept past. Somehow it became entangled with my glasses. For a moment I thought I was going to lose them – I imagined my glasses being whisked away to the end of the stand. But the moment, and the flag, passed, and I righted them on the bridge of my nose. Next time I will know better: don't get involved.

The Geordie on my right was good company when my ear at last became attuned to his accent. But I heard his prophecy clearly enough. Newcastle were awarded a free-kick close to the Luton penalty area. "I'll just watch them score this then I'll go to the gents," he declared. Sure enough, Luton failed to clear the ball and after a sequence of ricochets it was bundled into the net.

I checked the orientation of Newcastle railway station after starting this report from Tyneside. It crossed my mind that the line through the Castle might have been heading south over the High-Level Bridge for London (or, at least, for Darlington, which seemed to be the go-to destination for Victorian railway engineers). But no, it goes to Edinburgh, where the castle remains intact.

Newcastle United 3 Luton Town 1
St James' Park, 6 January 2018

Newport County

As my clueless antipathy to satnav grows, my sense of direction deteriorates. Hence, on a dark and windswept Friday night, I am driving up a track on a Welsh hillside (it could be a mountainside) looking for the road to Caerleon-on-Usk.

It isn't pitch black or, to be more Welsh, Bible black. Golf buggies would wheeze up this narrow road by day; at night it is lit at knee height by what appear to be garden lamps. The lighting is helpful but the fact of it being a golf course is not. Also, I am losing faith in the idea that anywhere 'on Usk' might be found at the top of a hill.

Materialising abruptly out of the darkness, like Coleridge's stately pleasure dome on a Star Trek Transporter platform, an international hotel appears. Not long ago there would have been crumbling stone walls and a rude shepherd's hut here, but the Hyde Park Corner hallucination persists and, as I get closer, resolves itself into the Celtic Manor Luxury Hotel. With its liveried bell-hops, courtesy coaches and shimmering civilisation, it isn't yet Caerleon-on-Usk but if the worst comes to the worst it will surely provide a bed for the night.

I park in a space reserved for limousines that would disgorge jet-setters and playboys. Liverish bell-hops move towards me. I sidestep them and enter the lobby. At Reception a young woman is patient, helpful and above all, Welsh. She gives me clear and definite directions. The sign I passed at the foot of the hill, to the effect that there was no access this way to Catsash Road, was intended to stop people driving through the golf course. I must drive on, she says, to the club house and turn left at the top.

Five minutes later I am on the Catsash Road driving into Caerleon. And that, children, is how we found places before we had satnav.

Caerleon is a very unusual place. The town is built on the site of a Roman camp, and its one-way system encircles most of the campsite. In the Wild West you would imagine whooping native

Americans charging around on horseback, firing flaming arrows into the wagons of hapless settlers. In South Wales, Silurian tribesmen might have run energetically across the vallum to attack the peat (later stone) walls. With the amphitheatre outside the walls, I like to think of them taking in a show on the way.

I am booked into a hotel called the Priory. The protocol in the dining room is almost Greek, from the early days of tourism on the more isolated islands. Instead of giving an order to a waiter, you approach a long chiller cabinet above which two boards tell you what the cabinets contain. You choose a dish, as though from a market stall; it is removed from the cabinet, cooked for you and delivered to your table. This being a Priory, I had monkfish.

Other memorable peculiarities of the Priory:

- At 3.45am for a period of about an hour there was a surprising amount of foot traffic in the corridor outside my room
- The mattress was of a softness to defy superlatives
- The bathroom was so clean that a guest not wearing photoreactive lenses might have been rendered snow-blind
- In the breakfast nook, leaded windows within ornate scroll-worked masonry contained images of Roman emperors. The pictures date from the 13th century, it seems, and may once have been a comprehensive record. Certainly the panes that survive include one or two very short-lived (literally) title-holders – Galba and Otho, for example.

The patio is populated by Tolkeinesque carvings and a troubling sculpture of a monk militant resting his hands on an enormous sword.

Down the lane to the left is the Roman amphitheatre. Artists' impressions of this entertainment venue depict banked wooden grandstands with seating for perhaps 6,000 bloodthirsty legionaries; the eight grassy mounds that remain in contemporary Caerleon look more suited to picnickers. It's a peaceful spot, with remnants of wall to the northeast and, away to the south, the river Usk making its stately and rather orange progress towards the Bristol Channel.

The setting is almost sepulchral, and it is difficult to imagine the violence that must have been enacted there. It's another instance, isn't it, of the absurdity of lumping Greece and Rome together as the Classics? Greek theatre passes down the centuries the drama of Aeschylus and the wit of Aristophanes; the Romans give us carnage as a form of proletarian pleasure.

Across the road, children are gathering for Saturday morning rugby. At ground level the amphitheatre feels circular but aerial photographs reveal it to be more of an oval in shape.

The road to the amphitheatre is apparently the Via Principalis of the old Roman settlement and it led back into the town through one of four gateways. These must be imagined, but sections of wall survive. Four metres high in places, with earthworks below and fortified turrets at intervals, they must have been a daunting prospect to an attacker with no artillery.

The road leads directly to the National Roman Legion Museum. At the desk is a young man who on another weekend might be storming a vallum. He is a re-enactor, though not exclusively of Roman era battles. He looks like a rugby player but this is Wales and such stereotyping is regrettably predictable. One might as well expect him to burst into song, as some of the men in the bar had done the previous evening.

The museum over which he presides is like the amphitheatre – a museum in the round. It is full of interest and works hard to spread that down the generations. The other visitors are families and it's noticeable that they stop at intervals to give the children time to play with the diversions set up for them.

For adults – for this adult, anyway – the smallest things are the most appealing. The collection of engraved gemstones is absolutely gorgeous, but the glassware, coins, gaming counters and so forth are also very evocative. This being a Roman Legion museum, some of the more prosaic exhibits are intriguing: a soldier's frying pan, for example, and detailed reproductions of uniforms.

Caerleon has some Roman remains that you won't see anywhere else: the only legionary barracks visible in Europe, for example, and as early an inscription as is to be found in the British Isles. But it's worth a visit in any case. In addition to the *spécialités de la maison*, there's the general breadth of the menu and the ambience to be enjoyed.

I started in Caerleon in case Newport had little to offer. A friend who was going there recalled being told by her dad to tape any banknotes she was carrying to the inside of her thigh. A mugger would be unlikely to find them. Ambiguous advice, certainly, but not a ringing endorsement.

I needn't have worried. And my own first impression of the city was wholly favourable. I sought to park close to the ground for a quick getaway later. Having lost all faith in my sense of direction I stopped and asked a passer-by. He said: "It's next left, just round the corner." I looked up and saw a sign 'Rodney Parade' attached to a lamp-post. "Where the sign says 'Rodney Parade'?" I asked. "Exactly," he said, grinning broadly.

From there it was a short walk into the city centre across the City Footbridge, which appears on the Visitor Map with a dolphin leaping beneath it. Storm Brian was blowing a gale up the Usk and there were no dolphins. Down the Usk the Transporter Bridge would surely have been closed to pedestrians, I reasoned. I doubt I would have gathered the nerve to climb 60 metres of open ladders to a perilous gantry on a calm day, but with the wind gusting at 70mph and occasional squalls sweeping through the city horizontally it was out of the question. I set out to enjoy Newport indoors.

On the way, there was street art to enjoy:

- A statue of an ox, or possibly an aurochs, bearing a large bell; supposedly inspired by the legend of Gwynllyw's conversion to Christianity, it was created by Sebastian Boyese. Gwynllyw is anglicised as Woolos and is the patron saint of Newport. The aurochs would never have occurred to me but one turned up later in the day in Newport Museum & Art Gallery.
- A mysterious shrouded figure with birds on the point of taking off from the arms of a frame surrounding him/it; the sculpture, by Paul Kincaid, is in honour of Newport poet WH Davies, who famously wrote: "What is this life if, full of care, we have no time to stand and stare."

- A monument to the Chartists, who staged the last armed rebellion in the UK. Their attempt to improve the lot of the working man and to extend democracy came to a bloody and disastrous end in Newport, outside the Westgate Hotel. A substantial and moving display in the Newport Museum & Art Gallery is devoted to it. The Newport uprising, in November 1839, came only 46 years after the execution of Louis XVI and just two years after the first publication of Thomas Carlyle's magnificent *History of the French Revolution*; those were significant, recent and still troubling events in a parliamentary democracy with a monarch as head of state.

From Westgate Square through the Market Sector and towards Newport Castle there's a large roundabout beneath which pedestrians are guided past the Old Green Mural, a series of mosaics. The subject matter is largely related to transport, mining and movement of coals to Newport.

It is worth the diversion, which is more than you can say for Newport Castle. Largely derelict and girded by fencing, the Castle appears impregnable until you look at the upper windows, where signs of rough sleeping are visible.

The Castle would once have controlled entry to the town across an elegant old bridge. Appropriately, it's where the riverside walk known as Town Gate begins. Along this promenade are more reminders of Newport's industrial heritage: the vast red metal sculpture called the Steel Wave; and further along an information panel that adds documentary detail to the imagery of the Old Green Mural.

Parallel to the Usk there used to be a dock and associated activities. Now there's a dual-carriageway, but beyond that Upper and Lower Dock Street and Canal Parade recall the past. Newport's Transporter bridge, the elevation of which was necessary to allow vessels to pass up the Usk to the city docks, also dates from that period. Now, one new bridge for pedestrians and two for vehicles mean that no more such vessels will be passing this way.

Commerce and not the weather drove me indoors for the first time. The bank had three ATMs on the street but nobody was using them. Inside, however, there was a queue at the single cash dispenser. Did the people prefer to use that machine because they could conceal their cash on the insides of their thighs more discreetly indoors?

A downpour coincided with my arrival at the Newport Museum & Art Gallery. This is a profoundly municipal building; the impression of utilitarian plainness persists up the stairs to where the exhibits begin. After an unprepossessing ante-chamber referred to as a café, you're served up Newport's justly famous tea-pot collections.

There are more than 350 items in the John & Elizabeth Wait Collection, not all of them immediately recognisable as tea-pots. Displayed in cases, on shelves or in reconstructed drawing rooms from various eras, they are a colourful thread from Britain's social tapestry.

The Iris & John Fox Collection includes ceramics of many other kinds, but the Waits will have softened you up and you won't be able to stop yourself being drawn to the tea-pots. Iris, known as the Queen of Wemyss, began collecting as a young child and paid for her first purchase by selling firewood. Her story is as colourful as her collection.

Other special galleries are devoted to the Chartists, a medieval ship and the Transporter Bridge. Of the gallery's collection of over 3,000 paintings and drawings, about 100 are displayed in a space that hints at what might be done with Amazon distribution warehouses when shopping online passes (with satnav, e-readers, tablets etc) into history.

On my way, eventually, to the football ground I had lunch at the Riverfront Theatre. This was a hive of activity: a community policing event was in progress and a drum band was warming up for a parade somewhere. I ordered the day's special, borshch, for its exotic appeal: the colour suggested beetroot or red cabbage or both.

There's a gallery here, too, on the ground floor. When I was there the exhibition was 'Case Study', by Stephanie Roberts, a collection of sketches, artworks and artefacts apparently relating to the artist's adjustment to her dyslexia.

At the Newport County ground, Storm Brian swept down Rodney Parade like a drill sergeant. Two youths sent out to erect flags in the centre circle gave up after less than a minute's struggle. A couple of dozen primary or nursery-school children formed a guard of honour and bravely stuck it out for 10 minutes.

The advertising boards from the side of the ground had been removed, leaving a plain reminder of the good old days: all it needed was the letters of the alphabet to identify the half-times.

In the stand, rows A to K were exposed to the storm but the hardy Welsh sat stoically through it. In possession of a ticket for row G, I retreated furtively to the rearmost row, which was reserved for occupants of the hospitality boxes behind. The boxes being empty, the only demand for their seats came from our side. Mysteriously, hardly anybody else encroached. The teams fought out a fretful draw. Football was not the winner.

Newport County 1 Mansfield Town 1
Rodney Parade, 21 October 2017

Northampton Town

In 1460 at the Battle of Northampton, the Lancastrians were betrayed by Sir Ralph Grey (who had his men change sides) and routed by Yorkist forces. At Sixfields Stadium, in 2018, the Lancastrians achieved a 2-2 draw but were relegated to the fourth division anyway, betrayed by a season's failure.

One more goal at Northampton would have saved them, but unlike the forces of Henry VI they had no artillery. Yes, the Battle of Northampton was the first in England in which artillery was used; but the history books go on to say that torrential rain made the Lancastrians' cannon useless.

The battle took place on land that is now a golf course, near Delapre Abbey a mile south of Northampton town centre. The Abbey tells a familiar story: a reflective order of blameless nuns, seizure by Henry VIII, passage into the private hands of one or two wealthy families, gradual decline, the poisoned chalice passed to the local authority, and finally a fight against development.

Now it's a popular place to take the children or walk the dogs on a sunny Saturday. In the walled garden on 5 May a spring fayre was in progress, and drawn up around the courtyard in front of the stable block were the vehicles of vendors of artisanal products, flowers, sweetmeats etc. It had a medieval feel.

The Abbey itself is worth a look for the restored décor. The penultimate private owner removed everything that wasn't bolted down, to stop it falling into the hands of a claimant he regarded as an imposter. But after restoration some of the rooms – the salon, the library and the drawing room ceiling especially – are very striking.

Set out around the library are toys of varying vintages, for children to play with. This is just one of the ways Delapre Abbey appeals to families. The Battlefield Room is almost entirely for children: artillery as a game of skittles, the components of gunpowder, family trees brought to life; but pride of place goes to an automated theatrical reconstruction with lights, commentary and rotating pictures.

The nuns, by the way, were perhaps not entirely blameless. According to legend two were disciplined for wearing sumptuous blue gowns. And the resident ghost, the Grey Lady (unrelated to Sir Ralph) is said to be a nun restlessly searching the house for the wounded soldier she nursed and fell in love with.

Northampton has another very striking interior to offer on the southern margins of the town centre, at 78 Derngate. This is said to be the only private home designed by Charles Rennie Mackintosh in England. "It is the only place in the world where Mackintosh's mature architectural and interior style can be seen in their original setting," adds the brochure.

The curators soften you up cunningly. First, you pass displays of the model trains and boats with which the owner, a Wenman Joseph Bassett-Lowke (people did like to make full use of all their names in those days, didn't they?) made his money. Expectations are raised when you are asked to put on blue plastic bags as over-shoes. The first couple of rooms are interesting – an inlaid rug, for example, so that people wouldn't trip on it – but in subtle, undra-matic ways. You'll find yourself examining the window fittings. And then abruptly you're in the Hall Lounge, a quite sensational room with shapes and colours that prefigure the computer age. Had you lived there, you would not have needed a television.

78 Derngate does an outstanding job of presenting its very specific subject, but it doesn't overlook the other functions of a heritage hub. There's an attractive café, with tables on a garden terrace; a gallery room; and display space that, on my visit, was occupied fittingly by the inheritors of Bassett-Lowke's passions, a society of model railway enthusiasts.

Its sophistication is at the opposite end of the scale from the Abington Park Museum. This is a short bus ride to the east of the town centre. It's a community museum: free, informal and, in places, charming.

The first exhibits are a cabinet of stuffed birds, the lid of an Egyptian sarcophagus and a large Buddha. The rest of the ground floor is military, charting the history of the Northamptonshire Regiment and culminating in a kind of chapel of remembrance, with names on the wall and Wilfred Owen on the soundtrack. With their chessmen made out of cartridge cases and their regimental badges carved from chalk near Loos, the old soldiers provide their own perspective 100 years on.

Upstairs is more quirky. A cabinet of old shoes evokes not only Northampton's industrial history but also the habit of concealing old shoes in construction sites, for luck. There are displays highlighting domestic water, drainage and lighting, and labour-saving devices. A cradle-to-grave sequence includes a wonderful collection of old toys. The Oak Room, the equal in its way of anything at Delapre or Derngate, is a reminder that this was once a fine country house. Then, after some porcelain and some portraits, you're back at the beginning in the main hall.

It's a most unusual place and well worth the trip. I'm not so sure about the adjacent Abington Park Aviary, though. The caged exotic birds seemed taunted on a sunny afternoon by their free domestic relatives.

Another bus ride out of the centre is the Roman Catholic Cathedral. If you find yourself spending much time at North Gate Bus Station, it need not be time wasted. Sit near the Colombiana coffee bar to enjoy the banter between the young woman serving and the bus drivers among her customers. Catching practice with satsumas was one of the diversions when I was there.

The bus station has history too. A plaque recalls the medieval synagogue that once stood on the site, and more recently it was a fish market. Also, look upwards: aligned with the struts holding up the glass (ETFE, strictly speaking, a fluorine-based plastic) roof, like text boxes snapped to guides, are Northampton highlights picked out in capitals. The lettering is reversed, as seen in a mirror; but the sun projects it clearly on to the wall of the public conveniences. 'Five Witches Hanged', 'Nobel Prize 1962' and, among many others, 'Thomas a Becket'.

Northampton makes the most of a rather slender connection with the famously turbulent priest. Accused by Henry II of contempt and embezzlement, Becket was tried at Northampton Castle in 1164. During the trial Becket 'lodged' in St Anthony's Priory, on the land of which the Cathedral of Our Lady Immaculate & St Thomas of Canterbury now stands.

It's a quiet, rather plain nave; in the colour of the pillars and their arches you may detect a hint of vanilla. But the mural behind the altar is very elaborate, and the decorated green panelling in the ceiling is eye-catching. Statues of the Virgin Mary and St Thomas a Becket stand on plinths on either side of the altar. The saint, lest there be any doubt over his identity, has a sword through his head.

You'll see other references to Thomas Becket in Northampton on the way out to Sixfields. The Becket Retail Park and the Thomas a Becket pub are on the left, not far from St James Church.

The town also works hard at providing tourist interest on the Northampton Waterside and in the Cultural Quarter. But you will see no signpost to Northampton Castle; the railway station is built on its site and a distinctive postern gate is all that remains.

The station was originally called Northampton Castle, but they dropped the suffix when it became the last remaining station in the town. The other stations were probably called Northampton Irreplaceable Iron Age Barrow and Northampton Exquisite But Bulldozed Art Treasures. Nor can I tell you anything about The National Leather Collection, which opens only on Wednesdays, or the Northampton Museum & Art Gallery, closed until 2019.

It's an unaffected town with some fine buildings, open spaces, a busy, colourful market and plenty to offer. And battle will be joined there again in the 2018/19 season, because Northampton Town were relegated too.

Northampton Town 2 Oldham 2
Sixfields, 5 May 2018

Norwich City

The colour palette of football is an undervalued aspect of the game's appeal. In football the contest itself is the spectacle, and the role of colour is purely to distinguish one set of players from the other. This isn't horse racing, which is so indescribably dull that the jockeys' silks are its brightest feature. Nor is it limited-overs cricket, where the colour of the players' outfits emphasises how distantly related this game is to its more demanding but monochrome progenitor.

On the other hand, a goalless draw will sometimes leave you searching desperately for extraneous points of interest. At Carrow Road in August 1969, the colours of the two teams' strips became a point of discussion at least as intense as anything happening on the pitch.

Norwich City against Portsmouth in the early part of the 1969/70 season set out as agreeable a selection from the chromatic scale as you might find anywhere in football. Norwich, in their canary yellow and emerald green, against Portsmouth, in blue shirts and white shorts with, around the cuffs, collars and turn-ups, details in red, white and blue. Under lights – for this was an evening game – the splashes of colour were particularly vivid.

The counter-argument was that Norwich and Portsmouth lacked two critical elements to be regarded as the last word in aesthetic impact. Theirs were primary colours, and in unbroken blocks. Not for them the delicacy of sky blue, the tang of tangerine, the lustrous hint of old gold or the cheeky piquancy of claret. They had not a stripe, a hoop, a sash, an epaulette or a quarter between them. (Norwich City had worn blue and white halved shirts in their earliest days, but that was because the team was composed of refugees from Blackburn.)

So the fixture had shortcomings. But it also had balance; the two strips complemented each other, with no internal or inter-necine clashes. Between them, they represented most of the colours commonly used in football strips, and did so harmoniously.

One aspect of the genius behind the marketing of the table-football game Subbuteo was that the basic set pitted a team in red shirts against a team in blue, both of them wearing white shorts. In those days coloured shorts (other than navy blue or black) were relatively uncommon. Most young players, then, could take the field with a favourite team. It might have been Manchester United against Everton, but it could as easily have been Swindon Town and Gillingham, or Nottingham Forest and Leicester City, etc, etc. Red and blue constitute a standard football combination, in opposition, but the spectrum offers so many more possibilities that they can be discarded in this context.

More distinctive, individual kits may also be discounted. Bradford City's maroon and orange, offered in recent years in hoops, stripes and a chequerboard pattern, certainly add to the rich tapestry but rarely look other than bilious except against a team playing in all-white. Scunthorpe United's light blue and claret halves were not so objectionable but, again, could not easily be matched with anything other than the simplest of strips. A shirt like Brighton's of years gone by, combining blue and white stripes with red shirt numbers, looked like a Tesco's carrier bag in the days before plastic carrier bags became disreputable.

In the mid-range there are combinations like the claret and light blue of Aston Villa, Burnley and West Ham, which are inoffensive but not easily complemented; the bold stripes of Newcastle, Notts County and, at a pinch, West Bromwich Albion, which are too close to monochrome to be worth considering. Red stripes, blue stripes, or in the cases of Reading, QPR and Doncaster hoops, and green at Yeovil, are attractive enough in their own right but again, limiting in combination on the field.

Blackpool's tangerine is a rare example of a distinctive colour retained by a club for generations. Another is the green of Plymouth Argyle, and I suspect that most football fans have a soft spot for Argyle for their commitment to a neglected colour, for using it in an interesting way over the years and for their unique name.

Then there are the colours that teams are remembered for long after they have been discarded. Most of these belong to the era of ambitious away strips: Coventry City's famous chocolate is an example, or Manchester United's grey, which had to be changed at half-time at Southampton because the players could not see each other.

Some shirts tried too hard, using too many colours: Arsenal's snakeskin away strip of the late 90s is an obvious example. Technology now makes a kind of linear blend possible: Barcelona led the way with a hellish away strip and impressionable executives at Manchester City and Liverpool have followed. At the other end of the spectrum, all-black strips have become popular, forcing the match officials to take the field in fuschia.

Oldham's contribution to the palette of football colours is limited but noteworthy. I believe Athletic were the first English team to play in pink, against Leeds United, in a televised match after which the shirts were auctioned for charity.

And on one memorable afternoon at Selhurst Park the match-day programme said Oldham would be in ecru, which added to the tension as 3pm approached; no-one in the crowd knew what ecru was until the team emerged.

Norwich City 0 Portsmouth 0
Carrow Road, 27 August 1969

Nottingham Forest

Rewberry, professor of Old Norse at the University of Mercia, was too concerned about saga trouble-maker Thorolf Halt-foot to notice that his taxi was about to stop. What was the nature of Thorolf's lameness? Might dinner with Thorstein Codbiter have been therapeutic for the sake of the omega-3? Unless Thorstein's taste was for a different kind of cod...

"Ere you are, boss," the cabby said agreeably.

Finance replaced fish as a source of confusion in Rewberry's mind. He had a £20 note, somewhere, but the fare was less than a fiver. Half in the car and half out, wary of the treacherous habit of kerbs to be an inch further away than expected, he patted down pockets in search of change. A fiver! From his left trouser pocket he detached a £5 note from a set of door keys, a linen handkerchief and a quantity of lint. Behind him, the tranquillity of the Notts County ground at 2.15pm on a Saturday afternoon escaped his attention altogether. Not so that of the driver, who accepted his note, kept the change and sped away.

Rewberry straightened himself, turned round and looked up. Ahead of him, the lifeless glazing of the club shop gazed back. No white-collar professionals headed for the Meadow Lane Executive Boxes to the right; three sets of closed shutters, with white lettering on a black ground, gave instructions on how to buy tickets other than on match days. Rewberry raised his eyes a little further and read: 'Notts County FC Ticket Office'. He had come to the wrong Nottingham football ground. A crumpled sheet of newspaper bowled past like tumbleweed.

Rewberry looked both ways along Meadow Lane. It was empty of pedestrians in both directions and largely devoid of traffic. On the other side of the road, low-rise low-density industrial units were as sullenly locked and shuttered as the football stadium. Grey clouds scudded across the cheerless sky. No meadows bordered the lane. It was not, Rewberry reflected, the kind of road along which taxis would routinely cruise.

He gathered his flapping overcoat around himself and began a process his mother would have referred to as 'taking stock'. This amounted to searching his memory for whatever he knew about Nottingham that might prove useful. To drill down to such seams, he found, he needed to discard a great deal of dross – not ordinarily dross, but not immediately valuable either. For example, knowing that JM Barrie and Graham Greene had both worked (in different eras) on the *Nottingham Journal* was of no help, beyond causing Rewberry to wonder whether the literary giants might once have stood, despatched to Meadow Lane to cover a County home game, on the very spot he now occupied. Equally useless, Rewberry's interest in politics yielded slight knowledge of Nottingham High School's contribution to 20th and 21st century parliaments (and tawdry terpsichorean entertainments): Ken Clarke, Geoff Hoon and Ed Balls.

At last, beneath several layers of such sediment, he detected a grain of possible value: lodged in a distant corner of his memory was the fact that Notts County belied their name by playing within the city of Nottingham, whereas Forest, who played at the City Ground, were outside the city boundary. One recollection prompted another: the grounds were not far apart. And a third: the Forest ground was very close to the home of Nottinghamshire County Cricket Club, which as the world – or, at least, that part of the world once coloured pink on maps and in atlases, denoting the never-setting sun – knows is called Trent Bridge. On a roll, Rewberry decided he needed to find the River Trent.

He knew in which direction the city centre lay – the taxi had recently brought him from there. It was logical to assume that, to find the City Ground, he needed to continue along that vector away from central Nottingham. At the same time he should take note of gradients: a slope should logically take him to the river.

Meadow Lane was more or less flat. He set off to his right, with Notts County unvisited over his right shoulder.

Almost immediately Rewberry came to water. The road crossed the canal that runs northward from the Trent into Nottingham city centre, where it turns sharply left to rejoin the Trent at Beeston.

This waterway he ignored. In the first place, the road rose slightly to cross the canal, in defiance of his theory of slopes; second, the canal could hardly be the mighty Trent, the third-longest river in the kingdom – it had a tired, suburban air, especially where a modest footbridge linked two sections of a modern housing development no doubt marketed as 'waterfront townhouses'. Besides, ahead he was coming to a main road on which the possibility of a taxi came back into the equation.

At the junction, right was sharp right and more or less back towards the city. Rewberry turned left. Immediately his spirits were raised by a startlingly well-preserved half-timbered building across the road; not by the faux-Tudor architecture, which was as convincing as a Morris Traveller, but by the name. It was apparently a pub and its name was the Embankment.

Rewberry pressed on, confident now that the Trent would be around the next bend. As in fact it was, flowing beneath a handsome Victorian bridge with a low cast-iron balustrade or parapet. To the left, on the south bank of the river, rose the floodlight pylons of the City Ground, not 200 metres away, and the ground itself was so close to the bank that the Trent End stand resembled the back of a precariously parked car.

Where the balustrade or parapet ran out and the last low lamp standard ascended from the last plinth, Rewberry turned left and made his way to the riverside walk.

By now he was thoroughly pleased with himself. The error over his instructions to the taxi driver was forgotten or, at least redeemed. By logic and ingenuity he had overcome a problem that would have defeated a lesser man. Deposited in the wrong place in an unfamiliar city, he had brought the knowledge garnered – unwittingly, in some cases – over the course of a lifetime to bear on the dilemma and resolved it. Would the youngsters with their utter reliance on digital aids be able to say as much? Yes, he conceded, they probably would; they would have satnav on their phones, and possibly Google Earth; they would in any case have been able to call another taxi. But if their phones were dead, or discharged or in receipt of no signal...

As Rewberry congratulated himself, admired the bridge from below, observed the dark (in the theatrical sense) floodlights of Meadow Lane a stone's throw away across the river and marvelled at the scale of the River Trent, he found himself absorbed into the body of a crowd making its way to a football match. He, chameleon Rewberry, was able to resume his ever so fine wool-gathering.

Nottingham Forest 2 Oldham 0
City Ground, 30 January 1993

Notts County

When your image of the city is formed from various film versions of the Robin Hood saga, Nottingham comes as a surprise. You expect a lot of forbidding masonry behind walls and palisades, and perhaps a gallows in a square milling with yokels. Instead it's a substantial, attractive modern city. The castle, like the legend, is thoughtfully maintained off to one side.

We'll get to that. But first, to reinforce the point about modern Nottingham's post-medieval appeal, I'd like to start at the National Videogame Arcade. Unfortunately I can't, because the Arcade has only been there since 2015 and my last visit to Nottingham for a football match was in 2011. I've been to the city since then, but that was a family visit with my 88-year-old father and he was not a devotee of videogames nor, in truth, of much technology since the Telex machine. All I can usefully say is that it's there now, and from the website it sounds fantastic.

On the other hand, the association of Nottingham with justice, through the ambiguous figure of the Sheriff of Nottingham, goes back centuries. It is an appropriate place, then, for the National Justice Museum. This is twinned on the Nottingham tourist trail with the City of Caves, so you may want to work out how much time you can devote to the pair of them before you commit to the joint ticket option.

The National Justice Museum is unusual in a number of ways. The premises are the exhibit, to a large extent; there's a form of role play beyond the costumed characters who patrol the galleries; and ghost-hunters who have investigated the building report that you'll never have a room to yourself, however quiet it may seem.

One of the abiding impressions of the Museum is the severity of Justice in days of yore; you can't help but be astonished at how easy it was to find yourself on the wrong side of a punitive sentence. The exhibits devoted to the era of transportation to Australia make this point forcefully. Robin Hood was some years ahead of his time.

If you move on to the City of Caves you'll pass close to the

Museum of Nottingham Life at Brewhouse Yard. This is twinned with the Castle Museum & Art Gallery. Is there scope for a passport-style ticket to the whole city? Someone must have thought of it and discarded the idea. And yet there are caves here too, almost an unexpected bonus after a more conventional series of period rooms, street scenes, shops etc. An unusual feature of the displays is that you're invited to touch some of the exhibits – the weight of the pans in the Victorian kitchen will renew your admiration for *Downton Abbey*'s Mrs Patmore.

Next door is Ye Olde Trip to Jerusalem, said to be the oldest inn in England; the sign says 1189. Ye Olde Fighting Cocks in St Albans claims to go back to the 8th century and says that the building on the site now is the 'oldest inhabited licensed house in England', dating from the 11th century. Those are disappointingly vague dates but well in advance of 1189: clearly the designation 'inn' is vital to the Trip to Jerusalem's claims.

I'm not sure about a pub with a gift shop and merchandise; on the other hand, the Trip has caves, which seems to make it an authentic tourist attraction in this undermined neighbourhood.

From the pub to the castle is barely a fighting cock-stride, and the footpath takes you past a famous statue of Robin Hood. Eventually, when a new generation of sprinters has taken the baton, the pose will once again look like England's favourite proto-socialist rather than Usain Bolt.

Nottingham Castle doesn't really call Alan Rickman to mind. Although the site is ancient, the building itself dates from the late Victorian era. A Norman motte and bailey castle, embellished and fortified by Henry II, was eventually demolished after the English Civil War in 1651. It was replaced later in the 17th century by a 'ducal palace', which rioters burnt down in 1831. The restored and remodelled palace opened to the public as a museum of fine art in 1878.

Today the building still houses art, and much else besides. Perhaps Nottingham Castle Museum & Art Gallery tries a little too hard: there is a lot to take in across a good many fields:

● Caves, almost inevitably. Edward III is said to have entered the castle surreptitiously through secret tunnels to take his mother and her lover by surprise. Their surprise may be easily imagined

- The Museum of the Mercian Regiment, covering almost 300 years of soldiering
- Fine Art, from medieval times to the present day
- Decorative Art, including the Gibbs collection of Georgian silver and the Ballantyne collection of 20th century British ceramics
- Carved alabaster panels and figures, a local speciality with stone mined in Derbyshire and Staffordshire
- Nottingham pottery, featuring especially salt-glazed stoneware pots.

After all that, you'll need to sit down. I found my eyes developing a tendency to salt-glaze over. Fortunately the Castle has an exceptional cafeteria, and attractive grounds in which to stroll off any excess.

In a comprehensive itinerary the Castle would be by no means the last call. Just out of the city centre to the west is Wollaton Hall and Park, including a natural history museum and the Nottingham Industrial Museum. Dotted around the city centre are the Nottingham Contemporary Art Gallery and several smaller galleries.

The day I went to Notts County, the city streets thronged with colourful ice-hockey fans heading for the National Ice Centre. There's also the possibility of watching sport of a high calibre at Trent Bridge, where Test Match cricket has been played since 1899.

But Meadow Lane is a fond memory for me because of the result. It was Oldham's first win in 13 attempts. During a dismal run of four draws and eight defeats (more than 25% of the league season) the team had scored just three goals.

By the way, if anyone ever asks you "What did the Normans do for us?" offer them the case of Nottingham in reply. The name originally had an 'S' on the front – the homestead of Snot's folk. The Norman habit of promiscuously dropping 's's did Nottingham no harm at all.

Notts County 0 Oldham 2
Meadow Lane, 2 April 2011

Oldham Athletic

What isn't widely known about Jack Sprat is that he was an Oldham Athletic fan.

This detail of the famously fastidious Sprat's private life came to light in the 1989/90 season. Oldham, then a Second Division team of such long standing that they might have served as a definition of second-rate, suddenly emerged on to the national stage.

They began to win cup-ties. In the case of the League Cup, the games took place in midweek; FA Cup ties were always played on Saturdays in that era, but replays also featured in the midweek highlights programmes. Oldham became regular stars of Wednesday night television in the winter of 1989 and early spring of 1990.

The club had no recent cup-fighting tradition to speak of. Exempt by status from the first round of the League Cup, they usually went out in the second (to Port Vale as often as not). Their FA Cup Third Round defeats were inflicted by more distinguished and geographically dispersed opponents but no less regular. In the 1989/90 season, by abrupt contrast, they overcame some very big names.

Arsenal were the first to go, defeated and ultimately demoralised on the artificial surface of the Boundary Park ground in the League Cup. Southampton, at that time in sparkling form in the old First Division, followed after a replay. Aston Villa and Everton succumbed in the FA Cup.

The team's exploits brought its manager to prominence. Joe Royle, already a figure of some physical stature, acquired matching figurative eminence. Week after week, it seemed, Joe would fill the screen with a beaming smile and a huge duffle coat. After paying a handsome tribute to his players he would add how overdue a reward the cup runs were for the Oldham faithful, who had stuck by the team through thick and thin.

'Thick and thin' was the expression he used and under the circumstances it might have seemed unexceptionable. It did not, however, bear close scrutiny. The win over Arsenal gave the clue.

Before that remarkable 3-1 win Oldham had not beaten a team from the top division in any competitive match for 60 years. The truth was that there had been barely any thick in living memory. It had all been thin.

True, Oldham had successfully applied for re-election, a triumph of sorts, in the early 60s. Having finally made good their escape from the Fourth Division they had won the Third Division title in 1973, which had to count as a good year. But those high-lights apart, and an occasional isolated result notwithstanding, Oldham supporters of more than six months' standing had experienced nothing but lean times. They all shared Jack Sprat's diet.

It is possible that Sprat would have noticed in 1990 that the fare from Oldham Athletic was putting on weight; he might even have changed his allegiance, moving down the road to Rochdale. Lean and fat, though, are relative terms. Even among football's elite, Oldham continued to present a lean outlook. Sprat would have had no difficulty remaining true to his convictions at Boundary Park.

Besides, it is the preference of his wife that suggests a fickle nature. Mrs Sprat, if she took any interest in football at all, would have moved between Tottenham, Liverpool and Arsenal in the years to 1990. Her subsequent leanings, it must be suspected, would be to the Manchester clubs. The uneasy coexistence in the Sprat household thus represents a truth about football in general. The fat get fatter and the lean get relegated.

When Athletic won the Second Division title in 1991, they did so as noted on an artificial surface.

In the preceding couple of years during their meteoric rise, the unnaturally flat and verdant pitch was the best-known fact about the club. Complaints of unfairness inevitably ensued. Not only was it suggested that Oldham could not play on grass but also that visiting teams could not play on anything else.

People associated with Oldham became very defensive, the centre-backs occasionally excepted. Statistics were adduced to prove that Oldham lost just as often at home as they did on real pitches elsewhere, but no-one was fooled. The surface at Boundary

Park produced something more akin to pinball than football. It occasionally had a comical element. Brentford fans may recall a very windy day there when their team was awarded a penalty: the ball had to be kept in place by a holder – a man lying flat with the tip of his finger at the end of an outstretched arm, stopping the ball from blowing away, as is needed from time to time in rugby union.

After the defensive statistics came the more positive assertion that the surface favoured skilful passing football. That was like saying that beach cricket favours a hearty slog in the direction of the incoming tide. Anyone with any grasp of tactics could see from the first two minutes of a match that the ball was out of control if allowed to bounce. Some sides like it that way – it isn't far removed from the guiding principle of the celebrated Route One long-ball style. A ball that might land anywhere is a random element from which a team of ferocious tacklers and tireless runners will expect to profit.

The Oldham team that won the Second Division title in 1991 was, indeed, a side of passing accomplishments. It added to Athletic's appeal that players would attempt to pass their way out of the deepest defensive trouble, gratuitously bringing to frantic life many a flat fixture. Late on in games when goals were needed urgently, however, Oldham could hoof the ball upfield with the best of them.

Some teams were visibly demoralised by the plastic pitch. Others were not. Why Hull City, for example, should succeed where Arsenal (champions and league leaders at the time) had so miserably failed is a mystery. The fact is, though, that Oldham were a strong home team long before the magic carpet was unrolled. Here the other well-known fact about Boundary Park may have come into play – its altitude. On a cold day, such as are not infrequent in the football season, Boundary Park is Siberian.

On the morning of FA Cup Final day, 14 May 1994, I was driving down the M6 from Manchester to Birmingham. Perhaps every third car that passed was showing Manchester United colours. Most had red scarves fluttering from the windows; others were yellow and green, some were black, and one was blue. There were not many colours that United had not turned out in during the past season. One car had a red devil stencilled on the rear window. There were fat-cat executive cars with tinted windows, 10-year-old Escorts with four burly occupants, nippy hatchbacks driven by girlfriends who would remain sober, mini-buses, coaches and even one or two motorcyclists. There was something of the sense of a people on the move, a migration, though with no overtones of Steinbeck's Okies heading west in *The Grapes of Wrath*.

It was a poignant morning. If football matches ended two minutes earlier, most of the town of Oldham would have been flying south down the M6 that sunny day. Instead Athletic fans would watch the match (if at all) on television, with the prospect in the following season of journeys down the M6 to second-tier away games in the Midlands, and on to Bristol, Reading and Swindon. Well, they had had their place in the sun, however briefly. Few of them could ever genuinely have expected it.

Manchester United would take the Cup back to Old Trafford, to match their Championship trophy. Players, interviewed on television, would remark that winning trophies for the fans was what playing for Manchester United was all about.

It must be a hollow kind of relationship that demands trophies to satisfy the fans. A kind of panic must attend a season without trophies. Not so in the Sprat household, where clubs who do not win trophies are honoured as the keepers of the spirit of the game.

Oldham Athletic 5 Accrington Stanley 2
Boundary Park, 11 February 1961

Oxford United

As the bus ground along Headington Road through the Saturday tea-time traffic, some of the passengers' nerves were fraying audibly.

"You sit there and don't move again. If you move again, there's no 'Strictly' for you this evening, young lady."

This dire threat evidently did the trick. "Good girl, Ariadne."

But temporarily. "You little minx, get back here! Ariadne! Sit down!"

Vainly trying to set Ariadne a good example was her smaller brother, who sat quietly throughout. I hoped he was called Theseus. But the family group left the bus without the boy doing anything to warrant being shouted at. Besides, on looking it up I find that Ariadne's brother was called Deucalion. Theseus was the hero helped by Ariadne to slay the Minotaur. A schoolboy error.

But that's Oxford for you. Even on public transport on one of its less favoured thoroughfares, you can't entirely escape the classical references.

Oxford is special and has been for close to 1,000 years. It claims to have the oldest university in the English-speaking world.

Unfortunately it can attach no firm date to its foundation. Such bombastic vagueness is suspicious. It's also worth noting that until 1620, the English-speaking world consisted largely of England. But you can see the point they're trying to make. Keeping the flame alight through the Dark Ages, first there were the monasteries and then there was Oxford.

According to legend, in 872 Alfred the Great fell into conversation with some monks in the vicinity of Oxford and a secular centre of learning was the result. The University of Oxford prefers flannel to legend: "Teaching existed at Oxford in some form in 1096 and developed rapidly from 1167, when Henry II banned English students from attending the University of Paris." That would have been the oldest university in the French-speaking world, presumably.

As a tourist destination Oxford is high on the list of UK cities outside London. Handluggageonly.co.uk puts it at number 6 and uses a picture of Oxford to illustrate its list of the top 14 UK cities other than the capital. It is a city for walking around, gawping or just people-watching. It teases, too: significant parts of it can only be glimpsed above high walls or through elegant gateways.

As a result, all over the city you get an impression of enormous open spaces seen through the wrong end of a telescope. On the other side of the wall that gives Longwall Street its name, for example, is the Magdalen College deer park. A deer park, less than a kilometre from the city centre!

You may be able to gain access to some of the college precincts at certain times, or on specific occasions, or accompanied by an undergraduate; others you simply have to accept must be admired from the outside.

Because there is so much to see – you truly can't turn round without something historic intercepting your gaze, whether it's contentious (the statue of Cecil Rhodes, for example, high on the wall of Oriel College) or celebratory (the plaque commemorating the achievements of Roberts Boyle and Hooke, on the same stretch of High Street) – I propose a short circular walk with visits and refreshments. I ought to say that my knowledge of and affection for Oxford is to be credited entirely to the account of Keith Barnes of the Oxford School of Photography. Before he put me right, I used to wish in my inverted snobbery for shale deposits to be found beneath Oxfordshire.

I'd start on the north side of the High Street, where a passage runs north between All Souls and the University Church of St Mary the Virgin. Almost immediately this delivers you to one of Oxford's great set-pieces: the Radcliffe Camera. Across the north side of Radcliffe Square is another, the Bodleian Library. Already you may be experiencing the tendency for Oxford's architecture to overwhelm. The solution is to break it down. Look at small sections of buildings, and at different levels. You'll find that the details are no less exquisite than the overall effect is stunning, but the whole becomes more manageable in the process.

By the way, if you're intimidated by the thought of the massive brains shifting through the gears all around you, consider: some of the earliest students here believed the world was flat.

In the Museum of the History of Science, just around the next corner, an orrery collection indicates the speedy progress made towards the elimination of such ignorance. Here, too, you'll find a first indication of an Oxford speciality: quirky museum pieces. An institution devoted to science is not so superior that it can find no place for the Enochian magic of 16th century charlatan Dr John Dee, who claimed to be in direct contact with angels.

If you go back to Catte Street (formerly Mousecatchers Lane) and turn north, you'll come to the Oxford University Museum of Natural History on your right, set back behind an oddly sterile expanse of sparse grass. The museum itself is another beauty, architecturally and for content. Its Victorian Gothic main hall, with dinosaur models below in the court and arching cast iron and glass above, is extraordinary, especially as the light changes through the day.

And it leads into the Pitt Rivers Museum of anthropology and ethnography – people and their outlandish artefacts. The Pitt Rivers is charmingly informal. Many of its display cases look as though someone has recently returned from a distant and exotic car-boot sale and turned out the proceeds for an impromptu police inspection.

The main attraction, thanks perhaps to *Lewis*, *Morse*, *Endeavour* et al, is the case containing the shrunken heads or, as the tag puts it, Treatment of Dead Enemies. This is handily placed close to the entrance; the floor in front of it has the weathered look of the inside lane of a motorway. But if, after considering your enemies' late ancestors, you then turn left instead of going back out, you'll find a wall of masks.

This is the Masks & Performance section. Make your way along it, towards the far wall (Transport & Navigation) and you'll find yourself detained by the intricate beauty of some of the pieces in the Amulets, Cures and Charms cases. And by now the Pitt Rivers has you hooked. Eventually, on an upper gallery, you'll find a selection of hooks.

The labels are exhibits in themselves. Many are ancient pieces of typescript on yellowing paper. Many more are written carefully on the items they describe, where flat surfaces are often at a premium. The evocation of Indiana Jones is almost palpable.

The bewildering variety of the exhibits is one thing; their sheer number quite another. You become aware that the display cases are only the start. Beneath them, in drawers and cabinets, are many more items; and in some cases there are racks above them too. On the galleries, above your head you'll notice collections of paddles and spears. It may take an effort to drag your attention back to the Tail and Buttock Ornaments at eye level.

Alerted by the Pitt Rivers, you'll notice that a similar determination to make use of every available inch of potential display space pervades the Museum of Natural History too. Along the arcade that separates the café from the museum floor, the columns are composed of different types of stone. If you've left your visit to the café to the end, you'll need to go back into the hall to see whether this applies all the way round. And it does. There are 126 columns fashioned from different British decorative rock, and their capitals and corbels are carved into plants.

It's time for a drink. Opposite the front of these two museums, Museum Road will lead you down to St Giles where, on the other side of the road, you'll find the Eagle & Child. This is famous as the pub where Tolkein, CS Lewis and others went for a drink, a smoke and a little light reading. They referred to themselves, oddly you might think, as the Inklings. I'm not sure how much fun Tolkein would have been over a pint. Hemingway, perhaps, but not JRR. As for the Eagle & Child, it doesn't inflate its prices to the extent of some of the Parisian haunts that claim to have hosted the author of *To Have and Have Another*. But the Inklings were apparently obliged to relocate across the road to the Lamb & Flag – not because of their smoking – and I was more comfortable there too.

If, fortified, you go south down St Giles towards the city centre, you soon come to Beaumont Street where the Randolph Hotel faces you and the Ashmolean Museum of Art & Archaeology stands slightly back from the road on the other side.

The Ashmolean is named for Elias Ashmole, an earthbound associate of angel-botherer Dr John Dee. It is quite exceptional and you might want to assign several hours to it. Of course that would probably cause you to miss a football match, but it will have dawned on you by now that Oxford is worth more than half a day tacked on to an expedition to a mediocre sporting event. Make a weekend of it, at the very least.

Much of the Ashmolean is free, although you'll pay for any special exhibitions: it was Warhol on the day I went. The impact of the name reinforces my point in the previous paragraph: when you look back on your visit to Oxford, will you think: "I saw a very moderate football match there" or will you think: "I saw the work of one of the 20th century's most inexplicably significant artists there"?

If you're thrifty you might prefer to see works by Dürer, Ucello, Pissarro, Manet and others for nothing. Or wander through the galleries devoted to Roman, Greek and Egyptian antiquities. There's a particularly fine collection of items from England, from the Dark Ages to the Middle Ages; and there are collections of coins and currency, statuary and Eastern Art that you won't find anywhere else. And one final comment about the Ashmolean: although it's very popular the galleries are on a lavish scale and you won't feel part of a crowd.

When you leave the Ashmolean, walk back to the junction with St Giles and to your right is the Martyrs Memorial. This is where some of the principle characters of the *Wolf Hall* era met their end: Archbishop Thomas Cranmer and Bishops Hugh Latimer and Nicholas Ridley were burnt at the stake here. Having survived Henry VIII they had the misfortune to be Protestants when Queen Mary ascended the throne and restored Catholicism. Three years later Elizabeth I imposed her father's Anglican writ again. To say those were difficult times for people in public life is a serious understatement.

The circuit is almost complete. You might return to the starting point via Broad Street in order to buy a book at Blackwell's, or continue down Cornmarket Street towards Carfax with the option of less cerebral shopping in the Covered Market. You might extend it with a short detour to Christ Church College and Cathedral, which make up for tedious centuries of dusty devotion by offering trendy and glamorous modern cultural 'experiences': Alice in Wonderland tea-parties, for example, and sets for Harry Potter films.

Of course there are many other corners of the city to look at. What of those towpaths and riverside walks, where Morse and Lewis were constantly hauling bodies out of the water? What of the exotic restaurants along Cowley Road? Punts, botanical gardens, a castle where Geoffrey of Monmouth wrote his *History of the Kings of Britain* and gave birth to the legend of Arthur... you've barely scratched the surface.

I can't leave Oxford without mentioning the winning goal. The ball was swept out to Frank Bunn on the right. Bunn, though not a winger, found himself in space and made a bee-line for the byline as Oldham striker Andy Ritchie and two or three Oxford defenders rushed into the penalty area. Bunn, by now directly in front of the visiting supporters section, looked up and noticed that Ritchie had slowed. The defenders hadn't. A gap had opened. Bunn whipped the ball into this gap flat and hard and it bounced to reach Ritchie at something like waist-height. Ritchie swivelled and hit the ball so hard that from square on, no-one was sure where the ball had gone... until it hit the back of the net. Still the most wonderful goal I ever saw.

Oxford United 0 Oldham 1
Manor Ground, 11 November 1989

Peterborough United

Beauty Parlour Syndrome (BPS) is an unlikely affliction for a football fan to suffer on a visit to Peterborough. But I almost blacked out in the Cathedral and, learning of the existence of BPS, can think of no other plausible explanation.

BPS, also known as vertebrobasilar insufficiency, is a condition associated solely with hairdressing salons. It is thought to be brought on by tilting the head backwards over a basin during washing and rinsing.

The term originates in the *Journal of the American Medical Association* in 1993, when a Dr Michael Weintraub treated five women whose neurological problems followed hair treatments. Their symptoms included dizziness, loss of balance, numbness around the face and, in four of the five cases, strokes (*Guardian*, 13 December 2016).

I was not, of course, having my hair done in Peterborough Cathedral. I was reading a plaque about Mary, Queen of Scots. The elevated position of the plaque obliged me to tilt my head backwards. After a moment's contemplation of the misery of Mary Stuart's last 18 years, I felt my eyes beginning to swim in darkness and my legs began to buckle.

In a cathedral there is no shortage of places to sit down and recover your wits. I rested a while, pondering this odd weakness. I had no knowledge of BPS at the time and inclined to a mystical explanation: Mary Stuart is, after all, an ambiguous and dramatic figure in history. Her execution, at Fotheringhay Castle a few miles from Peterborough, was hurried and botched. The executioner, having failed to sever her head with his first two strokes, eventually held the head aloft – and then watched as it dropped to the ground, leaving him holding a rich auburn wig. Mary was buried in a Protestant service at Peterborough Cathedral in July 1587 and later moved to Westminster Abbey.

Undisturbed here are the mortal remains of Katharine (this is the local spelling) of Aragon. The first wife of Henry VIII died in exile at Kimbolton Castle and was buried in Peterborough Cathedral in 1536. Her tomb has a low railing that bears the lettering (in capitals, lest there be any doubt) KATHARINE QUEEN OF ENGLAND. This is at shin level. You won't gete BPS looking at it, although who knows what other ailments lie in wait in beauty parlours. Peterborough has a Katharine of Aragon Festival in 2018.

One last reference to BPS: you should risk it to admire the ceiling of the nave and, at the East End of the cathedral, the ceiling of the 15th-16th century 'New Building'.

As for the spectacular accomplishment of the West Front, even JMW Turner apparently thought it better to let the architecture speak for itself – his drawings made in 1794 on a tour of the Midlands are notably sketchy.

What else does Peterborough have to offer? The museum is outstanding. Peterborough's proximity to such archaeological sites as Flag Fen get it off to a good Bronze Age start, but it is the more recent items that really mark it out as special.

The prisoner of war camp material from the Napoleonic Wars is marvellous, and kids with a taste for the gruesome will enjoy the Victorian operating theatre (the museum is housed in an old hospital building). It is in general a great family attraction, with plenty of interactive exhibits, a giant version of Twister and some dressing-up.

Across the River Nene from the museum is Railworld and the Wildlife Haven, an offshoot of the Nene Valley Railway. This is an unusual enterprise: model railways, indoors and out, combined with a former industrial site that is now home to invertebrates, birds and bats, 250 trees and plenty more flora and fauna in a number of habitats. It's very beautiful and constantly surprising.

The river itself gives Peterborough a certain distinction. It flows across the southern edge of the town centre; riverside paths, particularly on the north bank, give you easy access to parks and water meadows and an unexpected sense of Peterborough as a rural market town.

Peterborough United 1 Oldham 2
London Road, 22 January 2005

Plymouth Argyle

For most English football fans, Plymouth is the most distant outpost on the league map. So too for me; and it's where my travelling around the country in pursuit of mediocre football changed in character.

Hitherto, I had generally gone to games that were either within easy reach of wherever I happened to be at the time or were on the way to somewhere I might wish to be. Plymouth was neither. It would have been within easy reach if I'd happened to be in Truro; but I never had reason to be there. And it was on the way to a wedding I went to in Falmouth, but that took place out of season and, in any case, on a Saturday afternoon.

So Plymouth called for a special excursion. What made such a trek worthwhile? Simple economics. Meandering aimlessly around the Internet in the wool-gathering way that is the Internet's great contribution to productivity, I discovered that train tickets booked sufficiently far in advance were an irresistible bargain.

Meanwhile the Internet also made it much easier to find and book a hotel room. Perhaps a steadily rising disposable income helped too, because a weekend in Plymouth would still have cost somewhere over £150 when a meal, a football match and other expenses are added. But the hotel made it a holiday and the rail fare made it a relatively cheap one.

I stayed in a modest hotel to the west of the Hoe. At first I thought the whole city looked modest, to say the least; the preponderance of undistinguished concrete buildings seemed depressing and colourless. Gunter Grass writes somewhere: "God shat and called it Calcutta; God shat concrete and called it Frankfurt." Then it was pointed out to me that Plymouth had been very severely bombed during World War II, and that post-war austerity in the UK didn't run to the painstaking recreation of medieval city centres. Chastened, I started to notice Plymouth's brighter side: and I didn't have to look far.

But I wasn't there as a tourist. That bridge would not be crossed for another couple of years. I was there to see a football match, and so I neglected most of the internationally-famous attractions of Britain's Ocean City:

- The National Marine Aquarium
- The Gin Distillery
- The *Mayflower* Museum
- The City Museum & Art Gallery
- The Merchant's House
- And the Royal Citadel.

This list, by no means comprehensive, shames me. Instead I ambled around the city with a bag of chips. To make it up to all these institutions, links will be provided from a *Towns of Two Halves* website at www.townsof2halves.co.uk.

It's worth noticing, too, that 2020 will be the 400th anniversary of the departure of the *Mayflower* from Plymouth, bound for the New World. If you plan a visit in that year, be sure to look out for events under the *Mayflower 400* banner.

And ambling with no particular purpose can present you with unexpected curiosities. Perhaps the ghost of Sir Arthur Conan Doyle, who believed strongly in the after-life, guided my steps to the west of the city centre. On an unexceptional street not far from the inlet known as Stonehouse Pool, a number of short quotations from Sherlock Holmes books are set into the pavement. "Good, Watson, you always keep us flat-footed on the ground", for example.

Eventually a plaque explains that in 1882 Conan Doyle practised medicine from a building (no longer there) at 1 Dumford (now Durnford) Street.

He appears to have lived there no longer than six months, and it isn't clear whether he did any writing in that time – the first Sherlock Holmes story wasn't published until 1887. He was obviously gathering material or, at least, inspiration: Baskerville Hall in *The Hound of the Baskervilles* is in Devon. The plaque concludes: "A Holmes cult arose and still flourishes today."

At Home Park it was an exceptionally windy afternoon and Oldham scored two goals with the gale behind them. Plymouth managed none, with or without wind assistance. It was rare to see

Oldham apparently comfortable and in control, and gratifying after such a long journey.

From the park towards the railway station – and, hence, the city centre – I walked along a street of Victorian terraced houses. At a number of doorways women stood, arms folded, as though to welcome their menfolk home after a shift at the mill or down the pit. I wonder in retrospect whether I had this the wrong way round and that it was the women who were beginning a shift; and whether, then, the result across the park made any difference to their prospects.

Plymouth Argyle 0 Oldham 2
Home Park, 29 November 1997

Port Vale

The bus from Stoke to Burslem stopped at Hanley bus station, where among others a man in an advanced state of inebriation got on. He was so many sheets to the wind he could have stocked a bedding department. With him were two women whom, since I was thinking for some reason about Chicago at the time, I would have to describe as molls or possibly frails. They spent their journey discussing how they would wile away the evening.

Their plans, shared uninhibitedly with the rest of the upper deck, involved feats of drinking and athletic sexual congress. The night was young – it was barely 6pm – and time was no obstacle, but the idea that they might remain conscious long enough to achieve the prolonged coupling they anticipated seemed unlikely. What's the expression about not writing cheques your body can't cash?

As our journey proceeded the population of the upper deck began to thin. The risk increased of making accidental eye-contact with the Lovers, or of otherwise attracting their attention and being drawn into their discussions.

Part of the appeal of Chicago, I had decided, was that first-time visitors could be quite specific about how they would reach the city from O'Hare International Airport. The Blue Line would deliver them easily to Clark and Lake, within the Loop, and they would emerge straight into the Chicago street scene their imaginations had promised them.

I had no such expectations of Burslem. None of the Six Towns generated a picture in my mind. It made no difference to me, then, to escape the *Kama Sutra* by getting off the bus a couple of stops early and experience the approach to central Burslem on foot.

Which, in a hurried fashion as though trying to shake off a tail, is what I did.

Waterloo Road is an odd jumble of shabby commercial premises: lower-league supermarkets, takeaways, auto workshops. There's an occasional building that recalls better days: the name of Cobridge Hall, for example, has echoes of a building first put up there in 1780 with gardens, a park and a drive. That was demolished in 1913; the building on the site now is a concrete-faced monstrosity with a corrugated roof; it serves as the hall for St Peter's Roman Catholic Church.

The Warburton and Blackwell families responsible for earlier, more elegant buildings, helped to finance the construction of a Catholic chapel there. Local historian John Ward noted in his book of 1843 that building work happened to coincide with the anti-Catholic Gordon Riots in London. "The alarmed Catholics of Cobridge suspended their building for several months," he wrote. "The chapel... is an unassuming building, almost concealed by the Priest's dwelling-house, and an adjoining school-house erected in 1822."

Hidden among the dusty shop-windows of low-rent 21st century capitalism are some decent examples of Victorian residential architecture. At 205 Waterloo Road is the house in which Arnold Bennett grew up.

His father Enoch, a solicitor, bought the plot in 1879 for £200 and built the house on it for £900. In the 1881 Census eight Bennetts and a serving wench are recorded as living there. Arnold, who later wrote of the Five Towns, was the eldest at 13.

(The discrepancy in the number of Potteries towns is odd. Tunstall, Burslem, Hanley, Fenton, Stoke and Longton are the modern six; Bennett changed their names to Turnhill, Bursley, Hanbridge, Knype and Longton but omitted Fenton altogether. As a result Fenton is chiefly notable as 'the town that Bennett forgot'. The author himself claimed that Five Towns sounded better than Six.)

Bennett drew on the neighbourhood in his work: further along Waterloo Road is the site of the building that was Dr Sterlington's house in *The Old Wives' Tale* (identified by a plaque on the wall announcing 'Dr Stirling's House'); in central Burslem there's a Clayhanger Street; and Osmond Orgreave, the architect in *Clayhanger*, was probably derived from George Ford, who was responsible for a good deal of development in the area and may have designed number 205.

Further up again, you come to what was originally the Waterloo & American Hotel, more recently just The American. It's an unlikely anomaly. The explanation for the name probably lies in the Potteries Emigration Society that used to meet there in the mid-19th century; the society bought land for a colony of potters in America, raising enough for 4,000 (some reports say 12,000) acres of farmland in Wisconsin.

The motivation was complicated. In the Potteries and elsewhere, potters were struggling to set up a union. Wisconsin was presented as a land of milk and honey where pottery could be made in peace, free of exploitation. If it creamed off large numbers of workers, improving the job prospects and leverage of those left behind, so much the better. The Chartist movement provided an important background; there were Chartist riots in the Potteries in the 1840s.

Richard Weir, in his *Six of the Best: A Potteries Companion* (1988), says: "However, like Potteries folk through the ages, many emigrants found the change from home too great and returned." Wikipedia lists six Pottersvilles in the USA today and none is in Wisconsin.

From the late 1960s The American became a focal point of Caribbean culture in the area. It was taken on by Jamaican licencees and hosted blues and reggae. More recently it has turned temperance and any American influence is more New World New Age: The American Clubhouse is a walk-in centre providing arts and educational facilities for the local community.

And so eventually I reach downtown Burslem. By now darkness was falling and Burslem *centre ville* seemed to have little to offer. The pubs looked unappealing to me and pretty much everything else looked closed. Finally I found an Italian restaurant and ate an unexceptedly good lasagna before heading for the ground.

Did I mention that this was a night match? If you planned to go to Burslem by public transport on a Saturday afternoon, use Longport railway station. That puts you on the right side of Burslem for Middleport Pottery and Westport Lake.

And I hope you have better luck with the match. I happened

to be wearing in a new pair of spectacles. Not only were they varifocals but also photosensitive. Under the floodlights they darkened, making it difficult to follow the play at the far end of the ground.

Well, it was a poor game between two sides unable to find a moment of inspiration that might have sunk the other. I wondered, though, whether any gloom in the impression Burslem left on me might be attributed to the glasses.

Port Vale 1 Oldham 1
Vale Park, 29 September 2015

Portsmouth

This was my second attempt to see Athletic play at Portsmouth. The first had been in May 1995, when I expected it to be the last opportunity to see the great Andy Ritchie play in an Oldham shirt: a significant day, then, by any standards.

But apart from Andy Ritchie and me, there was one more person to be taken into account. And because she took such an unbelievably long time getting dressed, made-up and whatever else she was doing, it was clear as we eventually headed for the tube at a slightly breathless clip that we would not get to Waterloo in time for the train.

I said as much, trying to keep the exasperation out of my voice. Apparently I was successful because no argument or recrimination followed. After asking whether I was sure – and there could be no doubt, given that the train had already left according to the timetable – she suggested we get a taxi.

"It won't make any difference," I said. "We still won't make the train."

"No," J replied, "I mean to Portsmouth."

I wasn't entirely sure how much a taxi to Portsmouth might cost. A tidy sum, I imagined. Nobody wants to look a cheapskate but the old joke about buying a couple of full-backs for that kind of money crossed my mind. I wheedled my way out of a three-figure commitment by pointing out that a car from north London would probably not outstrip a train, and that there would always be another day.

For J there wasn't, as it turned out. We eventually went our separate ways, slowly and by stages.

Oldham played at Portsmouth twice more in the late 90s, but in the depths of winter each time and without Andy Ritchie in the team. The two clubs did not meet again until a brief revival in Portsmouth's fortunes found them once more in the same division in 2012. With no-one else to consider by then, I set off early to make a day of it.

I left the car beside Milton Park, in Fratton, and walked into the city centre along the roads and paths that follow the railway line. For much of the way this route is called Canal Walk, as though the engineers left it until the last minute to decide whether to build a waterway or a road for an iron horse.

In Guildhall Square, under the stern eye of a typically portly late-period Queen Victoria, a fanzone for the Paralympics was laid out. Two rows of folding chairs faced a big screen, and crowd control barriers decorated with sky-blue London 2012 banners cordoned off the area. Bags of ballast freighted the barriers, presumably in case the banners gave them aerodynamic qualities. The bags looked like unattended packages waiting for a controlled explosion. It was a more innocent time.

On the screen, Richard Whitehead came home for Britain in the 200 metres in a world-record time. Only one person watched from the chairs but a dozen or so paused in their Saturday morning pursuits. At a souvenir stall beneath Victoria's statue commerce too stopped for a while – 24.38 seconds, to be precise.

I walked on through what is a surprisingly green city, westward towards the harbour. The Spinnaker is a simple landmark to aim for; when you get there the Historic Dockyard is to your right and most of the eating and drinking places are at the base of the Spinnaker.

I turned right and bought a ticket that entitled me to visit various of the dockyard's attractions. That would be even better value now, with the *Mary Rose* Museum added to the list and the National Museum of the Royal Navy greatly extended.

I started at *HMS Warrior*, the first vessel you come to, and worked my way along the quays to the *Victory*. The *Warrior*, built in 1860, was the nuclear deterrent of its day. It never fired a gun in anger. Iron-hulled and armoured, powered by steam and sail, the vessel was apparently so fearsome that no dissenter to Britannia's rule ever tackled it.

The life of Riley for the crew, then? Probably not, especially if they were much over 5ft 6ins tall. Here (and even more so on the *Victory*) the miserly headroom below decks will catch your eye and possibly your forehead. A member of the Marine Voluntary Service, recalling a celebratory dinner on *Victory*, commented "they still haven't improved the headroom on the lower decks (there must be something in the Health and Safety regulations about that!)". When the press-gang dragged its net around a district, were short people were at greater risk of being pressed into involuntary naval service than their lanky fellows?

HMS Victory also has more to offer now. The poop deck has been opened to visitors and, with new suggested routes, 80% more of the ship is apparently accessible to them. To a certain extent it doesn't matter how much of *HMS Victory* you want to look at; it's enough simply to be on board, breathing its dusty, historic air.

After peering through the railings at the embryonic *Mary Rose* Museum I retraced my steps. Finding a place on The Hard where I could look across the water to Gosport, I enjoyed a bag of chips in the fresh air.

The day prompted reflections on empire building. Superior technology confers an obvious advantage, even at the most basic level – Pizarro and his 13 companions conquered the Inca Empire thanks in no small measure to their mastery of horses and gunpowder. Boldness is obviously important too, especially when the numerical disadvantage (as in the conquistadors' case) is so marked; Castro deposed Batista after at one point being reduced to just 19 followers. But luck and quick thinking and, perhaps, strategy will also make a difference. The 2,500 troops of the British East India Company defeated some 40,000 Bengali troops (with French artillery support) at Plassey and gained India, with just 80 casualties. The turning point in the battle was a torrential downpour, through which the British crucially managed to keep their powder dry.

As for the match, by delaying my visit I missed a 1-1 draw in 1995 and instead enjoyed a rare Oldham away win. But poor Portsmouth were on their uppers by 2012. They named only five of a possible seven substitutes, and not because their bench wasn't long enough.

Both teams had a man sent off with the game about an hour old. Oldham's Cliff Byrne was subsequently exonerated on the grounds of mistaken identity; his three-match ban was passed on to the full-back, Connor Brown. It was an odd mistake for the referee to make; apart from the coincidence of their initials, Byrne and Brown had hardly any characteristics in common, including skin colour.

Having delayed my arrival in Portsmouth by 17 years I delayed my departure to enjoy a half-pint of Gales Ales HSB while the traffic cleared. Then I delayed my departure again to be sure my head had cleared.

Portsmouth 0 Oldham 1
Fratton Park, 1 September 2012

Preston North End

I have real difficulty justifying this entry. I can hardly say anything with conviction about my one visit to Deepdale. I remember nothing of when it took place nor who was playing. The fixture recorded below is what they call in the print media a place-holder. It may have to hold its place for quite a while, because there is little prospect of my memory supplying anything more reliable.

After all, it was 50 years ago or more. I grew up on the Fylde coast, not far south of Blackpool, and two of my schoolfriends were bussed in from Preston. One was a fervent North End supporter. A group of us went to at least one match, at his invitation.

When? It might have been any time between 1966 and 1969. North End were a fixture in the old Second Division in those days. They had dropped out of the top flight in 1961 and spent a decade failing to get back, until (apparently exhausted) they slumped to the foot of the Second Division in 1970. They never did make it back to the big time, but by the same token they never played in the fourth tier either.

What there might have been to do in Preston in those days was not a question that detained me for long. Preston was somewhere you went through (or around) on the way to somewhere else. It was no accident, in my childish view, that the first motorway in the UK was built to spare people the trouble of going through Preston.

It had a railway station at which passengers for the lines to Blackpool arrived from more or less exotic places. The station is immortalised in a song by Jethro Tull, *Cheap Day Return*, off their album *Aqualung*: "On Preston platform, do your soft-shoe shuffle dance, brush away the cigarette ash that's falling down your pants, and you sadly wonder... does the nurse treat your old man the way she should? She made you tea, asked for an autograph, what a laugh."

Preston – a mere town in those days, but the county town of Lancashire – also had what was the largest enclosed dock in the country when it opened in 1892. The Albert Edward Dock featured in geography lessons and then appeared in real life, like a rogue dinosaur from *Jurassic Park*, as an obstacle to be circumnavigated in the drive south through the town. In the mid-1960s Preston acquired a notorious Brutalist bus station. And it had a hospital, the Preston Royal Infirmary, in which I spent most of the 1966 summer holidays, recovering from a mystery illness.

That too was related if peripherally to football. It came on soon after the World Cup final. A previously healthy 12-year-old, I began to experience headaches, dizziness and loss of balance, as though overwhelmed by the extent of England's achievement. I was whisked off to an isolation ward at Blackpool's Devonshire Road Hospital so that I would not transmit whatever I had to anyone else. Time passed. When nothing happened – except that the symptoms began gradually to ease – I was transferred to the Royal Infirmary 'for observation'.

It must have been a bad summer for juvenile illness. There was no room for me in a children's ward so I went into a ward with a group of friendly and hospitable men. I was subjected to various tests – I remember a Barium meal procedure, electroencephalogram sessions and at least one examination that involved a general anaesthetic.

More time passed with very little to add to the chart at the end of my bed. I developed a taste for hospital food (junket food), fell in love with staff nurse Shirley Bailey and watched a great deal of televised athletics.

The British Empire & Commonwealth Games, as they were still known, took place in Kingston that summer. A bespectacled Trinidadian athlete called Wendell Mottley stays in my mind, perhaps because of the euphony of Mottley, Shirley and Bailey. Another sign of the era: Wendell Mottley won the one-lap sprint, which in those days was the 440 yards.

Taking its own sweet time, the mystery illness disappeared as inexplicably as it had set in. The Royal Infirmary discharged me after about four weeks' increasingly tedious observation. For a while, in adult life, I owned up to this period of hospitalisation on application forms – for insurance, for example – but eventually stopped doing so. An unexplained headache sometimes makes me wonder what might be coming next, but I've found that 10 minutes submerged in a hot bath does the trick as reliably as four weeks in a hospital.

One day, perhaps I will go back to Preston to see what it has to offer. For now, I feel as if I have spent enough of my life there.

Preston North End 1 Charlton Athletic 1
Deepdale, 14 September 1968

Queens Park Rangers

Very few are the football fans who wouldn't, given the chance, have reached for the Baldwin's Nervous Pills at one time or another. "Cures nervousness, irritability of temper, fear, dread, neuralgia, hysteria, disturbed sleep, melancholy, insomnia and all nerve pains and diseases," the advertising proclaimed.

Unfortunately, these miraculous pills were last available as a medical resort when Glossop, New Brighton and Gainsborough Trinity were in the football league. The poster in the Museum of Brands, Packaging & Advertising dates from about 1900. You can still buy a reproduction of the poster for £7.49p – the pills themselves, 120 years ago, would have set you back less than 14p a box.

As with any good pharmaceutical product, there's so much to enjoy about Baldwin's Nervous Pills:

- The fact that the pills themselves are described as 'nervous'; this is unintentionally hilarious, and it prefigures the contemporary tinkering with parts of speech through which advertisers now urge us to 'Find your happy' or 'Think different'
- They call to mind the scene in *The Outlaw Josey Wales* where the carpetbagger is trying to sell Clint Eastwood a bottle of universally efficacious elixir, upon which Eastwood gobs from his plug of chewing tobacco on to the man's white lapel and asks: "How is it wi' stains?"
- Finally, of course, the cheerful disregard for truth.

G Baldwin & Co, Purveyors of Natural Products Since 1844, are still in business. A search of their website for 'nervous pills' yields nothing that would obviously tackle fear or dread. Still, they must have been doing something right to be approaching their 175th anniversary.

The Museum of Brands, Packaging & Advertising, at the top of Ladbroke Grove, is the closest museum to the home of Queens Park Rangers. Eventually it will come to symbolise English football in general as a triumph of packaging over content. The layout of the Museum is essentially a timeline; you are led as though through a labyrinth between display cabinets in which a history of consumer culture is recreated, from the earliest times.

It's a great museum and, in places, an art gallery too. There was a time when famous names produced artwork for advertising, and their posters were signed: Paul Nash, for example, and Ben Nicholson. Progress along the passage becomes more difficult as the displays reach the 1950s and older visitors recognise items from their own pasts: ah, the soothing pleasure of 10 Joystick cigarettes! The emergence of pop culture follows, and the growth of merchandising associated with films and TV shows, and the development of celebrity culture.

Room will have to be made at some stage to mark the successful promotion of English football around the globe. There was a time when QPR would have deserved their own annex in such a display. With the profile of the sport around the world now, the identity of QPR and the qualities of their personnel would have made them global superstars.

As far back as most living memories stretch, QPR were the archetypal underdogs. As a Third Division team playing in 1967 in the first League Cup Final staged at Wembley, they came back from a 0-2 deficit to beat First Division West Bromwich by 3-2.

That was the day Rodney Marsh became a household name (beyond households in the vicinity of Fulham and Shepherds Bush, at least). Marsh set the tone for a different kind of archetype at QPR – the maverick genius. When he left (to Manchester City, where it was said he cost them the 1972 championship), the baton passed to Stan Bowles. These people were not only brilliant footballers; they were wits. Bowles, told by QPR's manager Tommy Docherty "You can trust me, Stan," is said to have replied: "I'd rather trust my chickens with Colonel Sanders." When City manager Tony Book tried to build bridges with a disaffected Marsh by saying: "If you think I'm effing useless it's not going to work. D'you want to take it back?" Marsh is reported to have replied: "No chance. In fact thinking about it more, you're not that good."

Marsh played for England nine times; Bowles just five. England managers were (and arguably remain) suspicious of brilliant, clever individuals. In the modern game they would have been international superstars, and QPR might have ridden the comet's tail.

Where else might you spend time in the vicinity of Loftus Road? The enormous Westfield shopping centre springs immediately to mind.

Here the lessons illustrated in the Museum of Brands, Packaging & Advertising are put to daily use, backed up by some optimistic hunches. Outside, a green wall, bunting and a listless water-feature may be intended to generate some sort of market-town High Street atmosphere. Inside, the sector called The Village will be unlike any village you've ever seen. Throughout, there are touches designed to extend your stay: play areas for the kids, strange assortments of upholstery in rest zones for the grown-ups, the largest and most linear food court you can imagine. Unoccupied retail spaces are not empty, they're where new neighbours will soon be arriving – almost as if a crop rotation system is in operation and some units will always be fallow.

As with English football, so with shopping mall retailing: one day, all of this will be distilled into a display case in the museum at the top of Ladbroke Grove.

Queens Park Rangers 1 Oldham 3
Loftus Road, 23 November 1991

Reading

If the citizens worry about their town getting ideas above its station, they have two options: they can appoint someone of the humility of Uriah Heep to look after the town's public relations; or they can pour money into building an exceptionally elaborate station. In Reading they've taken the second course.

Reading is another in a long series of 'home' teams. My family's move to the town coincided with my own departure for university, so Reading was where I spent holidays for three years. Later, I lived there briefly as a commuter. I had no great affection for Reading but I was never one to ignore league football.

All that was more than 40 years ago. The Reading fixtures I attended were at Elm Park, a charming but decrepit reminder of Reading's origins in the lower leagues. The club that currently yo-yoes between the Premier League and the Championship is unknown to me, and the Madejski Stadium sounds absurdly grand.

Soaring above any risk of delusions of grandeur, Reading's new railway station opened ahead of schedule in 2014, at a cost of £897m. Her Majesty Queen Elizabeth II did the honours – it would have been a journey of about 40 minutes for her, up the branch line from Windsor & Eton to Slough, then on to a mainline train to Reading.

The structure she opened is quite something. Access to the platforms from the north side is via an escalator modelled on the set of *A Question of Life and Death*. You ascend into the clouds. Raymond Massey would not be out of place greeting you there in rather pearly monochrome.

At the top, there's a walkway the size of a football pitch. Down the centre, the inevitable retail opportunities; to either side, more escalators descend to the platforms. Canopies cover the platforms: from below they might be repurposed from a water park, from above they look curiously like steps leading down from an old-fashioned sweep of terracing. They are held in place by what appear to be gigantic steel Nike swooshes.

It is a remarkable railway station but its modernity presents some problems. Chief among those is the insistence on the part of railway operators to imitate the airside/landside distinction of airports. Moving about the station with a ticket would be simple enough if the barriers read the tickets reliably; and even then, there's usually one gate manned to compensate for the shortcomings of the technology. But if you don't have a ticket – if you're seeing someone off, or meeting someone, or just trying to get from one side of the station to the other – it's not straightforward. If you're meeting someone off a train there I'd advise you to add 10 minutes to your planned journey time to allow for Reading station.

As for the town itself, the Reading Museum has a rare treasure: a replica of the Bayeux Tapestry. You'll find it on the first floor, and after such a slight climb it won't be the stairs that take your breath away.

The Tapestry occupies the walls of a gallery laid out, in a figure-of-eight fashion, around a well through which float the sounds of the café below. It's an intriguing contrast: the everyday life of modern Reading, especially its children, providing a background to a record of one of the most significant events in the nation's long history.

The Tapestry was embroidered by 35 Victorian gentlewomen. They completed the 70-metre project in 1885. Their labours provided Britain with a full-scale replica of the Bayeux original, and it came to Reading in 1895 when Alderman Arthur Hill bought it and presented it to the museum.

The gallery opened in 1993. The Tapestry and accompanying translations and text snake around the walls within a continuous series of beautifully designed and lit vitrines. There are notes about individuals named in the tapestry, the contributions of individual embroiderers are identified, random pieces of ironmongery recall the savagery of the era. The embroidery itself is gorgeous and the display does it full justice.

Those Victorian stitchers worked from hand-coloured photographs. Their work, then, is not necessarily true to the original colours. Nor can it be said to be entirely true to the spirit of the

11th century: at some stage in the process of reproduction (so to speak), censorious Victorian hands removed a couple of candid depictions of genitalia. (In one bowdlerised case the man's penis is more detailed in the original than his face.) And the Norman cavalry appeared to prefer mares.

Is a replica Bayeux Tapestry the embroidery world's equivalent of a tribute band? I've never really seen the point of tribute bands, given that the musical output of the real thing is so readily available in so many forms. And if you can't see the real thing perform for one reason or another – price, distance, retirement, the Grim Reaper etc – how will a bunch of people who pretend to look and sound vaguely similar be an acceptable substitute?

So with a historic tapestry: if you can't make the journey to Bayeux, the publishing industry can offer you a variety of alternatives. It would spare you a trip to Reading, which may be a recommendation in itself, and you can take them anywhere with you.

And yet... The Reading replica is very special. If the choice facing you is between the Reading Bayeux Tapestry or a football match involving Oldham Athletic, go for the life and vitality and sheer beauty of the Tapestry. The game in April 1997 was the penultimate in Oldham's 23-year spell in the top two divisions. Their performance was so woeful that a visit to see a carefully printed T-shirt would have been more exciting.

Reading 2 Oldham 0
Elm Park, 26 April 1997

Rochdale

Did you know that Gracie Fields was born in Rochdale? No? That can only mean you've never been to Rochdale. It's hard to imagine anybody spending much time there without encountering her image, or a recording or a memorial of some kind.

Her statue is in front of the Town Hall; the Gracie Fields Theatre is on the western margins of the town; there's a special display and soundtrack at the Touchstones local museum; and eight commemorative plaques mark the Gracie Fields Heritage Trail.

And why not? She would have been a credit to any town. Born[1] over a fish and chip shop, Gracie Fields became a huge international star and at one time was the highest-paid actress in Hollywood. There can be no doubt that she was much loved. Among the Gracie memorabilia in Touchstones is a bush hat to which the troops she entertained contributed badges; not much hat is visible.

Gracie was a practical Rochdale FC supporter. In the 1930s, during the peak of her popularity, she helped the club financially. Her assistance bore fruit and 35 years later the club achieved the first promotion in its history.

The other Rochdale institution you can hardly miss is the Co-op, represented by the Rochdale Pioneers Museum on the site of the first store set up by working people. This is so highly regarded around the world that in Kobe, Japan, there's a replica of 31 Toad Street, where it all began. 'Toad', incidentally, is a contraction of 'The Old' through 'th'owd' and 't'owd'.

It's a fine old Georgian building in a well-preserved row in Rochdale's Heritage Quarter. The name is almost superfluous: heritage is never very far away in Rochdale.

The Museum's ground floor tells the story of the origins and growth of the co-operative society. When the pioneers opened their first shop, on 21 December 1844, local wholesalers wouldn't sell to them, so they had to go to suppliers in Manchester. The gas

---

1 She was born Grace Stansfield, which by coincidence is the surname of another great singer born in Rochdale.

company wouldn't supply them, so they bought candles. A panel emphasises the importance from the very first day of bookkeeping, for the calculation of the divi.

Within a few years, more such shops opened and by the late 1850s the pioneers were looking at doing their own wholesaling. The Co-operative Wholesale Society followed soon afterwards.

It's a very human museum from the moment you open the 'shop' door. The store is laid out with produce on a counter composed, as in the original, by planks across two barrels. A bold modern wooden structure, perhaps modelled on a tower or on the circular ascent to a car-park, encloses the stairs.

On the first floor the focus was on tea memorabilia and traditions in May 2018. The second floor has a viewing room and a selection of films running from 3.5 to 38 minutes, including a young Bill Owen (Compo from *The Last of the Summer Wine*) and a Stanley Holloway monologue.

A barrel and Rochdale's social conscience also feature in the Touchstones local history museum. The American Civil War did the Lancashire mill towns great harm, especially when the Union blockaded the Confederates' ports preventing the export of cotton. But the Rochdale mill workers nonetheless supported the North's opposition to slavery. In 1863 the citizens of New York and Philadelphia sent supplies including 15,000 barrels of flour to the starving people of Lancashire. The barrel in Touchstones is the last surviving relic of that cargo.

Touchstones is an excellent cultural centre. The museum genuinely brings history to life with some outstanding exhibits – I defy you to listen to the exchange of letters between Gladys and, at the front, her soldier Jim without sharing her anxiety. The collections combine local with general memorabilia and celebrate a number of great Rochdale citizens.

One such, John Collier, turns up again in the Touchstones' galleries as the Lancashire Hogarth. Using the pseudonym Tim Bobbin, he wrote Lancashire dialect poetry and produced satirical cartoons – a display is devoted to him in the museum section. Upstairs in the gallery some of his cartoons appear alongside prints by the London Hogarth, Rembrandt, Whistler and John Martin's work for *Paradise Lost*.

There are five galleries: four numbered and one described as the Heritage Gallery. The fourth had a very challenging display linking a food riot in 18th century Manchester to the 50th anniversary of the Paris uprising of May 1968. 'While England Mourns', by Magnus Quaife, is the kind of work that makes you feel irredeemably bourgeois just to be looking at it. The images should be taken, the notes say, as "an inducement for finding, through contact with the masses, new levels of action, both on the cultural and the political plane".

Downstairs in the Heritage Gallery, among the Egyptian artefacts local worthy Charles Heape acquired from his chum Sir Flinders Petrie, it was a relief to be back on safer ground where the art wasn't shouting at you. Next door, the Art Café is very good and has some glazing that looks old and French.

The Greater Manchester Fire Service Museum, on the road out towards Rochdale railway station, opens only on Fridays and that isn't likely to coincide with many home matches.

Which is a pity, because it too is a fine museum. The equipment on display goes back to the 1740s but the information boards describe fire-fighting much further back. In the process they explain issues like water supplies, insurance, respirators and so forth.

Early respirator technology involved soaking your beard, gripping it between your teeth and trying to breathe through it. Early appliances are illustrated in full sets of cards issued by John Player, whose products must have been responsible for some of the fires that needed dousing. In the background, real fire-fighters are on hand to pass on their own memories of the service.

Public infrastructure provides other things to admire in Rochdale. The bus station is quite something and the town has two notable bridges.

One of these is now known as the Lviv Bridge, with a plaque in English and Cyrillic to record the twinning of Rochdale and the Ukrainian city.

The other, more recently refurbished, is the medieval bridge lost to the town when the River Roch was confined to a tunnel in the early 20th century. The bridge reopened in 2016.

Rochdale 1 Aldershot 1
Spotland, 29 April 1961

Rotherham United

I'll be honest. When I went to watch Athletic at Rotherham I planned to spend the preceding couple of hours looking around Sheffield for old times' sake. There was only one old time spent in Rotherham in my university days: a trip to the cinema to see *The Good, The Bad and the Ugly*. My companion on that evening, wary of the facilities from the very beginning, complained of itching throughout and eventually wore me down: we left early.

I have a distant memory of calling into a pub called the Puddlers' Arms on the way back. My memory is clearly faulty. According to one of those intriguing specialist websites, there has been such a pub close to the Sheffield-Rotherham road; but it was barely a mile outside Sheffield city centre and it closed in 1870.

The Internet doesn't let you off that easily. In return for information of such questionable value, it demands a couple of hours of purposeless browsing. Trying to give my research meaning, I turned up some very good names. Rotherham has or had pubs called:

- The Cat and Cabbage, a reference to the crest of the York & Lancaster Regiment.
- The Comedian, commemorating Sandy Powell, who was on hand in 1970 to open the pub. Powell, born in Rotherham in 1900, belongs to the Golden Age of Comedy, when all that was required for people to collapse insensible with laughter was the utterance of a catchphrase. In his case "Can you hear me, mother?" did the job all over the world and for many years.
- The Rifleman's Rest, which name did the application for a licence no good at all. The pub was close to the Volunteer Rifle Butts and some feared that the aim of the marksmen might be impaired. The pub very quickly became the Eastwood Inn. The licensee in 1889 was fined 20/- and costs for the mysterious offence of harbouring a police constable, who was promptly dismissed from the Force.
- The Foljambe Arms, named for a family that came over with the

Norman Conquest. It means 'a person with a limp'.

- The Merry Heart, which comes from the Bible (Proverbs) by way of Shakespeare (*The Winter's Tale*). The pub seems to have lived up to its name. When its landlord applied for a spirits licence in 1869, opponents cited the noise of music (fiddling, especially) and carousing (involving some persons only 16 years of age). A manager at Guest & Chrimes brass works (the name of which is prominent on a building adjacent to the football ground) reported that "on Sunday night about 8.50pm he heard a man in the Merry Heart play what he believed was the 'Cuckoo Solo' with variations, loud applause following the performance". Nobody was drunk, it seems, but the application was refused. Five years later the Merry Heart became the Grey Horse, a name sober enough to gain it a music licence after another 10 years. It closed in 1962.
- The Moulders Rest. This pub closed in 2009. Its name comes from an occupation related to industry, if not necessarily steel, and it is fairly close to the town centre. This could be the place my memory has converted to the Puddlers Arms.
- The Reindeer Inn, inexplicably.
- The Rhinoceros, one of two Wetherspoon pubs in the town. This being a relatively new pub, the name may simply be a piece of contemporary trendiness; or someone is an admirer of Jean Anouilh.

I am indebted to the Clifton Local History Group for much of this information. They published two booklets about Eastwood in 2008.

All this is by way of a digression, because I went straight to Rotherham in the event and visited no pubs. Instead I took a look at Clifton Park, surely one of the most versatile public gardens in the country.

Clifton Park has everything from a mini-golf course to a museum. I didn't spend much time at the water splash, the skate park or the play area; I didn't ride the Clifton Express land train; but the museum and café in the grand old Palladian mansion at the southern corner of the park passed the time very agreeably until kick-off.

Clifton House has been the home of Rotherham Museum since 1893, so they've had plenty of time to work out how to present themselves. Like the rest of the park, it's designed to appeal to families. Those exhibits you might expect to be slightly dusty – the history of Rotherham, the story of the York & Lancaster Regiment – turn out to be beautifully done, either through the stunning quality of the pieces (especially some of the Rockingham pottery) or through interactive gizmos.

Rotherham's past turns out to feature not only steel but also glass, pottery and other metals. The museum makes the most of the diversity that implies, but it isn't above playing obvious crowd-pleasing cards. Pride of place, in its appeal to children, goes to Nelson the stuffed lion and a European Brown Bear called Marco. Marco is a reject from Warwickshire County Council; he represents the bear on the Warwickshire crest, but apparently they disliked him and he came to Clifton Park instead. As part of the school loans service for almost 20 years, Marco must appear in the nightmares of a generation of Rotherham schoolchildren.

Attached to the museum is a gallery. This too has echoes of Rotherham's industrial heritage. The largest single component is a group of watercolours produced by the local metalworking firm George Wright to demonstrate and promote its products.

Rotherham United 3 Oldham 2
The New York Stadium, 14 September 2013

Scunthorpe United

This is a rare birthday treat, isn't it? An away-day in Scunthorpe – how much more vigorously could a man push the boat out?

But Scunthorpe in the eight-bit footprints of the Millennium Bug held more for me than the visit of Oldham Athletic. It was also the home of a young woman – middle-aged, by then – to whom I had attached myself at university a quarter of a century earlier. Let's call her N. She deserves the shelter of anonymity.

It had been an irregular relationship. N took me on early in the second year; in the middle of the first year my first love had broken my heart and I allowed many months to waste away while I fed a voracious appetite for self-indulgent misery. By the time I fell into N's embrace, I was not so much healed as exhausted. I was no bargain.

N was a pleasant, attractive young woman. She was on the same course, attended the same lectures, frequented the same coffee lounges as I did. Even so, there was nothing preordained about the gradual approach of our gravitational fields; there were scores of people on that course, many of them pleasant and attractive. But I was wounded in my self-esteem and found something appealing in N's homely qualities. N was cuddly and her embrace was like a comfort blanket. I can't usefully speculate on what she ever saw in me.

The contrast I make, 40-odd years later, between N's girl-next-door charms and the more vivid young women visible at the hotter end of the thermal imaging scale, may help to explain the chaste nature of our relationship. At a time when young people were supposed to be at it like rabbits, with the restraints of family and society cast aside in one way or another, N and I restricted ourselves to canoodling – I choose the word carefully, for its overtones of innocence and immaturity.

On reflection, I can't even be sure how much kissing and cuddling can have gone on, knowing how reliably one thing would lead to another. I had three sisters, she had a brother – it's possible we

sensed the proximity of a taboo, through a strange kind of sur-
rogacy.

Once again, I fail to see the thing through her eyes. Looking
back it seems certain that she wanted more. Innocent and inexperienced, she could find no way of letting me know beyond increasingly broad hints that I doggedly ignored. I wanted a girlfriend; N
wanted an adult relationship. She may have begun to suspect that
the girlfriend I actually wanted was the one who had finished with
me a year earlier. Perhaps exasperated and almost certainly insulted,
N in turn dropped me during a field trip to Cromer.

To her further credit she held no grudge (whereas I still struggle to find a good word for Cromer). Never on the warmest terms
imaginable, we remained fairly good friends. It's a testament to the
tepid nature of our 'relationship', isn't it?

The early days of the Internet era helped greatly in tracing
people and renewing contact with them. N was not hard to find: a
distinctive surname makes some difference, even if it is no longer
the one by which a person is known. I set out to arrive in the southern suburbs of Scunthorpe by midday, to take N out to lunch and to
apologise. Apologies for historic faults were just coming into vogue
with the new century. That done, I would go to watch a football
match.

I was over-confident. My researches had revealed the presence of someone sharing N's maiden name, age and qualifications
at an address on the south side of the town. When I arrived I found
it to be the premises of a nursery school which, this being Saturday,
was firmly shut.

I found myself alone in Scunthorpe with three hours to spare.
There was no real prospect of tracking down N from where I stood.
I doubted Scunthorpe would have an equivalent of the clock at Victoria Station, beneath which everyone I knew would pass by if I
stood there long enough. Besides, I only had three hours.

If only I (or someone else) had written this book 20 years
earlier. It could happen to anyone, to find themselves in Scunthorpe
with three hours at their disposal. Equipped with this book I would
have turned away from the nursery school door with a clear plan of

how to make the most of the time before kick-off. Instead, I wandered aimlessly through Scunthorpe's shopping precincts trying to kill time.

Time was surprisingly "tenacious of life", as Julian Barnes once observed in a quite different context. But I stuck at it, and eventually headed off... to the wrong football ground. Scunthorpe United had moved out of the Old Showground in 1988, relocating to a new stadium called Glanford Park.

A Safeway supermarket stood on the site of the very Old Showground. Apparently there was a plaque at the deli counter to show where the centre-spot had been. I had no time to waste on the deli counter. After frittering away three hours, I eventually arrived at the right place with only minutes to spare.

What should I have done, on that lost Lincolnshire afternoon? The North Lincolnshire Museum is close to the town centre and gets decent reviews on TripAdvisor, although an inflatable dinosaur exhibit disappointed some visitors. Another reviewer implied harshly that the place would be perfect for a visiting football fan, because infrequent visitors would not notice that the displays were not refreshed very often.

Not far away is the 20/21 Visual Arts Centre at St John's Church, and this too gets enthusiastic reviews from the TripAdvisor faithful – with one priceless exception: "A good venue but spoilt with uninspiring so-called art. Definitely not my cup of tea, although the tea bar does a reasonable brew."

As for the game, I was rewarded with an away win and a fine goal by perennial favourite Paul Rickers. Oldham fans have always loved an honest trier. Or a dishonest one, if it comes to that. It's the effort that counts.

Scunthorpe United 1 Oldham 2
Glanford Park, 25 March 2000

Sheffield United

Sheffield, like Bristol and Nottingham, is a city with two rather mediocre football teams. Unlike Bristol and Nottingham, both Sheffield's clubs are widely regarded as sleeping giants.

It sounds impressive, doesn't it, like King Arthur biding his time, waiting for the moment to return and make Britain great again?

In football, however, a 'sleeping giant' is merely the cliché applied to clubs that, were they not confined by incompetence to the lower levels, would surely attract larger attendances to top-flight matches than do the likes of, say, Bournemouth or Watford. It is a versatile, multi-purpose designation that patronises two sets of clubs at once.

'Sleeping' in this context calls to mind the mocking lines of James Joyce in *Ulysses*: "In Innisfail the fair there lies a land, the land of holy Michan, a land where great heroes sleep in death as in life they slept." As for 'giants', Sheffield United and Sheffield Wednesday nowadays are giants mainly when the random nature of cup competitions pits them against non-League opposition, making them susceptible to an act of giant-killing.

Nonetheless, both clubs go back a very long way. Wednesday's roots penetrate football's bedrock to the depth of 1867, just five years after Notts County – the oldest club currently playing in the Football League. Five years further into history you reach the foundation of the club that claims to be the first ever, coincidentally from Sheffield and perennial amateurs. Sheffield United, relative upstarts, celebrated their centenary in 1989.

Cricket looms large in the histories of both. Wednesday was originally a cricket club; United's Bramall Lane ground used to open out along one side on to a cricket pitch, where Yorkshire CCC played home games until 1974.

When I was a student in Sheffield in the early 1970s, Bramall Lane would have been high on the list of places to take visitors. A football pitch as the outfield of a ground on which a Test Match had been played... It wasn't something you could see just anywhere.

Unusual or even unique attractions were a feature of Sheffield in those days. Some survive; some are gone forever; one or two have adapted to the new century; and many new ones have emerged. In June 2017 Sheffield was named Emerging City Destination of the Year by *The Luxury Travel Guide*. It already had individual establishments winning awards in such awards categories as Coolest Hotels, Best Coffee Houses and 50 Best Breakfasts in the UK. Even the bar at the railway station has won an award. The city has a lot to offer.

It hardly matters, then, that most of the itinerary I would have devised for visitors is no longer available. Gone, to my regret, is the Stone House. This was a city-centre pub that looked from the outside like a Dickensian bank and turned out, once your eyes had accustomed themselves to the dimmed artificial light, to be decked out as a medieval village square or perhaps courtyard. Drinkers stood like untidy peasants on the cobbles and flags or sat on benches and at tables around the margins. Replica shop fronts arose convincingly on all sides (and, now that I think of it, from various eras, although half-timbered is the dominant look in my mind's eye) and above, a painted ceiling mimicked the night sky. Walking into the Stone House was like walking out of, say, Nottingham's Trip to Jerusalem in its heyday.

Theme pubs were very rare in 1972 and I had little experience of pubs of any description at the age of 18. The Stone House, then, left an abiding impression. I'd like to add that the beer was served foaming in tankards by buxom wenches. After all this time, who's to contradict me? Although there were many pubs in the area of the University, and on the route to the city centre, it was a favourite destination.

Still there, but not necessarily easy of access, is the University of Sheffield Arts Tower. The last time I went into the Arts Tower, in 2013, it happened to be an Open Day. Prospective students and their parents were looking the place over, and so it was possible to wander into just about any building you chose. Perhaps it still is, as long as you don't mind posing as a mature student, or perhaps security personnel would step in to stop you. That would be a pity.

The Arts Tower has a particular sort of lift called a paternoster. The name (literally 'our father') may come from the quiet prayer you mutter to yourself as you remain in the car beyond the top floor or, for that matter, below the lowest. For the paternoster is a conveyor belt of open cabins circulating eternally through the spine of the building, going up on one side and passing down in the other.

To ascend, you simply step into a cabin as it rises up the shaft and step out again at the appropriate floor. If you have difficulty with an escalator you might want to calm yourself and breathe deeply for a while before attempting this. You might take comfort from the knowledge that a paternoster lift is very much slower than a conventional elevator, precisely to avoid problems getting in and out.

Even so, no new paternosters were installed after the 1970s, for safety reasons. Sheffield's attachment to the Arts Tower's model may be, as elsewhere, largely a matter of sentiment but its defenders point out that any risk is surely greatest where very young or very old people are concerned, and these are the least likely users of the Arts Tower.

If you go over the top you'll glimpse graffiti left by the Vasco da Gamas of the lift-riding world, and the sight of the mechanism is a startling reminder of the simplicity of the principle. Some, knowing there were gullible first-year students about, would emerge from transition standing on their heads.

The Arts Tower's paternoster, by the way, is said – and not only by Yorkshire people – to be the biggest in the world. The building has 20 storeys and the lift 38 cars. You do not have to wait very long for one.

The gap between the Arts Tower and the University Library used to be called the Wind Tunnel and perhaps still is – no breaks or baffles have been erected. The Library is worth visiting for two reasons: one, its foyer now has a display space; and two, having gained entrance to view the artwork you might be able to sneak off to the floors below ground, where archived copies of ancient newspapers and magazines are stored. The dark ranks of stacked shelves are utterly silent, as though the newsprint has absorbed all the sound and fury that the journalists once generated.

If the thought of lost generations of journalists makes you thirsty, the Star & Garter on Winter Street is within sight of the Arts Tower. This previously unmissable stop on the Sheffield circuit of surprises is still there; but it is much diminished. In particular, no trace of garter stays.

A huge mural used to command the lounge bar's north-east wall, on which were depicted three can-can dancers snapping a mean garter. The dancer in the centre had her back to the audience and cheekily revealed her frillies; but the artist, coyly, had painted no suggestion of separate buttocks, giving the impression that the dancer had a pillow in her pants.

Recently (summer 2017) deceased is the second-hand book and music store Duodecimo Tomes, also known as Rare & Racy. This unique store first opened in 1969; "guaranteed to make any bookworm giddy", said one admirer, who admitted he'd gone in primarily to look at the jazz records. The block that housed Rare & Racy will make way for new shops, and student flats above. Will one of the new shops house a lively, independent second-hand book and music store? Don't bet on it.

Perhaps it takes a little time for the character of a place to reassert itself. The developers sweep the old away, replacing it with computer-generated blandness. But character, like a sleeping giant, shakes itself periodically and awakens long enough to revitalise the streets. A cityscape is in constant transition, then, as the living and the soulless exchange the upper hand.

If the Sheffield I remember no longer exists, the city still has character to spare. Visit the museums and galleries by all means – the steel industry at Kelham Island, the city at Weston Park – but don't miss the boats on the lake of Crookes Valley Park on the way.

From there, make for the Eccleshall Road and buy a bag of chips the first chance you get. Heading towards the city, you'll pass the former site of Wards Brewery on your right. When a previous generation of students approached this after dark from the direction of the University, the letters 'WAR' were illuminated in vibrant red against the night sky – the 'D' and 'S' were obscured by the buildings of William Street. Reflecting on the relationship (if any) between war and beer (good God, you all), continue to the A61, here known as St Mary's Gate, turn right to Bramall Lane and watch a football match in a fine, four-sided stadium.

Sheffield United 1 Arsenal 0
Bramall Lane, 7 October 1972

Sheffield Wednesday

A visitor to Sheffield at almost any time from the mid-Victorian era to the third quarter of the 20th century would have found a city in noisy, malodorous thrall to heavy industry.

Guided by a pillar of smog by day and the hellish halo of furnaces by night, the traveller would have found the city standing proud on its hilly skyline and perhaps a shade smug in its smoky vales, for Sheffield, like any city built upon hills, stops counting them at seven. The Rome of the North? Sheffield is better known by another name.

Metalwork, especially the forging of a cutting blade, was a typical Sheffield activity for hundreds of years. Chaucer refers in *The Reeve's Tale* (late 14th century) to 'a Scheffeld thwitel', which is to say a short, pointed knife with a rounded blade. But the monks of Kirkstead, eight miles away near Rotherham, held a grant for iron-working 200 years earlier, and in Chesterfield, 12 miles to the south, a street called Knifesmithgate still cuts through the centre of the town; Sheffield was the focal point of a region in which the production of sharp, cutting or sawing blades was of national importance.

Steel City, then, is a relatively recent name. The Bessemer process that allowed ironmasters to mass-produce steel more economically didn't come into widespread use until the 1860s. City status came even later to Sheffield in 1893.

Still, people growing up in Sheffield in the 20th century would think of themselves as citizens of Steel City. That would make some impression on the psyche, wouldn't it? Quite apart from any physical demands of working in such an industry, the sense of self would surely be tempered in some way.

It doesn't necessarily carry overtones of violence. The city's historical association with knives and blades turned into a focus on cutlery, from which you might as plausibly argue that Sheffield's citizens would have unusually elegant table manners. But table manners bespeak sophistication and Yorkshire folk would have no truck with such frippery. The blade, the sharpened blade is the thing. It's no accident that Sheffield United are known as the Blades, and to their detractors as the Blunts.

According to the theory known as nominative determinism, a name has associations towards which people of that name tend to gravitate. Hence a man called Bolt becomes an extremely fast runner; or, if he had been slothful by nature, he might have gone into the security business.

A simple citizen of Steel City would surely regard himself as tougher than, say, a Mancunian (Cottonopolis) or an inhabitant of York (Chocolate City). There might be some pride or sense of distinction to be derived from belonging to the Workshop of the World (Birmingham), but it hints at Dickensian drudgery; or the City of Arcades (Cardiff), which actually sounds like an invitation to go shopping. But steel – or granite in the case of Aberdeen, iron in Middlesbrough and, to a lesser extent, tin in Llanelli – is unequivocally hard and unyielding. To be born and raised in the Steel City must be to absorb a sense of oneself as being made of stern stuff.

'Steel' isn't a name with entirely positive qualities. In Russia at some point in the early years of the 20th century, Josef Vissarionovich Djughashvili changed his surname to Stalin. His birth name meant 'son of Djuga', and 'Djuga' is possibly a proper name or more tenuously means 'shepherd'. Either way it has a gentle, pastoral sound. 'Stalin', by contrast, is more clearly related to the Russian word for steel. And the original man of steel (the character of another notable man of steel, Superman, wasn't sketched out until 1938) became one of the most merciless tyrants in the history of the world.

Trotsky, not Stalin's greatest admirer, claimed that the Bolshevik leaders chose nicknames that made them sound menacing. Not only Stalin, then, but also the famous cocktail-shaker Molotov (from *molotok*, meaning 'hammer') and Kamenev (*kamen* = 'rock'). Lenin and Trotsky, what you might call the intellectual wing of the movement, pointedly did not follow this trend although 'Lenin' itself was a *nom de guerre* and Trotsky was born Bronstein. The origins of 'Trotsky' are disputed, but some critics have pointed out its similarity to *Trotz*, the German word for 'defiance'.

Of course it would be ridiculous to propose that Stalin behaved so badly towards his fellow man simply because of the name he had chosen. It was, however, his choice and it is charged with potential. Some of his worst behaviour recorded under the name Djughashvili was talking in class at school.

Stalin is widely discredited now. The reputation of steel, too, is in retreat in this country, where native steel producers battle high energy costs, falling demand and unfavourable tariffs. According to Government statistics Sheffield makes more steel products by value now than at any time in its history, through moving into specialist areas. The heavy engineering has largely departed and taken its jobs and its smog with it; the largest employers in Sheffield now are in the public sector – universities, government and health agencies.

The nickname of Sheffield Wednesday, the Owls, is a perfect fit for changing times and shifting employment patterns. The owl has symbolised wisdom since the heyday of classical Athens. In a city with two universities, the image of owls celebrates the present focus on education rather than Blades recalling former glory.

In fact Wednesday are known as the Owls because their stadium is in the district of Owlerton – which is pronounced locally as 'ollerton', but the Olls would make no sense atoll.

Sheffield Wednesday 1 Oldham 1
Hillsborough, 14 December 1974

Shrewsbury Town

Britain's first TV gardener, the avuncular Percy Thrower, was Parks Superintendent in Shrewsbury from 1946 to 1974. A notably floral town, Shrewsbury takes care to make Percy prominent in its tourist brochures. But Percy, a balding, Brylcreemed pipe-smoker, presented his last television programme for the BBC in 1975 and he died in 1988; his name will mean very little to people under the age of 60. You would have to wonder at the demographic Shrewsbury imagines it attracts.

The Shrewsbury Flower Show usually takes place in mid-August. If the fixture computer or the League Cup draw gives your team an early-season visit to the Shrews, you may be in luck. The Show, according to its own publicity, is one of "the country's Premier Flower Show events". The capital letters are intended to suggest not that the show is a German event but that it must be taken seriously. Sure enough, it has a small permanent staff and over 100 volunteers dedicated to "ensuring that our visitors have an extraordinary experience with value for money".

It sounds a good deal better than anything you might expect at the Greenhous (now Montgomery Waters) Meadow, although 'greenhous' was a promising start in a horticultural context.

Throughout the year Shrewsbury's various festivals might supplement the unreliable 'experience with value for money' represented by lower league football:

- In late August the Shrewsbury Folk Festival runs over four days, with multiple marquees and stages
- In October and November there are guided ghost tours
- February highlights the origin of Charles Darwin in Shrewsbury with a festival that spans almost two weeks
- In April, the Shrewsbury International Cartoon Festival fills The Square in the centre of the town
- The Children's Bookfest, in early May, boasts Michael Morpurgo as its patron.

In short, there are not many points in the football season

where Shrewsbury will not be hosting an event of great local, regional or even national significance. Instead of a one-off visit you might consider buying a season ticket.

Perversely, my elderly father and I went to Shrewsbury for a match on a Tuesday evening when the town was not overrun by visiting Darwinists, cartoonists, children's authors nor ghost-busters. Shrewsbury was simply its usual calm, agreeable self.

It is a particularly lovely place to spend a late spring after-noon. We ate at the Boat House, beside the Severn, and it was warm enough after dinner to drink a coffee on the terrace across the water from Quarry Park, where runners and dog-walkers took their exercise. Rowers periodically went by in multiples of two – the Shrewsbury Regatta is usually in mid-May.

The idea of ambling across the footbridge and roaming around the town for an hour or two was tempting. The church of St Mary the Virgin is well worth seeing for its world-famous collection of stained glass. But don't overlook a memorial by the west door, where an 18th century 'flying man' is honoured.

Robert Cadman was a showman whose speciality involved ropes and high places. He entertained people around the country by 'flying' – more accurately, sliding on a grooved wooden breast-plate down an inclined rope – in a death-defying manner. For example, in Dover he 'flew' from the top of the cliffs to the road that now runs alongside a marina; in Lincoln he set off from a cathedral tower to a point near the castle; and in Derby from All Saints.

Shropshire-born, he was apparently a regular flier from the steeple at St Mary's to a meadow on the other side of the river. When he covered short horizontal distances, the speed of the descent caused the rope to smoke. Before longer flights on milder inclines, he would walk up the rope, lie across it, hang from it by his chin, play a trumpet or fire a pistol. But death, taunted by Cadman's preliminary stunts, would not long be defied; in February 1740 the rope snapped and Cadman fell to earth.

The University of Nottingham's archives note that "this dra-matic death... ended the golden age of flying", as though a plush Short Sunderland flying-boat had disappeared on the London to

Singapore route. The Churches Conservation Trust is more laconic. Observing that Cadman attempted to slide from the steeple, "head first, using a rope and a grooved breastplate," it adds simply: "His engraved obituary stands outside the west door."

Further random facts that demonstrate what a singular, interesting place Shrewsbury is:

- It was briefly Charles I's capital
- It has some magnificent timber-framed buildings
- The 1984 film of *A Christmas Carol* was filmed in Shrewsbury, and the gravestone of Ebenezer Scrooge can still be see at St Chad's
- Its alleys, known locally as 'shuts', include Grope Lane.

We drove back out towards the edge of town to where Shrewsbury Town's new stadium opened in 2007 (just down the road from Percy Throwers' Garden Centre, coincidentally).

This otherwise unremarkable fixture marked the end of 50 years of attending football matches with my dad. It had become apparent that at the age of 86 he was too frail to walk any distance, to climb up through the staircases of a grandstand or to cope with crowded spaces.

Never having been to Gay Meadow I can't comment on the ease of parking for away supporters at the club's previous home. But it's hard to believe the New Meadow is an improvement. A vast car-park sits alongside the stadium but not for the use of away fans, however doddery their fathers. It turns out that a Park & Ride is available on Tuesday evenings now, but I'm not sure it was in 2013. The only remaining option was described by the club as 'Park and Walk', which sounds like a catchy description for what most motorists do anyway.

The closest parking we could find was in front of a neighbourhood parade of shops that included the Meole Brace Fish Bar. Had we not recently eaten I would have been tempted by a chippy whose name I couldn't even pronounce. Instead, we set off for the stadium. It wasn't far away – perhaps half a mile, most of which was taken up by a large roundabout – but it was revealing of my father's diminishing range. The last football match we will attend together, it was the end of an era. How appropriate that it should be topped off by a characteristically inept Oldham performance.

Shrewsbury Town 1 Oldham 0
Greenhous Meadow, 23 April 2013

Southampton

Vade mecum sounds like something unpleasant to be taken twice a day, or the botanical name for a particularly dangerous mushroom. In fact the expression is Latin for nothing more complicated than 'go with me'. It implies a guidebook but in 2018 it could just be another term for a smartphone.

In days gone by, towns produced booklets to show residents and visitors what was on offer. They still do, but now with website, hash-tag and @ links sprinkled through the text. I have a chronic weakness for this sort of publication. The one I picked up in Southampton was called A *Guided Talk around the Old Walled Town of Southampton*. The title runs on a bit but it lets you know what to expect.

My copy of the booklet was produced by the Southampton Tourist Guides Association (STGA), perhaps in 1991. Granted, desktop publishing was still young then and digital photography wasn't even a pixel in Kodak's eye, but publishing in general was hundreds of years old. People paid to do that sort of work had a fair idea of how to make something attractive to a reader. This booklet's design, or rather the complete lack of it, raises the possibility that the STGA provided work experience to Girl Guides and that someone failed her badge with it.

The layout artist had no truck with any trifles that might have made the brochure at all appealing. There are a few black and white photographs of indifferent quality, one inexplicable drawing and a couple of apparently contradictory maps.

The relentless march of text is broken by no sub-headings. On several pages there are blocks of text and nothing else. If you lose your place on such a page, perhaps by glancing up to look at the historic scene you're reading about, you may never find it again. The type is italicised throughout and the leading (space between the lines) is tight.

You could not say the same for the editing. The opening sentence is 55 words long, and 19 of them have staggered past before you reach the main verb. Three subordinate clauses create a thicket in which the meaning is concealed and on which the reader's energy is wastefully expended hacking through it.

All this matters for at least three good reasons.

- First, if you're proud of your city and want to show it off, it is careless to pay no heed to the window-dressing
- Second, in addition to your responsibility to the city there's history to be considered, and the interest of the reader in both; you risk stultifying it
- Third, if you're paid to produce brochures you really ought to do as good a job as you can.

The thought occurs that perhaps the STGA were volunteers. There's still very little excuse. An enthusiastic amateur would only need to spend five minutes with a half-way alert journalist to learn how a publication might be improved and at no extra cost, beyond perhaps the price of a pint.

The *Southampton Pocket Guide*, a contemporary guidebook, is a bright, superficially attractive contrast. Full colour, lively lay-out, creative but disciplined typography... It's hard to imagine that so much progress can have been made in barely 25 years.

In one respect, though, standards have gone steeply down-hill. The earlier brochure was, at least, well-written in a literary kind of way: plenty of the passive voice, an aversion to hyphens and numerals, instructive if long-winded. The *Southampton Pocket Guide*'s tone is light and chatty, and the proof-reading is hopeless.

In 2017, we learn, Southampton celebrated "it's historic connections" to Jane Austen. "The Austen's took boat trips on the River Itchen", they lived in an "old- fashioned" house, "you can still stand in the be The Mercure Southampton" and you might pick up a *Jane Austen Walking Trail* leaflet at "160 Hight Street". An enthusiastic amateur would only need to spend five minutes etc etc.

The effect of such laxity is cumulative. When you factor in the frequent exclamation marks, it's like being harangued by a numpty. I'll stick with the older model for my recollections of Southampton.

Predictably, the STGA booklet takes a page and a half to reach the stage of the narrative at which the tour begins. The more helpful of the two maps is not notably explicit on this point. Assuming, though, that you can find the Bargate, you're away.

Because the brochure is essentially a guided walk, the text skips about chronologically. You must imagine a person with a bright red umbrella shepherding a party of camera-clicking Orientals around, stopping at intervals to explain what can be seen from particular spots.

The explanations roam freely through the ages. With no thematic structure and no layout style, fascinating details have no means of forcing themselves on your attention: you simply have to read it all.

The Jane Austen connection was news to me, and it was helpful of the writer to specify "Jane Austen, the novelist" to avoid confusion with any other Jane Austens who may have hung around the waterfront for a few years from 1806. At the Civic Centre, you may want to hang around for at least 15 minutes to see whether the clock still plays *Oh! God Our Help in Ages Past* as its chimes. Just north of West Gate, marvel at "the only example in this country of machicolated[1] arcades". This is a word so rare that Microsoft Word throws up its cursor in despair and puts a cursory red line underneath because it knows no better.

One final example of this neutral presentation of interesting facts: Southampton was the port from which the Pilgrim Fathers departed, but because one of their two vessels was barely seaworthy they had to put in at Plymouth. There they abandoned the *Speedwell* and set sail all together on the *Mayflower*.

Sadly, the brochure assigns no more prominence to such nuggets than it gives to a review of the dimensions of the Western Docks.

There are some compensations: in reading of the Western Docks the reason emerges for a key disparity in the maps. In 1611 the walled town looked out to the west over water, but that area has been reclaimed and now accommodates hotels, superstores, cinemas and other extramural features.

As you reach the end of the walk and turn the final page,

---

1 "A projecting parapet or gallery with openings for pouring molten substances upon an attacking force below." *Chambers 20th Century Dictionary.*

there is a possible explanation for the modest production values of the booklet. It was printed by Portsmouth City Council Printing Service. Even so, it could still hold its own against modern phone-based or other digital versions. Its batteries won't expire; it won't try to side-track you into commercial transactions; and it won't attract the attention of muggers. There's a lot to be said for a brochure, even a poor one.

At the Dell, Oldham Athletic achieved their penultimate win in the Premier League. Three days later they beat Queens Park Rangers. Thereafter, from eight games they took just three points and were relegated. It's as though they'd left Southampton in high spirits and soon afterwards had to put in at Plymouth in reduced circumstances.

Southampton 1 Oldham 3
The Dell, 30 March 1994

Southend United

There's talk of Southend United moving to a new stadium at a place called Fossetts Farm. That has a pretty, rural sound – but it could never match the name of the club's present home, Roots Hall.

Can there be a more appealing address among the English leagues' 92 clubs? Roots Hall sounds like the home of one of Mr Toad's dissolute cousins. Australians might speculate on the nature of the dissolution (*Eats, Roots and Leaves* was a wonderfully ambiguous book title in the Antipodes), but in simple, innocent English it has an earthy charm.

You could say the same about the town. Presumably, in years gone by, Southend was the first experience of 'seaside' for generations of Londoners. Sarfend-on-Mud is how it was known – unkind, perhaps, but Southend's position on the Thames estuary makes the 'on-sea' sound a little forced.

My own first experience of Southend was an attempt to open up new markets. Having failed to sell any encyclopaedias in Colchester, a group of us was sent further afield. It made no great difference – Southend was equally resistant.

That was in 1975. Thank heavens for the Internet, which makes such humiliation unnecessary. Now, clearly, I would find the town greatly changed too. Busy arts organisations have revitalised the cultural life of Southend and it has more than its share of events, exhibitions and festivals. The Film Festival is annual, as are the Village Green, Carnival and many other festivals; and every other year there's the Estuary Festival.

In my day, a walk along the sea-front was enough. I'd be willing to bet that for most visitors it still will be: it's a fine promenade, smooth and level, good for small kids on unsteady legs or for bigger ones on scooters. There are flat and undemanding cycle paths and ramps. On one side, at all times, is a fine sweep of beach.

At the pier end of Marine Parade, Adventure Island is the main attraction. It's no more an island than Southend's City Beach is in a city, but the adventure is the point, isn't it? The beach then extends eastward past Sea Life Adventure, past an 18-hole crazy golf course, towards the town's eastern margins and into Thorpe Bay, where bathing huts appear.

The Western Esplanade is different in character. From the beach, across the prom and the road, the land rises steeply. A funicular called the Southend Cliff Lift carries a dozen passengers at a time up to the higher level, an ascent of about 17 metres. There's an odd historical peculiarity about this conveyance: when it was built in 1912 it replaced a moving walkway, essentially (in 1901) a forerunner of the escalator.

Southend has another, more famous, mechanical conveyance. The Southend Pier Railway runs for a mile and a quarter out towards Kent on the largely featureless structure that is Southend Pier. Here too there were forerunners: a horse-drawn tram from the mid-19th century, followed in 1890 by an electric railway that ran all the way through to 1978.

The current diesel trains date from 1986 although fire and emergency engineering works have interrupted the service on occasion. The trains are named after Sir William Heygate, instrumental in the construction of the pier, and Sir John Betjeman, who had obliging things to say about it.

At the Essex end of the pier, beneath the shore station in the Old Pier Workshops, is Southend-on-Sea Pier Museum. Run entirely by volunteers, it's a quiet contrast with the commercial life going on at ground level. The exhibits are largely railway-related, although there are also original, working slot-machines and a collection of models, photographs and postcards.

Is it worth the 1.3-mile walk to the other end of the pier? If you opted to take the train out and walk back, you could always change your mind. But is it really worth doing either? Yes, to say you've been to the end of the world's longest pleasure pier. Apart from that... There are reports of seals having been seen from the end of the pier, the views back to the shore are good, there's an odd little crazy golf patch and beach-huts masquerading as shops and a bar, and the lifeboat station, museum and shop invites visitors. Since it's said to be one of the UK's busiest lifeboat stations there's a reasonable chance of seeing a boat launched. The end of the pier has no restaurant, however; just snacks and ice-creams. You also pay for the privilege of walking along it – £2 for adults, the last time I looked – but it's a listed structure and it needs maintenance.

Facilities at the town end of the pier are typical of an English seaside resort. The beach is more shingle than sand, although according to the locals it used to be authentically sandy. Still, you can hire a deck-chair if you don't care to lie down on it. Along the front there are the usual fleece-me-quick operations: arcades, slot machines, takeaways, ice-cream parlours and the like.

If you go as a tourist, the weather is probably crucial. If you're there as a football fan the result might be more important. Best, then, to go as both.

Southend United 1 Oldham 1
Roots Hall, 27 April 1996

Stevenage

Stevenage New Town is more or less what you would expect: concrete in profusion, sharp angles, overconfident lines, ambitious statuary and a church that looks like a swimming baths with a fire station's lookout tower attached.

Around the Town Square the discount trinity Primark, QD Stores and Wilco mark their territory. Within the square another tower, this time with a clock rather than a bell, rises out of a water feature which, from above, might be taken for a Mondrian. At the base is a cute mosaic, a kind of town plan but one that anticipates the age of computer icons. Tiles of different design indicate how land-use is planned for the New Town: a bat and stumps for sports facilities, a spade and root vegetable for allotments, a blackboard for school, and so on. The distinctive church has its own tile.

An energetic sculpture here evokes the famous bull-leaping fresco from the Palace of Knossos on Crete, but rather than an acrobat and a bull Stevenage has a mother and precariously balanced child. Called *Joyride*, this is by Czech sculptor Franta Belsky. Belsky had no time for elitism in the art world. Although he sculpted busts of four generations of the Royal Family, he is equally celebrated for work at the Arndale Centre in Manchester.

Appropriate to Stevenage, Belsky found a way to sculpt in metal-coated reinforced concrete. He also left a form of time-capsule in his work: a copy of that day's newspaper, an empty Guinness bottle, a coin and a note identifying himself as the artist.

Around the square above street level the buildings have those multi-purpose frontages that in the 1960s might have meant offices, polytechnics or carefully-disguised car-parks. You can imagine officers of the Stasi beavering away at their work of repression behind the dark ranks of windows. Some have vertically louvred blinds, some roller blinds and some, apparently, no blinds at all. In all other respects the windows, dozens of them on two decks, are identical.

Not far from all this – separated from it by several hectares of car-park and a supermarket of similar proportions – is Stevenage Old Town. In this, Stevenage resembles Hemel Hempstead closely: a modern blob of concrete deposited alongside a genuinely attractive village high street. This, in Stevenage, is the restaurant, crafts and New Age quarter. It extends only a little way to the north of the town but it is an inspiring contrast. In 1901 the population of Stevenage was 4,049; 100 years later it had risen to 79,715.

The old town – or village, strictly speaking – made its living as a coaching stop on the Great North Road. When the Railway Age forced stagecoaches off the road Stevenage's fortunes sagged. Charles Dickens, perhaps on his way to Blackburn for a reading, noted: "The village street was like most other village streets: wide for its height, silent for its size, and drowsy in the dullest degree. The quietest little dwellings with the largest of window-shutters to shut up nothing, as if it were the Mint or the Bank of England."

When you read of the reception given to the Government minister who cut the ribbon on the New Town in 1946, you'll feel better again. The Labour Government's Lewis Silkin, despatched to Stevenage to respond to opposition to the New Town plan, arrived at the railway station to find the sign-boards changed from 'Stevenage' to 'Silkingrad'. Silkin bluntly told a largely hostile crowd: "It's no good your jeering, it's going to be done." Indeed it was, and although the locals had been assured that the Old Town would be left intact, the Old Town Hall did not survive forcible renewal for very long.

For a town where most of the history is relatively recent, Stevenage has a fine museum. Underneath the church of St Andrew & St George (a pairing to warm the cockles of Unionist hearts), it is particularly good for children. There are 'trails', interactivity, films and craft activities, and many of the exhibits are shown in carefully arranged settings – a 1950s kitchen, for example. The Vincent motorcycle recalls a significant name in Stevenage's recent past. The church, since you're in the vicinity, is said to be the largest built in this country since WW2. The stained glass window installed to conceal a view of a neighbouring office block is quite something.

Also worth a look in Stevenage is the frieze celebrating the town's notable sportsmen and women. This lines the pedestrian walkway through the Arts & Leisure Centre into the town centre. Ashley Young of Manchester United and England but born in Stevenage, cut the metaphorical ribbon in November 2014. Young, Lewis Hamilton and Ian Poulter feature on the last panel to be completed.

On the opposite wall a second frieze was unveiled a year later, with Stevenage's contribution to the worlds of theatre, film, art and literature. Ken Follett, Vicki Michelle and, from Uriah Heep, Ken Hensley were on hand to add real-life glamour.

Even in the dead centre of the town there's a persistent echo of popular culture. The film with one of the best lines in cinema history was set in Stevenage. In *Here We Go Round the Mulberry Bush*, the central character, played by Barry Evans as a lustful teenager, reflects sadly: "This is how the world will end; not with a bang but with a Wimpy."

Stevenage 1 Oldham 0
Broadhall Way, 13 March 2012

Stoke City

At football matches, even in this liberal, tolerant era, you will still find young men whose anger is effectively unmanageable.

Provoked beyond endurance by the slightest obstacle to their team's success – an opponent feigning injury, perhaps, or a manager straying infinitesimally from his technical area – they will rise from their seats and bellow in the direction of the visiting supporters or management, often brandishing the universal hand signal.

Fascinated despite yourself, you may allow your eye to dwell on this extravagant display of what it is fashionable to refer to as 'passion'. You must resist the temptation. Because when the castigators of the unworthy have finished berating the opposition they will turn and scan the home fans for signs of backsliding.

Your eye contact, given that you are sitting down, casting aspersions on nobody's sexual preferences, keeping a lid on your emotions, your eye contact will mark you out as someone whose laissez-faire attitude might exclude you from the congregation of true fans. Future outbursts – and they will come, sooner or later, regardless of how well the game goes for the team – will be at least partly directed at you.

Better by far to pretend the furious young man isn't there, in your line of sight, compromising your very integrity by sharing at least some things in common with you. But until these people either grow up or find something else to do on a Saturday afternoon, your soul will shrivel just a little through association with them. If top-class football is trying to price such men out of the game, it isn't working.

In all other respects, Stoke-on-Trent was thoroughly agreeable: challenging, from time to time, but in a good way. Being in a city of half a dozen towns is disorientating, but it's easier if you try not to worry about whether you're in Stoke, Hanley, Longton or wherever. How the locals manage is a mystery; presumably they have more pressing problems.

In Stoke itself I visited the Minster and a pottery exhibition.

The Minster is another consequence of Stoke's dispersed character; although it's a city it has no cathedral. A minster is simply a church of rather more than average importance. It does not, however, betoken a city – the east coast in particular is a cabinet of minsters, at Sunderland, Grimsby, Kings Lynn and Great Yarmouth. Some of the towns in which 'minster' survives as part of the name are even smaller: Axminster, Leominster etc.

Stoke Minster forcefully makes the point of how old the settlement is. Its Anglo-Saxon font is still in regular use; and outside the church a carved Anglo-Saxon stone pillar is the oldest monument in the city.

Within are signs of Stoke's more recent distinctions: Josiah Wedgwood's tomb, memorials to members of the Spode family and a memorial to Sir Stanley Matthews.

Sir Stanley, by the way, has two statues locally: one in the centre of Hanley and the other outside the Stoke City football ground. The latter is more ambitious artistically, portraying the man in three phases of leaving a full-back on the seat of his pants; but the statue in Hanley, passed and perhaps acknowledged by thousands of people everyday, is somehow more successful.

The Minster is also clearly 'of the people'. When I entered the church I found myself immediately in a small nursery class. Two mums (or teachers) were chatting brightly and three or four children were deeply engaged in purposeful play. I picked up a leaflet about events at the church, to justify my intrusion, and moved on into the nave.

It's an interesting interior. The church has a second tier running as a balcony down the length of the nave, ending at an arch beyond which is the choir. Despite a generally low ceiling (and artificially low ones beneath each balcony) it is surprisingly light. The memorials, of course, catch the eye, but also worth a look is a carved wooden eagle serving as a secondary lectern across the nave from the pulpit.

Not far from here, in the old Spode works, the Biennial exhibition of the work of young sculptors was taking place. My untrained eye was unfit to pronounce on their quality. But the notes alongside their exhibits strayed reliably into Pseuds' Corner. Some took inspiration from Dostoevsky's letters, others from obscure Victorian or earlier Welsh volumes. Most of the work represented the artists' "playful but challenging" approach to things like "rich iconography", "aesthetic potential" and, inevitably, the "indefinable space between landscape, body and object".

The Potteries Museum & Art Gallery is up the hill in Hanley. There are plenty of buses, of course, but a walk will take you through Hanley Park. This is a fine, old-fashioned English park, with a lake, a bandstand, a pavilion, play areas and sports fields and, bringing the Industrial Revolution to the party, the Caldon Canal. No, that isn't a spelling error. The Caldon Canal runs the 18 miles from Stoke to Stafford, and is not to be confused with the Caledonian Canal, which snakes through the Great Glen.

The Potteries Museum & Art Gallery isn't to be missed. Its ground floor is largely given over to the local and natural history of the Potteries, including objects from the Staffordshire Hoard – the largest collection of Anglo-Saxon gold ever found. There is also a special gallery devoted to the Supermarine Spitfire, designed by Hanley High School graduate Reginald Mitchell.

On the first floor are ceramics from the Potteries in all their former glory: the oriental exhibits are breathtaking, the design eras and art pottery beautifully explained and the big set-piece productions for royalty etc sit alongside display cases highlighting a golden age of elegance. The idea that people – a very few people, admittedly – might have owned such treasures and possibly eaten off them inspires either awe or mean-spirited reflection, depending on your point of view.

After that, the art and craft galleries may seem overshadowed. But the PMAG has an interesting collection, with works by diverse artists: the war artists, British surrealists and Scottish colourists, for example, plus a few Lowrys, if that's to your taste.

By contrast with the spectacular ceramics of the PMAG, the Gladstone Pottery Museum, in Longton, is mainly about the people. The Gladstone works produced relatively run-of-the-mill goods. There are, of course, some exquisite decorative items on display but this museum is primarily concerned with the working lives of the people employed in the Potteries. It was a hard life.

You're left with the impression that the men running the works would stop at nothing to avoid paying their workers. They deducted money for breakages or other imperfections, they laid off youths as soon as their apprenticeships were served, they employed women and, with the connivance of men, paid them less. Above all they obliged their people to work in such dire conditions – temperature, dust, toxins, burdens – that they were not long a drain on the payroll.

Workers were paid piece rates, by the completed dozen. When the employers conceded payment pre-kiln it was a huge step forward; before then, potters had been penalised for anything that went wrong in parts of the process that were well beyond their control.

Even so, the generosity was restricted. The production of 10 items would not qualify for payment. But in some instances nor would many more, because the interpretation of 'dozen' was very loose. A dozen cup handles, for example, might be as many as 36. When a new item was produced, the time it took to make was calculated and the relevant setting for a dozen was determined. A dozen might occasionally have meant 12 but not often.

The great beauty of the Gladstone Museum is that the clearly marked progress through its exhibits takes you around the actual premises in which the processes described took place. Including the kilns. Cold and dark, now, they are some of the very few bottle ovens surviving in the Potteries.

Two are preserved as tableaus, illuminated and stacked with the 'saggars' that protected the pottery during firing. In one, a mannequin poses for eternity with a pile of saggars on his head.

Needless to say, when a batch was ready for removal the interiors of the ovens were fiercely hot. Regulations said workers should wait a certain time for the temperature to fall to a safe level, to enter and remove the batch; employers encouraged them to wait half the time.

The museum makes good use of quotations from the people

who actually did this kind of work. It does not find room for one of the texts from the Biennial which might have been appropriate here, from Neil Brownsword: "The appropriation of by-product structures salvaged from the factory production line, were an attempt to reference the identity, knowledge and actions implicit in a variety of anonymous labour."

In summer 2017 the Gladstone's demonstrations included pot throwing and pottery painting. Younger visitors were encouraged to take part, and the volunteers – with great patience and good humour – helped them to produce items that were then boxed up and taken away.

The terminology was a treat to take away with you too. An early exhibit, explaining saggar making, introduced plenty of words. The saggar maker was assisted by a frame-filler and a bottom-knocker, who employed a wooden mallet known as a 'mawl' (pronounced 'mow'). The items placed in the saggars were 'reared' or 'dottled' to prevent them coming into contact with each other.

Before then, of course, they had been made. Of the various ways of creating pottery, most will be acquainted with throwing and molding. Jiggering and jollying will be less familiar; and fettling is one of those multi-purpose Midlands and Northern words used here to indicate tidying up the pot.

> **Stoke City 1 Arsenal 0**
> *Britannia Stadium, 19 August 2017*

Sunderland

Ideally you would want your team to share a division with Sunderland for several years. Then, with repeated visits, you could do full justice to this unusual seaside city. Also, you might regard its football team as something of a soft touch and a reliable source of six points each season. I couldn't possibly comment. But if sharing a division is akin to living in the same building, let it be in different flats; on the evidence of recent years Sunderland AFC are looking like basement dwellers.

It's a slightly disorientating city. Arriving on the Metro from Newcastle, you pass through the air over the majestic Wearmouth railway bridge and are immediately ushered underground for Sunderland's central station. Accustomed perhaps to the north of England's magnificent Victorian railway buildings, you may feel slightly lost – it feels more like a stop on the Northern Line. Upstairs, you emerge not on to an arcing forecourt with a colonnade, taxi ranks, fountains and a down-at-heel Station Hotel, but into a modest shopping street where the sense is of a market that has recently packed up for the day.

You might worry that you will be unable to find the station on the homeward journey. You need not concern yourself, and on two counts: first, Sunderland's street signposts are plentiful and reliable; second, you won't be leaving from this station if the football match is your last call. And although the Metro station two stops down the line is called Stadium of Light, you probably won't be leaving from there either.

But to return to the exit from the station, where briefly you are as lost as if a 'grand taxi' (shared, like a dolmus in Turkey) has just dropped you in a Marrakech souk. That brief visit to the underworld may have unhinged your sense of direction. Take a moment. To your left is a post pointing the way to Tourist Information and the Museum, Art Gallery & Winter Gardens. It's as good a place to start as any.

Or, arguably, a better place than most. As the name suggests, it has a lot to offer. At first glance, however, it doesn't even have a front door to offer; if you approach from the Borough Road side you will probably take a short excursion into Mowbray Park and enter through the cafeteria. The main door, shop, information desk etc is on Burdon Road.

The beauty of the circuitous approach is that it brings you straight to the Winter Gardens' main attraction, although from the outside. On the other side of a lot of glass is a recreation of rain forest, with a treetop walkway, dinosaurs lurking in the undergrowth and a pool with enormous and energetic (leaping) koi carp.

Inside, the temperature and humidity are high and, according to a warning sign, even higher on the elevated walkway. There's something similar in the middle of Kuala Lumpur airport, but here in Sunderland it is somehow more exceptional. If Kuala Lumpur airport had a gallery devoted to shipbuilding, with walls decked out in plates and rivets, and with the bow of a ship breaking through a stairwell, the comparison would be more apt because Sunderland Museum & Gallery has that too. Actually, since Malaysia builds about 1% of the world's new ships, it may have. I bet it doesn't have many Lowrys, though. And if it has a textile gallery, I bet you'd look in vain for an explanation of the garment known as the 'gansey'[1].

Variety is the hallmark of this Sunderland institution. Among the arts I haven't mentioned so far: decorative ceramics, glass, Victorian artists who aren't pre-Raphaelites, Thomas Maria Madawaska Hemy (though not his famous picture of a Sunderland v Aston Villa[2] fixture from 1895, said to be the first ever painting of an association football match – that hangs at the Stadium of Light).

Then there's a fine natural history section where the contrast between Lost Worlds (dinosaurs etc) and Living Worlds makes the point very subtly about conservation. Here is an animated gliding

1 According to the museum, a pullover knitted in the round (with five needles), patterned on the chest and upper arms. It was worn by working men and they generally liked to own four: one for summer, one for winter, one for evenings and one for best. In Manchester, on the other hand, a gansey was a cardigan, not necessarily decorated and certainly incorporating seams.

2 If you can, find an image of this painting and count the number of Sunderland players defending the corner. It looks to be 11. If one of them is the goalkeeper he's disguised as an outfield player.

dinosaur, extinct, and here is an actual, living and very weird creature called an axolotl. The main attraction for children, by the way, is said to be a stuffed lion called Wallace, but for me the axolotl beats Wallace into a cocked hat. Wallace, whose skin would probably yield several cocked hats, is in fact in third place for me, behind the stone head of a seal (or other animal) in the archaeology section.

Apart from the ceramics gallery, which is austere, the rest of the sections are inviting, imaginatively assembled and not forbiddingly large. There's a substantial exhibition space on the top floor – devoted to the 300th anniversary of the Port of Sunderland when I was there – but apart from that the museum and gallery dispenses its largesse easily and in manageable portions.

A shabby shopping street leads you towards Sunderland Minster, but the right turn at St Michaels Way suddenly presents you with Victorian Sunderland, an illusion broken only when Bridges Shopping Centre and the Travelodge hove into view. The Minster, despite promising on a large board to be open daily from 9am to 3pm, is closed.

Keel Square, round the corner, is open. Part memorial, part public art installation it celebrates the city's maritime heritage in a list of the most significant vessels built on the Wear back to the 18th century. The Keel Line, running through the square, also includes the names of people who worked in the shipyards. It is the length of the *Naess Crusader*, the largest ship ever launched on the Wear.

Across the Wearmouth Bridge, Monkwearmouth Station Museum is supposed to be open on Saturday – perhaps, as in the city centre, I was simply approaching it from the wrong side. But to approach from the other side would have involved trespassing on the railway.

Further round this easterly digression along the north bank of the Wear, St Peter's Church is also closed. Its website reveals that it opens only on Mondays, Wednesdays and Fridays. That's a pity, because this is a church sufficiently important to have been a candidate for World Heritage Site status.

St Peter's is one of the oldest stone churches in Britain,

dating from 674AD – the western wall, porch and lower tower survive from the very earliest building. The first coloured-glass window in the UK was produced to decorate the church, and the famously venerable Bede lived and worked here.

Your trip to St Peter's won't have been entirely wasted; just across the car-park from the church is the National Glass Centre. This is in equal parts an educational resource, a viewing platform, museum, exhibition space, restaurant, shop and events venue.

The first aspects of its multi-faceted character to be presented to the visitor are an exhibition (Wearable Glass on my visit) to the right and a brief history of glass-making in Sunderland to the left. In the exhibition, some of the items were wearable only if you employed bearers; and some perversely gave glass the appearance of other materials – pottery, metals and, inexplicably, plastic; but most of the exhibits were simply gorgeous.

The history section referred back to St Peter's and noted Sunderland's often unsung contribution to the world's users of glass products. In particular, the world's cooks, because Pyrex comes from Sunderland.

Once again, it's the language that stays in the mind after the sparkling exhibits have caught the eye. 'Friggers' were pieces produced in their spare time by glaziers with left-over bits and pieces; 'rummers' may have contained rum, or indeed any other liquid, being very strong, straight-sided souvenir vessels often celebrating Sunderland's proudest moments; and conversely 'disaster glass' referred to engraved or etched pieces that were originally produced to raise money for the families of victims of accidents.

I lunched in the Centre's restaurant, the Glass Yard. My jacket potato with tuna came on a glass plate: the waitress told me that originally all the crockery had been glass, but time had taken its toll.

The restaurant looks out across the river. Occupying the site of a former shipyard, the Centre gives you a view of gentrification creeping along the south bank of the Wear. For now it has reached a pub called the Boars Head, which appears to be reliant on scaffolding to sustain its position.

From here it's a 25-minute walk along the river to the Stadium of Light. The view, the life of the river and a sculpture trail are laid on to keep you interested. The pretension of Sunderland AFC giving such a name to their ground may also give you pause for thought as it comes into view.

It isn't the only Stadium of Light or even the first. Benfica's Estadio da Luz has hosted matches in the Euro 2004 championships and a Champions League final, and it was named the most beautiful stadium in Europe by *L'Equipe* in 2014. Are Sunderland giving themselves airs?

The odd thing that strikes you first about the Stadium of Light is that it is surprisingly dark. From the back of the West Stand you'd think the ground was covered, like Centre Court on a wet day or the Millennium Stadium, Cardiff, arbitrarily. It does, however, have exceptional tiling in the Gents; you could almost be back in the ceramics gallery.

After the match head for St Peter's Metro station. It's simpler to find, and you've probably scouted part of the route on your way to the ground. Resist the temptation to try to use the station called Stadium of Light: it's further away and the route might be described as 'intricate'.

But if Sunderland are still in your division next season, go again and try some of the places I lacked the time for: the Roker Park conservation area and beach, for example, or the highly-regarded Donnison Heritage, Education and Media Centre, which is just along the road from the Sunderland Maritime Heritage centre.

Sunderland 1 Cardiff City 2
Stadium of Light, 23 September 2017

Swansea City

When a railway station has the word 'Parkway' in its name, you can usually rely on two things: there will be no sign of a park, arboretum or parterre of any kind; and any town or city mentioned will be miles away.

Alfreton & Mansfield Parkway springs to mind, or perhaps Bristol, or Bodmin. Port Talbot Parkway is an anomaly, conforming to only the first of these rules. The train pulls into a station with an unparalleled view of Port Talbot, and especially of the industrial plant for which the town is known. It isn't a pretty sight; miles away might have been better. On the other side of the carriage a child pipes up to his father: "Are we in the back of beyond again, daddy?" Was daddy quietly disparaging Port Talbot on an earlier journey? Certainly most of the carriage hears on the return.

That would make Swansea, being next down the line, some way beyond the back of beyond. And in truth it isn't the most attractive city you'll ever see but to be any more dismissive would be harsh.

The locals seem to share that assessment. I set Sunday aside for sight-seeing. In the morning I asked the young woman at the hotel's reception desk what I shouldn't miss, given that I had only the day to look at Swansea. "The Mumbles," she replied distinctly and without hesitation.

I was struck by the reply. Asked for Swansea's main tourist attraction, someone who might be expected to know would propose something not in Swansea. Well, I wasn't going to hire a car so the Mumbles was (were?) out. "Anywhere in the city?" I asked. And God bless her, she responded with the Dylan Thomas Museum, which proved to be good advice.

I made my way to the Marina area by a roundabout route that took in Vetch Field, the earlier home of Swansea City. The Swans moved into the Liberty Stadium in 2005, leaving the Vetch to apparently listless property developers.

Nothing much had happened in the meantime. It was still

recognisably a football ground, though boarded up and neglected. Peering through a gap in the fence, I could see the playing area on which such giants as John Charles bestrode the football world. The stadium clock eventually found a new home in Swansea Museum. The centre circle was apparently to be kept in the development plans, because people's ashes had been sprinkled there. The rest of the playing surface was colonised by a vigorous weed that might have been vetch. It had not previously occurred to me to wonder what vetch was – it sounds like something from Keats: "The vetch is withered from the lake, and no birds sing."

The Marina looked far from its best under a leaden sky but the Dylan Thomas Museum relied neither on looks nor weather. Its first appeal was, appropriately enough, to the ears of passers-by. The unmistakable voice of Richard Burton declaimed lines from *Under Milk Wood* to the pavement at large. Even if I had not been heading that way the voice would have lured me in.

Inside, it was possible to hear the poet himself. Would you go for the cover version or the real thing? It's interesting to hear an author read a piece in which rhythm is so important; Thomas was apparently an admirer of the work of Gerard Manley Hopkins, and although he didn't use the expression 'sprung rhythm' himself his phrasing occasionally suggests it.

On the other hand, as the satirical crime fiction writer Edmund Crispin wrote: "Isn't sprung rhythm just putting familiar words in an unexpected order?" And the grammarian GH Vallins referred to *Under Milk Wood* as an "incantation".

A whole museum devoted to a writer (whose life was not long) sounds potentially dry and possibly excessive. That's not the case here. The variety of the presentations – plenty of visual and audio treats, as well as exhibits in two and three dimensions – is constantly interesting. One of the impressions you're left with is of industry: how busy, how assiduous he was and how much work went into the various projects in which he was involved.

A feature of which the poet might not entirely have approved was the museum café. The furniture was informal and comfortable: armchairs and sofas that would seem to invite sprawling, beneath book shelves along which coffee drinkers might browse. But as far as I could see it was not licensed. No doubt the champions of Dylan Thomas would prefer to downplay their man's enjoyment of a drop every now and then – indeed some of them appear to be in denial on the subject – but I don't think there can be much doubt he would have swapped the sofa for a bar-stool given the choice. Had I gone to Mumbles, I believe I would have found a Dylan Thomas Pub Crawl.

In the end my reaction to Swansea was largely conditioned by an entirely different factor, and my enjoyment of the town from yet another. The Welshness of Swansea is important in both.

I had booked a hotel almost directly opposite the railway station, to be close to the city centre for looking around. That left me with quite a trek to the Liberty Stadium but it does no harm to see something of a place on foot, does it? I walked out of the city up the Neath Road.

It's not the most scenic walk. There may be a more pleasant alternative along the east side of the River Tawe, through woodland. On the west side, separated from the river by a railway line and commercial property, there's a good deal of dull beige pebbledash on the homes and small businesses, many of which are takeaways of questionable nutritional value or hairdressers or off-licences. Occasionally the terraced houses are set back from the pavement far enough for an enclosed space at the front, but these cannot be called gardens – none has so much as a planter, but the kitchen waste caddy in one is a welcome splash of green. If a railway station were to be built here, they might call it Swansea Parkway. The houses themselves are completely plain except for eye-catching Ionian Greek-revival front doors.

Further along, the character if not the colour changes, and there are gardens with lawns and swings. Across the road commercial premises sit in more expansive grounds. And then you reach two railway bridges and a roundabout and the Liberty Stadium is in front of you.

In Swansea I had neither in-laws along for the ride nor friends to meet for a beer. I chose to sit among the Swansea fans, for no good reason I can remember. But it was not a bad idea. Swansea won and the fans were in good humour; the Welshmen around me were very agreeable company. My Oldham allegiance amused them, but the mere fact that I was English gave them much more enjoyment. At Twickenham that afternoon, kicking off at 4.30pm, England were playing Wales in the Six Nations.

This was an early stage in the steady rise of Swansea City. Roberto Martinez was in charge, and Barcelona might have been the model for the style of play. Beating Oldham by the odd goal might not sound like the dominance Barça would have exerted, but Swansea were never really threatened and there was something routine about the win. Sure enough, they were promoted at the end of the season and from 2011-18 played in the Premier League.

It didn't ruin my day. From an Oldham fan's point of view there the defeat was certainly routine. I made my way back to the hotel to watch the conclusion of England putting the Welsh in their place. Wales had not won at Twickenham since 1988. As Kenneth Wolstenhome might have said: "They have now!"

Perhaps Wind Street, the main thoroughfare in Swansea, is a boisterous place on any Saturday night. Or perhaps the win over the English disposed the locals to celebrate immoderately. Either way, my exploratory walk down Wind Street persuaded me that a drink in the hotel bar and dinner in its restaurant would be a quieter, more relaxing evening than I was likely to find elsewhere in the city that night.

The hotel bar was very quiet and the restaurant held only two other diners. They were a couple engaged in an intimate tête-à-tête, and when the maître d' made as though to put me alongside them I suggested we give them some privacy. Nodding at my consideration, he found a place for me at the far end of the room; if not at the back of beyond, certainly at the back of the north Wind.

Swansea City 2 Oldham 1
Liberty Stadium, 2 February 2008

Swindon Town

Until recently my chief football-related memory of Swindon had nothing to do with the 1973 West Bromwich game and very little to do with Swindon. On 25 October 1989, I was on the M4 in the vicinity of Swindon when I heard the news that Oldham Athletic had beaten Scarborough 7-0 in a League Cup tie, and Frank Bunn had scored six. I had to pull on to the hard shoulder for a moment to recover.

Ten years later Scarborough dropped out of the league and disappeared. On that night at Boundary Park they were a modest Division 4 side, and Oldham were a good Division 2 team. To that extent, you might say, Oldham would have been expected to win. But by seven goals... And in the previous round Scarborough had beaten none other than Chelsea, 3-2. Even in those days, pundits were apt to reflect sagely: "There are no easy ties beyond the first round," meaning after Rochdale had been knocked out.

It is Oldham's misfortune to feature in one of English football's most enduring records. The highest aggregate score in a game in the history of league football was their 13-4 defeat at Tranmere Rovers in 1935. The 7-0 beating of Scarborough is some way short of the League Cup record, 10-0, shared by West Ham and Liverpool at the expenses of Bury and Fulham respectively. But Frankie Bunn's six is still the highest individual achievement in the competition's history.

In the following round Oldham beat Arsenal. Southampton, at the time the form team in the top division, went the same way in the quarter-finals. Their victims in the semi-finals, West Ham, went down 6-3 on aggregate. By this time it was 1990 and Oldham Athletic were clearly the Team of the Nineties.

They lost the final 1-0 to Nottingham Forest. My recollection is that they performed rather tamely, but I have no means of checking. When I left the house to go to Wembley I set the video recorder but failed to move the indoor aerial into the right position for the channel. I recorded two hours of interference and fog.

To make good the deficit in the Swindon memory bank, I treated an old friend to a game at Swindon Town and a look round the town. Keith and I drove down from Oxford, had lunch at the College Farm pub in Watchfield and continued into Swindon to see the sights.

My plan had been to spend an hour at the Swindon Museum & Art Gallery and another hour at the Museum of the Great Western Railway. The timings were tight, especially with navigation of an unfamiliar town thrown in, but I felt that with discipline we could make it.

Thanks to the miracle of Google Maps I was able to drive almost straight to the first stop – almost, because at our first attempt at a Hemel Hempstead-style Magic Roundabout I came off one exit early and had to go round again. That aside, we found the Museum and parked on a side street and were rewarded by a shopper who illegally transferred her ticket, with 50 minutes left, to us.

At the Museum reception I said to the young woman at the reception desk: "We're first-time and possibly only-time visitors: what should we not miss?" The collection of modern British art, she said, without having to stop and think, adding cryptically "and the crocodile".

The modern British art was largely the gift of a local businessman; it seems that he had some very big names in his collection but, by and large, only one example of each. Hence a Lowry, mercifully low on matchstick figures; a Lucian Freud etching; a Gwen John pencil and wash; a Graham Sutherland landscape; and so on.

In one mysterious case, the gift appeared to have been made to the gallery before the work was undertaken – an amusing typographical error, no doubt. Still, admission was free.

We were well on course for an hour at the Steam Museum. However, there was still the crocodile. This proved easy to find; a series of footprints is painted on to the floor and stairs, leading to the upstairs room within which the so-called crocodile (identified by one baffled TripAdvisor reviewer as a 'sculpture') basks.

Whether a sculpture or an example of the taxidermist's art, or indeed whether it is a crocodile at all are questions that it would take another visit and forensic examination to resolve. We gave it a glance and we left. Its long, thin snout suggests an animal called a gharial.

The Museum is in Swindon's rather attractive Old Town area. The Steam Museum and the football ground are not. We went to the football ground to check out the parking before committing ourselves to another cultural visit. By mutual consent, the Steam Museum slowly slid off the end of the itinerary.

For your information, parking at the County Ground is fairly straightforward. St Joseph's Catholic College makes available its substantial parking space (do students all drive cars to school these days?) and it's no more than a 10-minute walk to the ground.

As for the stadium itself, one of its distinctions is that it claims to have been the first football ground in the country to be equipped with floodlights (in 1951). They were not necessary for the tedious 0-0 draw we sat through – or, at least, most of it. We left early to beat the rush out of the car-park. On the way back through the small park to the east of the ground we found two youths kicking about the ball that had gone over both bar and roof in the second half. One of them let me have a kick and made my day.

Swindon Town 1 West Bromwich Albion 0
County Ground, 8 September 1973

Tottenham Hotspur

During Oldham's three-season stay in the newly-formed Premier League, they achieved a goalless draw at Spurs in January 1992. Although the result was memorable, I remember very little about the game. Two seasons later Oldham lost 5-0 at White Hart Lane and my recollection of that game (especially of its opening eight minutes) is vivid.

In the first eight minutes Spurs raced into a 3-0 lead. This came about largely because Oldham's centre-backs repeatedly passed the ball back to the goalkeeper on his non-kicking foot. His scuffed and visibly panic-striken attempts to hoof the ball upfield sent it no further than the all-too nimble feet of the pack of forwards, whose baying was easily imagined.

The metronomic clicking over of the scoreboard was troubling. I can't have been the only member of the crowd doing mental arithmetic. Clearly, a double-figure tally was comfortably within Spurs' reach and the league record 13 goals conceded by Oldham at Tranmere was not beyond the bounds of possibility.

Worse yet, 90 divided by eight multiplied by three comes out not very far short of 36, the total famously achieved by Arbroath over the hapless Bon Accord in a Scottish cup-tie in 1885 – still a British and international record. The Arbroath goalkeeper is said not to have touched the ball during the entire match; a further story alleges that he watched much of the match from beneath the shelter of a spectator's umbrella when unseasonal rain fell. These were sobering reflections for the ninth minute of a professional football match.

As a result, the fact that Tottenham won the remaining 82 minutes by only 2-0 felt like a victory. When it became apparent that Tottenham were not, in fact, going to rack up a cricket score it was possible to relax and, to a certain extent, enjoy the game.

This was, after all, Tottenham Hotspur, one of the most famous clubs in the world, and Oldham were playing there on equal terms in a the self-proclaimed best league in the world. Such a magnificent event had not happened (until Oldham's promotion in 1991) since 1923. I'm certain that most of the people at the visiting supporters' end were there to enjoy the experience on just those terms. Throughout the club's time at the highest level of the English game, three seasons in the mid-90s, there was the sense that this must be savoured because it might never happen again.

Besides, it was a very warm September afternoon early in a new season, and a defeat at a big club was not the end of the world. As it happened, three draws in the last four games of the season marked the end of the world, and Oldham were relegated three points from safety.

Not all visiting supporters will be as star-struck. They might want more out of a day in London than to feel privileged to be playing against Tottenham.

For them, then, the attractions of the West End will beckon; or, not far from the ground, Bruce Castle Museum and Park. This is a lovely and surprising place. It's pretty thorough on the history of the area but it doesn't overlook legend.

For example the Ghost of Bruce Castle makes herself known during the football season, choosing November to walk abroad. This is Constantia Lucy Hare, Lady Coleraine. She is said to have displeased her husband, Henry, who reacted by banishing her "to the top of the house". If that was intended as a conciliatory gesture it didn't work, and Henry felt it necessary to lock her into a small room beneath the clock. She killed herself and her child, by jumping either out of a window or off a balcony.

Two centuries later, Bruce Castle was a school. Rowland Hill, originator of the penny post, worked there as a teacher; Charles Dickens is known to have visited; and the computer pioneer Charles Babbage sent his sons there.

Babbage's early calculators were called Difference Engines. They sound quite appropriate to the memory of a heavy defeat. But afternoons like that September day at Tottenham also provide a perspective for other results in much less distinguished surroundings: 5-0 at Hereford United, for example, or 7-0 at Milton Keynes Dons. It helps, as you mooch morosely away from such hideous mismatches, to be able to remember seeing defeats of similar scale on much better days. It was almost a privilege to be given a sound thrashing by Tottenham.

Tottenham Hotspur 5 Oldham 0
White Hart Lane, 18 September 1993

Tranmere Rovers

Tranmere Rovers, by hook or by crook, are the last in this book. The distinction is theirs neither alphabetically nor by the date of the fixture, but their win in the National League play-off on 12 May 2018 makes Tranmere Rovers the last club to be confirmed as a member of League 2 for the 2018/19 season.

On 7 August 2010 I set out to watch Oldham play at Tranmere. And the game I actually watched was on 15 October the following year. Did it take 14 months to reach the Wirral? Sometimes it felt like it.

Our transport on that August day was a VW Campervan called Tango[1]. Had we paid money for it, to buy or rent, we would have been royally tango'ed. But we hadn't, and in fact it completed the journey in just under five hours. But that was still too late to be anywhere near Prenton Park, Tranmere, in time for kick-off.

The Campervan was a loan. S, long-suffering veteran of the trip to Brighton & Hove Albion, had procured it from an advertising client of her publishing business. A man setting up a VW rental agency proposed that we borrow a Campervan for a weekend and then print a review in S's modest but surprisingly influential local magazine.

That plan began to unravel on the Friday evening when we picked the van up. S had forgotten her driving licence and so could not be registered as one of Tango's drivers. She therefore only had my word for it, as I wrestled the thing home, that you could never be sure quite which gear you were in.

I exaggerated only a little. Tanking along at top speed – about 50mph – and the fillings not being shaken loose in your mouth, you could be fairly confident you were in fourth gear. But those were the good times. On all other occasions, anxiety was your co-driver.

Especially, for example, when you tried to turn right from

---

1 All orange Campervans are called Tango. This one should not be confused with any actual VW Campervan, living or dead.

a junction into a main road, from a standing start. If there was any approaching traffic in sight, however far away, you'd rev the van like fury in case you were in third gear, and hope for the best as you let the clutch in; because until you tried to move forward you wouldn't actually know. Only when the vehicle stalled halfway across the junction could you be sure.

Restarting, and searching frantically again for first gear, all you could rely on for protection was the van's vivid colour – surely nobody would pile into a stationary bright orange box slewed across the carriageway?

Reversing out of trouble was not an option because reverse was the most difficult gear to locate. In car-parks you could allow for that by finding a space from which to drive out forwards. In general it was wise to behave as if the vehicle had no reverse gear.

If you ever had the misfortune to drive one of those original models (not the more recent Brazilian versions) you'll still shudder at the memory of that spindly, high-rise gear-stick. It may just have been Tango, but my guess is that in all early Campervans, changing gear was like trying to pin the tail on the donkey, at arm's length, in the dark, and with the donkey fidgeting.

The following day, in the course of a 200-mile journey, Tango introduced us to his other idiosyncrasies. (Although vehicles are traditionally female I think of the VW Campervan as a rather spiteful male, like Caliban.)

The driver's side wing-mirror – more important in this kind of vehicle than on a standard car – would steadily drift out of position in response to vibration. The windscreen wipers were inadequate. The sun visor on the driver's side was missing, inconvenient for when it wasn't raining. And did I mention that it was a left-hand drive van? Yes, yes, it's a style icon. So put it on the fourth plinth in Trafalgar Square and let people admire it. Just don't ask me to drive one again.

What with one thing and another we reached the Wirral too late to go to a football match. Instead, we drove to the campsite to experience the more idyllic part of the Campervan experience.

Sure enough, our orange VW Campervan drew admiring

glances and comments. But the people paying lip-service to that kind of nostalgia returned to their six-bedroom awnings and their HD home entertainment systems; we settled into our cosy, slightly claustrophobic accommodation without even a radio.

The question of dinner arose. When you've parked and set up for the evening, you can hardly drive off to a restaurant for dinner. Experienced Campervan users would not make this mistake more than once. The saving grace for us that evening was that a fish and chip van visited the campsite on a Saturday evening. Cheap it was and, through gritted teeth, cheerful.

After dinner S and I sauntered along a lane and watched the sun go down over the estuary of the River Dee. Small yachts bobbed at anchor. In Liverpool Bay the wind-farm was still. A dad and his two boys arrived on bicycles and sat amid the grass and darkening wildflowers a little way away; we caught fragments of the story he was telling them.

As the twilight leached the colour out of the scene, a bunch of thistles caught a last glancing ray of sunlight and became fulgently, imperially purple. Is a VW Campervan conducive to romance? Without the Campervan works just as well.

On the Sunday morning we left the campsite and drove to West Kirby. Taking care to leave room to move out forwards, I parked beside the promenade. We shopped and S made a traditional Sunday breakfast.

Again, people (including a couple on a tandem) stopped and chatted. This time there may have been a little envy – I could see the aspirational appeal of the thing at last. When we had eaten, washed up and cleared away I headed home prepared to give the vehicle the benefit of the doubt.

We had made just a handful of miles when, on the slip-road to the M53, the clutch pedal parted company with the mechanism below the floor. A weekend of struggling to find a gear had taken its toll. But I was in fourth gear by then, on a motorway, so we decided to see how far we could go without a gear-change before we sought help – a service area, at the very least, would be preferable to a hard shoulder in the middle of nowhere.

Three hours and no changes of gear later, the motorway element of the journey home was done. We pressed on, keeping the gear-changes to a noisy minimum in completing the 15 miles to Tango's base. I hope never to drive such a vehicle again, and our magazine published no review.

Tranmere Rovers 1 Oldham 0
Prenton Park, 15 October 2011

Walsall

Walsall are known as the Saddlers and the town will be associated with leather for as long as lasts last. How nearly the nickname might have been different, though, if the flow of industrial history had followed a slightly different course. Walsall could easily have been the Loriners.

The Loriners... It sounds like a sitcom that wouldn't go into a second series. Laughs at the expense of a family who couldn't even spell their own name properly would quickly begin to feel awkward. But in fact a loriner is a craftsman, and a Worshipful Company of Loriners is still one of the ancient Livery Companies of the City of London. Skill in lorinery in Walsall goes back to the early 17th century and it probably opened the door for the saddlers.

A loriner makes equestrian metalwork: parts of the harness, bits, bridles, stirrups and spurs – and sometimes the saddle tree, on which the saddle is built.

"The national centre of the craft today is mainly in and around Walsall where the [Worshipful] Company has in recent years established strong links," the Company says. It points out that lorinery predates leatherwork in Walsall and it cites a trade directory of the town in 1813 when 29 different companies turned out specialist metalwork.

The balance shifted in the following decades. By the mid-19th century Walsall had become the main source of saddles in the country. It seems the town was full of loriners who turned their hands to leatherwork. The first manufacturer of saddles may have been a man called Thomas Newton in about 1830, "whose family had been producing bits, stirrups and spurs for several generations", according to the Workshop of the World website www.workshopoftheworld.co.uk.

In 1900 the leather industry employed nearly 10,000 people, many of them women whose hand-stitching was key to the quality of the product. Leather and lorinery thrived side by side until the arrival of the motor car.

Just to the north of the town centre you'll find the Walsall Leather Museum and this holds lorinery-related exhibits as well as leather. Most of all, though, it is a working museum, meaning that there are demonstrations by real leather-workers. It makes the point that leather-working is still an important industry in Walsall, not only in the history of the town but also in the present, with more than 40 leather companies based there, still doing business all over the world.

Aside from saddles there's a second leathery link with the club. Leather was the material from which footballs were made in the good old days. Walsall had six manufacturers of footballs listed in a trade directory in 1925. When Walsall beat the mighty Arsenal 2-0 in the FA Cup in 1933, the match ball was almost certainly a local product.

In the 20th century Walsall branched out and apparently became known, at least locally, as the Town of a Hundred Trades. The Museum reflects this by staging events related to other forms of craft activity. It has become a widely admired community centre of sorts, and if you go you should expect to spend more time there than you intended.

If that means your visit threatens to run beyond 3pm, you might seriously consider giving the first half a miss. Besides, there's still the Aston Manor Road Transport Museum, the New Art Gallery and the Walsall Arboretum to think of. Perhaps you'd better plan a separate journey. Who would have thought it: making plans for a day's visit to Walsall?

The Bescot Stadium has a historic distinction, too. For generations, many football grounds were sited in old residential areas of towns. Football was a product of the Victorian era and it matured amid terraced housing of the same vintage. The grounds were often a very snug fit.

When the Taylor Report made its report in 1990 into the Hillsborough disaster, the Football League responded by insisting that all stadiums in the top two divisions be all-seater by 1994. It's likely that clubs across the country reviewed their accommodation.

At some clubs the process was already well under way. Walsall's preparations to move from Fellows Park began in 1988 and the Bescot Stadium was ready (less than half a mile away) by the 1990/91 season. It was only the second such move in the entire Football League; Scunthorpe United were first a couple of years earlier. But Scunthorpe look likely to move again in the near future, so Walsall's will become the oldest new stadium in the country.

The *Daily Telegraph* described the Bescot (now, with a change of sponsor, the Banks) Stadium as "serviceable but charmless" and identified a Wonder Stuff concert as a highlight of the club's first 25 years there. Fellows Park, meanwhile, became the site of a Morrison's supermarket.

Walsall 3 Oldham 1
Bescot Stadium, 1 May 1999

Watford

Some date the origins of the Internet to 7 April 1969. On that day, according to *Wired* magazine, the first Request for Comment documents came out of a US academic project called Arpanet. The purpose of Arpanet was to create a network of computers that might become a kind of library.

Very few people at Vicarage Road, Watford, that night would have doubted where the more significant events were taking place. A goalless draw with Hartlepool United was good enough to guarantee Watford promotion. It was an awful game, but the outcome was adequate and a few weeks later Watford went up as Third Division champions.

Now, of course, I can reconstruct that season through the agency of none other than the Internet. The Internet has changed the world, while the team Ken Furphy built (skipper Keith Eddy, goalkeeper Micky Walker, players as talented and charismatic as Barry Endean and Stewart Scullion) returned to the Third Division in 1972, after two seasons of scraping through at the higher level and one of failure. When Elton John became involved in 1976 the club was in the Fourth.

Consigned to history, that 1969 team appears in a black-and-white photograph in Watford Museum. On the opposite wall is a shirt from the club's 1904-09 period: red, yellow and green hoops. The museum's celebration of its local football club is easily the most gaudy room in the building – not only with the preponderance of Watford FC's lurid yellow, but also such exhibits as a suit designed for Elton John to wear to the footie.

While you're there, look out for pictures:

- A reproduction of the woodcut made in 1534 of the execution of St Alban. According to legend the executioner's eyes popped out when Alban had been beheaded. The woodcut is not for the squeamish in that regard, but the saint's ability to maintain a kneeling posture while his head dangled from a nearby bough is a welcome distraction

● Two portraits by Joshua Reynolds in the Cassiobury Collection, which also includes a familiar portrait of Elizabeth I's favourite Robert Devereux, Earl of Essex.

The museum is housed in old Benskins Brewery premises, but brewing is just one of the Watford industries to be highlighted. Papermaking, printing and Premiership football are other features. Generic local museum presentations of various aspects of the town's past are colourful and creative: an illuminated display of where and what kind of bombs fell on Watford in WW2 is exceptional, and the samovar presented by twin-town Novgorod is hilarious.

What contemporary industry will the museum of tomorrow focus on? The signs at Watford Junction station pointing to the Warner Bros Studio Tour and the Harry Potter bus are probably a reliable indication. The Studio's website says the average visit is about 3.5 hours, and with ticket prices as they are you would probably want to make the most of it. I haven't been and can't comment. But the word used by people who have done the tour is 'magical', and they say it has as much for people interested in how films are made as for Harry Potter fans.

As for the rest, I really ought to be able to do better. I have lived within 15 miles of Watford on and off for a combined total of 25 years. What have I used it for in all that time? A trip or two to the Palace Theatre; a few visits to Vicarage Road to watch Oldham; a panic-stricken Christmas Eve shopping expedition; and sadly, a number of journeys to the hospital, for old friends.

Watford represents the remorseless passage of time for me. When I first went to the football ground the Vicarage Road terrace was open to the elements and there was a dog-track around the pitch. Now it's a handsome Premier League stadium and they call it the Vic. In the town itself the High Street has been remodelled and populated by a different kind of business. From the train it looks like a medieval walled town. From within, it feels transitional.

Watford 0 Hartlepool 0
Vicarage Road, 7 April 1969

West Bromwich Albion

West Bromwich Albion was my father's team. Not that he came from the West Midlands; far from it. His family, for generations, had been tethered to the mill towns of North Manchester. No, he liked West Bromwich Albion because he found the name exotic.

Or so, at least, he said. Perhaps it is. 'Albion' has dramatic, historical overtones; 'west' somehow invariably sounds better than 'east'; and 'Bromwich' suggests castles or possibly orchards with druids snipping mistletoe from conveniently drooping boughs. It is not, obviously, the most exotic name he could have chosen: Plymouth Argyle, Crewe Alexandra and Sheffield Wednesday all spring immediately to mind. But it does seem to have been a positive choice. Some people take on a football team through force of geographic circumstance; others through peer group pressure; very few, I suspect, by looking at the available candidates and selecting one that sounds good.

And that is another oddity of his choice. My father claims to have pledged his allegiance to West Bromwich just before the 1934-35 FA Cup Final. He would have been eight at the time. He and some friends were discussing the forthcoming match in which WBA were pitted against Sheffield Wednesday. His friends were all of the view that Wednesday were the better team. My father, not by nature a contrarian, took a different view, apparently arbitrarily. Wednesday won 4-2, but my father's loyalty never wavered on that or on any subsequent day.

He applied the same unswerving commitment to other areas of his life. He was 23 when he married my mother and had reached the age of 86 when her death left him a widower. I wouldn't say they never had a cross word – they bickered occasionally – but I doubt he ever gave her cause for serious anxiety.

Similarly, he found a white-collar job when he left school at 18 and remained with the same employer until his retirement 42 years later, at a gratifyingly elevated level. He probably never so much as thought about his CV, far less put one together.

The institutions of marriage and career rewarded his devotion handsomely. The same can hardly be said of West Bromwich Albion, although he saw them win a Wembley Cup Final eventually and that's something not all of us can say about the team we follow.

Tenacity applied to opinions and institutions prompted him to maintain some difficult or even false positions. Having completed his National Service in India, during Partition, my father never knowingly ate curry in later life. I say 'knowingly' because the occasional kedgeree may have got past him, and in nursing homes at the end of his life he had more or less lost the ability to make that kind of judgement. A gentleman robbed of his wits by dementia, he ate what was put in front of him simply to be agreeable.

He sustained a similar aversion to garlic, which for many years put much Continental cuisine beyond his appreciation too. Until the early 1970s that hardly mattered; exotic restaurants were only just beginning to appear on his radar and he saw little use for them. When the family ate out, to celebrate birthdays or anniversaries, it went usually to country pubs that could be relied on for a glass of Liebfraumilch and a plate of chicken dégueulasse. As his career advanced, the need to dine out at galas or residential conferences must have increased, but the menus would almost always have included chicken or some more or less decorative version of fish and chips. That's after the prawn cocktail starter, of course, and before the crème brûlée.

He remained a dogged non-swimmer throughout his life but added a swimming pool to two successive gardens so that my mother could take her daily exercise. He was generous not only with money but also with time: maintenance of the pool from which he took no benefit added to the list of his regular household duties.

Where his employer was concerned, his loyalty took some barely rational forms. Towards the end of his life, in charge of his finances, I found he had no fewer than six accounts with his former employer and generous pension provider. Two were current accounts and four were fixed-term bonds of one kind or another. Three paid no interest at all and none of the others paid anything like the rates quoted on comparison websites. There's a possibility that such perverse financial planning was an early indication of something amiss, but I believe it was simply firmness of commitment.

Such dogged adherence to one financial services supplier is entirely consistent with lifelong support of a middlingly successful football team. For brief periods during my father's lifetime West Bromwich have been among the best teams in the country; by the same token, they have been among the third-rate for some of that time too. Apart from the second-tier Championship in 2008, they haven't won anything since the FA Cup in 1968. And for much of the time they haven't been especially attractive to watch, either.

None of that matters. You pick your team, by whatever divinatory means, and you stay with them. In the absence of greatness you take pleasure in small triumphs – for example, it pleased my father that West Brom in recent times became a byword for prudent financial management. You follow the careers of players who move on.

And very occasionally you go to watch the team and you remember better days. Inevitably, that will make you feel old. And one day you actually are old and can go no longer and one more candle must be lit at the altar of the Corinthian past, which lives on in ever fewer memories.

West Bromwich Albion 1 Bologna 3
The Hawthorns, 8 March 1967

West Ham United

Mount Ararat, as any Bible scholar will tell you, is where Noah's Ark came to rest. Greater Ararat is the highest mountain in what is now Turkey. In neighbouring Armenia it looms from across the border over the capital, Yerevan, where it is held in great affection and appears on the country's coat of arms.

The Bible legend contributes to that affection: there exists a Loch Ness or Bigfoot-style fascination with the upper snow-covered slopes of the mountain. Some say that the so-called Ararat Anomaly, a shadowy feature of photographs of the area around the summit, is evidence of the Ark – shades, literally, of the Turin Shroud. In the name of a football club it clearly indicates high achievement.

Ararat Yerevan in the mid-70s competed at the top-level of football in the Soviet Union and had won the USSR Cup earlier in 1975. That was how they came to be in East London on Bonfire Night for a European Cup-winners Cup tie.

I was living not far away in Colchester at the time, and sharing a house with a West Ham United supporter. "D'you want to go to the match?" he said that afternoon. Life was so much easier then. If you wanted to see a football match you simply went along, paid at the turnstile and walked in. If the ground was full you might have to go to watch Leyton Orient instead, but that would happen only if the visitors were Manchester United. So Pat, the Hammer and, as I recall, a builder, my partner D and I drove into the East End, parked, had a drink and presented ourselves at the ground in good time.

The man at the turnstile may also have had a drink. In admittedly indifferent light he took D, who was not tall, to be a small boy and said: "You just hop over the turnstile, son, you'll be all right." I went through first, helped D over and Pat followed. We found somewhere to stand – this was almost two decades before all-seater stadiums – and for a while we revelled in the atmosphere of a big European night at a famous old ground.

The West Ham team that night included some great names:

Trevor Brooking, for example, Billy Bonds, Frank Lampard Snr and more. Another sign of the times: every member of the team was English.

As the kick-off approached the suspicion grew that our friend on the turnstile may have mistaken rather a lot of people for small boys. The terracing became astonishingly crammed. According to official figures the attendance that night was 30,399, and the notional capacity of the Boleyn Ground was more than 42,000 (a record set at the visit of Tottenham in 1970). In other words there should have been plenty of room; but there wasn't, and D became first agitated and then claustrophobic.

At half-time we tried to move through the crowd to see whether the crush was less severe anywhere – further from the middle, perhaps – but movement of any kind was difficult. Shuffling sideways, we eventually found ourselves not far from an exit. We took this to be a Sign, like Noah's rainbow, or, at least, an easy way out. It was impossible to resist and if I'm honest, once outside again, all three of us breathed a heartfelt sigh of relief. That was for many years the earliest exit I made from a football match.

It wasn't my last visit to West Ham but I'll include it here for the exotic quality of the opposition, for my only experience of a Bogof at a football match and for the warmth of the memory. But I've also seen Oldham win there, comfortably. The fans sustained the chant of "Joe Royle's blue-and-white army" throughout the second half. Towards the end, as their voices deteriorated, it began to sound more like "Joe Royle born on a Monday" but if Joe's day of birth was not the Sabbath I'd be astonished.

That too was at Upton Park. Living in north London by then, I knew the capital better. I used to work for a magazine that used typesetters with premises in Hoxton. If you have time on your journey from your London rail terminus to the Olympic Park, stop off there at the Geffrye Museum.

The full title is the Geffrye Museum of the Home. For that reason people occasionally pigeon-hole it as being about interiors, which to a certain extent it is; but that's like saying the Science Museum is about electricity. The collections in the Geffrye are arranged in a series of rooms and gardens that give snapshots of life at intervals, going back to the 17th century. Set in 18th century almshouses and surrounded by its own gardens, the Geffrye feels less like a museum, more like a particularly well-appointed hotel into which you would make a booking if you could. It has all the things a museum should have: a library and archive, a formal set of collections, a changing programme of events and, of course, a shop and an outstanding café. But there's something about its structure and the way the rooms are organised that feels less like a museum, more like a review of middle-class aspirations down the ages.

The Geffrye is free, which is a bonus. It's also close to public transport. I doubt it's still close to any typesetters. Typesetters might warrant their own museum by now.

On a press visit to Budapest in the late 1980s I thought for a while that such artisans were indeed honoured in the Workers' Paradise of the Eastern Bloc. On a coach tour of the capital, our guide kept drawing our attention to statues of famous Hungarian 'compositors'. The compositors' names were understandably unfamiliar to our Western ears until that of Franz Liszt was clearly enunciated and the penny dropped.

West Ham United 3 Ararat Yerevan 1
Upton Park, 5 November 1975

Wigan Athletic

Wigan would not strike many people as the most glamorous destination on the Football League map, but if they want glamour they probably shouldn't follow a lower league football club in the first place. Besides, glamour and football have rarely coincided.

I almost talked myself out of the trip to Wigan. According to the weather forecast it was going to be a penetratingly cold February day, the journey would be long with an early start and I had a backlog of work building up. The train tickets, reeled in online three months previously, had cost £32. It didn't seem an excessively high price to pay to avoid a trip to Wigan that morning.

What would I have missed? On the face of it, a 0-0 draw between two ordinary teams. Not to mention a return exotically delayed by track-side explosions in the Tring area.

On the other hand... It is in towns like Wigan that this form of tourism really comes into its own. On the strength of a few hours' acquaintance, you would be sure to develop at least a sneaking regard for Wigan: its mysterious Egyptian connection, its handsome civic park, its public art, a football ground that can be approached, like that of FC Venezia, by water, and finally its unjustly overlooked cuisine.

On a cold day, the Museum of Wigan is as good a place to start as any. Its Egyptian collection is the first thing you see, assuming you follow the directions of the receptionist or you instinctively turn right rather than left on entering an exhibition. I suppose it's the swag of another Victorian tomb-raider, but it's unexpected, incongruous and well-presented.

The rest of the museum, in a handsome Victorian building, displays Wigan in all its variety. You can almost smell the greasepaint as you admire a poster from the Leigh Hippodrome introducing Lena Brown, 'Lancashire's Premier Whistling Comedienne', and 'The New Naturally Funny Comedian Fred E Taylor, Who Acts Daft'. A seat in the upper circle cost 5d (2p) on a weeknight, 1d more on Saturday.

There are also exhibits relating to Wigan at War (a Zeppelin raid), Wigan at Play (happy faces on a Wakes Week chara') and Wigan at Work (mining, predominantly).

The museum has relatively little to say about one of the world's foremost Rugby League clubs. If you imagine that this shortcoming will be made good at the stadium, make the most of what you see here because it's all you're getting. A national rugby league museum is planned for 2020... in Bradford. You can almost hear the gnashing of gum-shields in Wigan, can't you?

Upstairs from the museum, by the way. is the reference library. This is a special and atmospheric place. Orwell is said to have used this building to research *The Road to Wigan Pier*.

The road to Mesnes Park takes you through the town centre. Here, a happy family scene turns out to be slightly deceptive. Small children circulate merrily on a merry-go-round. Their doting mothers stand with pushchairs to one side. On every rotation, the infants are treated first to the encouragement of their mothers and then to the sight of winos on an adjacent bench.

But there's art, too: in the public gardens towards the top of Millgate, a massive mask rises above the height of a streetlight. This is *The Face of Wigan*, a statue by Rick Kirby. On Google Earth Streetview the face is blurred out to defend its right to privacy – apparently the software decided it might be recognisable.

Mesnes Park is full of more young women with pushchairs and people with dogs. A group of lads is showing off with wheeled accessories. One, on a bicycle, performs extreme airborne cycling, Steve McQueen-style, off the bank stepping down from the pavilion. Three more lurk on skateboards opposite the Boer War memorial. But when a passing dog fails to chase a ball and, indeed, gives up entirely leaving the thrower a walk of perhaps 60 metres to retrieve both ball and dog (which is by now inert and unresponsive beside an ornamental bed), the lads hurry to the rescue.

This is an attractive corner of the town. The tree-lined road alongside the park's western flank has handsome bay-fronted Edwardian semis. On the north side, by contrast, there's a derelict mill. Gentrification proceeds unevenly all over the country.

I had no time for visits to Haigh Hall, Mab's Cross and other Wigan tourist attractions, and Trencherfield Mill (with the world's largest working steam engine) doesn't open on a Saturday. I imagine it did when capitalism depended on it. But my route to the football ground would take me past it, and within a stones' throw of a notable anti-capitalist's monument.

Wigan had more surprises first. The bridge carrying the railway over the main road south, out of the town centre, is a work of art. Its coloured tiles, arranged in strata up the supports and in large blocks across the span, represent different aspects of Wigan life.

The football stadium is about a mile away through a maze of main roads, service roads and retail parks. To cut all that out, the Leeds-Liverpool Canal towpath handily makes itself available. You join it precisely at Wigan Pier.

Because there is, famously, no pier, it's hard to be sure at first. But the pub across the water is called the Orwell and, in smaller letters, its address is given as Wigan Pier; and to the right, protruding from tunnels in a scummy little annex, is the prow of a narrowboat on which waterborne tours of the pier are offered in better months than February.

The pub, incidentally, doesn't look bad but it proves to be closed up and the barricaded door is plastered with notices that someone – the proprietor, perhaps – might find menacing.

The pier appears to be no more than a wharf or two. On the opposite towpath a life-size metal statue of a workman rests his arms on a wall and contemplates it, contributing historical perspective. A little further along, a similarly statuesque Wigan pit-brow lass skulks beside the reconstruction of a coal 'tippler', and an information board displays a verse commemorating their work. The pit-brow lasses stood at a conveyor belt, sorting the coal by size and getting rid of stones or other foreign bodies at the same time.

It's a pleasant walk along the canal to the DW Stadium, where there proves to be no museum to honour the achievements of Wigan's rugby players, Warriors or otherwise. I fill the time with the worst cheeseburger I've had in quite a while. Actually, since Mansfield, when I think about it.

And that had been another goalless draw, but this one was a rare example of a stirring 0-0 draw. More important, coming after the Mansfield fiasco it was reassuring to see Oldham looking like a football team again. Wigan started the game in third place in the league table, Oldham next to the bottom, so it was an encouraging afternoon.

Contributing to the positive charge of the day, something mystical happened at half-time. Through a gap between the stands at a corner of the stadium, a distant red-brick industrial skyline with rooftops and a chimney caught the declining sun. The rosy glow very briefly suggested Tuscany with town-houses and a campanile. And the temperature seemed to rise several degrees in the second half.

After the match I had an hour and a half to kill before my train. This had been the trade-off from saving about £12 on the return ticket. Naturally, I found no difficulty donating much more than £12 to the Wigan economy in passing the time. Once again, food was part of the transaction.

First, Wigan tapas. It's three smallish pies – meat, cheese and chicken and mushroom – served with mashed potato, mushy peas and rich gravy. Magnificent.

As I paid the bill I asked the patronne: "I've got 40 minutes to kill before I catch a train. Can you tell me where's the quietest pub round here?"

She looked nonplussed. "Okay," I said, "how about the least rowdy?"

She smiled but still had no recommendation. "It doesn't have to be a pub," I said, to be helpful.

"On the other side of the bridge from the station," she said, "there's a bistro you'd get a glass of wine in."

I thanked her, left a generous tip and entered the first pub I came to. At 6pm on a Saturday evening it was full. The barman could find no wineglass for my 175ml of red. He handed me a small tumbler and I complimented him, saying that was how it would be done in France. He looked pleased and I felt more comfortable about making it last more than half an hour, occupying a small table, watching Chelsea thrash Newcastle United on a large screen in the corner. Glamour, indeed.

Wigan Athletic 0 Oldham 0
DW Stadium, 13 February 2016

Wimbledon

No longer underground but overground and Wombling free, AFC Wimbledon have pitched up (for now, at least) four stations along the line in Kingston-upon-Thames.

They could have done much worse. According to newspaper polls, Kingston is one of the friendliest or happiest places to live in London. If you think of it as a poor man's Richmond you probably come from Richmond. If your impression is formed by the concrete canyons that conduct the A3 around the town you need to break your journey there one day.

What will you find? The clue is in the name – this is a town of kings. Legend has it that seven Saxon kings were crowned here in the 10th century. In support of legend Kingston has Exhibit A, the Coronation Stone; and the first-hand testimony of St Dunstan on which, he being a saint, we can probably rely.

The Coronation Stone is a sandstone block equivalent perhaps to Scotland's more famous Stone of Scone. It stands in a tasteful enclosure in the grounds of Kingston's Guildhall. The railings and the stone piers match those of the decorative bridge that carries the High Street over the Hogsmill River in the background: this is an unexpected corner of old England.

The stone rests on a seven-sided base on which are inscribed, in suitably steampunk script, the names of the magnificent seven. Below are their dates in Roman numerals. Through the generosity of the British Museum, examples of coins minted during their reigns are inlaid in the base.

One of the seven was King Eadwig (ruled 955-959), known as All-Fair. St Dunstan, then the Abbot of Glastonbury, attended his coronation and played a part in unusual proceedings. The young Eadwig, who may have been only 14 years old at the time, had the reputation of being something of a lad. At one point in the coronation feast it was noticed that Eadwig was missing; Dunstan and the Bishop of Lichfield, sent to find their king, tracked him down in what the tabloids would call a three-in-a-bed romp with a young woman and her mother. They dragged their king back to his duty, possibly with an earlobe gripped firmly between finger and thumb.

By and large the English don't pay much attention to pre-Norman Conquest kings. There are several reasons:

- The kings had such foreign-looking names. A good proportion of the Kingston Seven bore names with quaint early-English ligatures or dipthongs: Æthelstan, Eadred, Æthelred (yes, the Unready) and Eadwig; not to mention the Danes and Vikings, some of whose leaders had easily memorable names (Ivar the Boneless) and some otherwise (Ragnvald Sygtryggsson).

- What were they kings of? The Anglo-Saxon Heptarchy had four main kingdoms, three smaller ones and a number of 'territories'. The first truly English king may have been Æthelstan in 924, or possibly Cnut the Great in 1016.

- If not here today, gone tomorrow, they were often subject to fairly rapid turnover. Two of the seven Kingston kings reigned fewer than five years – more a shower than a reign.

All in all, it's like regarding William the Conqueror and his successors as the leading characters in *The Lord of the Rings* and then trying to memorise the names of a bunch of hobbits. Hardly anybody bothers. Perhaps that's why, for centuries until about 1850, the stone was not treated with the dignity due such a significant monument; apparently it served riders as a mounting block in the Market Place.

By contrast one of Kingston's most famous commoners, the photographic pioneer Eadweard Muybridge, clearly set plenty of store by the town's heritage. Muybridge was baptised Edward Muggeridge. He changed the Christian name to what he regarded as its Anglo-Saxon form, as used by King Eadweard the Martyr crowned in Kingston in 975. The surname looks like a whim.

One of the photographic feats that made Muybridge famous was his proof that all a horse's feet come off the ground when it gallops. When you say 'Eadweard', are all the vowels in his Christian name in the air at any one time?

Kingston Museum is free and the Muybridge exhibition, though small, is informative and very well put together. Besides explaining Muybridge's importance and versatility, it includes hardware – perhaps the only surviving example of an early device (called by Muybridge a zoopraxiscope) for displaying moving images, for example.

The museum is also notable for some fine stained glass. There's a rather startling mannequin of Æthelstan; and aside from conventional archaeological finds there are samples from a Forger's Hoard. Imagine the disappointment of the metal detector wielder who unearths... a pile of forgeries.

Other local worthies include Nipper, the dog associated with His Master's Voice. Among the industries commemorated are aviation pioneer Sopwith, later Hawker, and the agricultural engineer Sherwin & Co which turned its attention to the homemaker market and became a manufacturer of mangles.

As elsewhere, the playbills for local houses of entertainment are hard to beat. Marco, Prince of Magicians, Hal Bert, the Elastic Comedian and Cleland, the Maddest of all Mad Jugglers, all on the same bill and some way below Lillie Langtry.

The Martinware – late 19th century/ 20th century salt-glazed stoneware made by the Martin brothers of Southall – is another unusual speciality of Kingston Museum, but the upper floor closes to allow for the preparation of new exhibitions on a regular basis, so you may be unlucky.

Out of doors, Kingston has plenty to offer. The Thames riverside has parkland walks north and west of Kingston, and where it runs alongside the town centre it bustles with beer gardens and alfresco dining terraces. There are boat trips to Hampton Court and Richmond, boats for hire and more swans that you could shake a swan-upping educational brochure at.

About 100 metres back from the river, through the suitably narrow and sombre Kings Passage, is the Church of All Saints and the Market Place. Kingston's modern shopping palaces are to the north of here, but this is the historic heart of the town. A nice touch: volunteers wearing Kingston Rangers t-shirts patrol the area, helping out with information and advice.

On the approach to All Saints, inlaid in a low wall, is a plaque marking where the south wall of the Saxon church of St Mary's ran. Once again you are close to Saxon royal history here: St Mary's may have housed the Coronation Chapel.

Many towns have a statue of Queen Victoria looking as though some syrup of figs might help; Kingston has a gloriously gilded statue of Queen Anne, in front of an Italianate former town hall. Within, connoisseurs may notice the "fittings inspired by the Choragic Monument of Lysicrates in Athens" (Historic England's listed building entry).

The queen, by the way, used to stand in a niche and had no need of a back. Now, free-standing on a plinth, she is fully 3D.

In the piazza in front of her and at a slightly lower level is the Shrubsole Memorial. The Shrubsole in question here is not Anya Shrubsole MBE, a World Cup winner with England Women's cricket team. This is Henry Shrubsole, three times mayor of Kingston and versatile capitalist (he turned the family undertakers business into a drapers and banking empire). The memorial is surprisingly beautiful. It's a woman with an urn on her shoulder, holding by the hand a boy who crouches at her side. Slightly weathered and surrounded by bustle, this statue is another unexpected touch of grace in Kingston-upon-Thames.

Not far away, between the railway station and the Thames, is another surprise: a walkway decorated with mosaics. It is inspired by the Austrian ecologist, artist and architect Friendensreich Hundertwasser and, put together with the help of 1,800 residents, uses recycled materials to brighten what might otherwise have been a rather drab space.

More public art embellishes an otherwise plain roundabout on the periphery of the town centre. *The Paper Trail* sculpture by Michael Antrobus and Thomas Kean mimics 'paper' planes to celebrate Kingston's association with aviation.

On Old London Road, David Mach's dramatic *Out of Order* has been dividing opinion since it went up in 1989. A line of 12 red telephone boxes apparently tumbles over like dominoes. Mach has called for more such installations to be put up elsewhere in the country, and he also proposed that the vertical box on one end be wired up so that people could use it to make phone calls. Plumbing in the one at the other end, people could use it as a hip-bath.

Some of the other aspects of the Kingston experience are less substantial. Above your head you may become aware of parakeets. In your nostrils, in the Norbiton Avenue area, the Mediterranean scent of oleanders is strangely prevalent.

At the Kingsmeadow Stadium, you'll be pleased to find admission remarkably affordable. On the other hand, if the northeastern corner of the terracing is the only space left, you'll be paying for atmosphere. You won't be able to see much – the steps are too shallow and the angle to most of the playing surface too acute. And if you don't, like Eadwig, leave at half-time, there's nothing to keep the rain off you in the second half. But for a 2-2 draw, twice coming from behind, who really cares?

AFC Wimbledon 2 Oldham 2
Kingsmeadow, 21 April 2018

also **Wimbledon 3 Oldham 1**
Plough Lane, 8 November 1983

Wolverhampton Wanderers

It was a dreary day in the West Midlands. The third round of the FA Cup is one of the most exciting days in the football calendar, but Wolverhampton in the distant afterglow of Christmas on a day of unremitting drizzle did not make for a vibrant prospect.

I didn't care. For one thing, I was going to a real football stadium again. Meaning no disrespect to the occupants of the lower divisions, I had been going to games in nothing but humble surroundings for some time. Molineux may have seen better teams and better days, but it has history, solidity and quite possibly some restricted views.

I also had a party in a West End bar to look forward to that evening. It was a friend's 30th. The prospect of a West End bar amid people 20 years younger did not, in itself, excite me beyond measure; but I liked the contrast between my arrangements for the afternoon and the evening. They meant, of course, that I would not be spending much time in Wolverhampton.

Not expecting much of the place, I found that I enjoyed it from the moment the train pulled in. It's a conveniently compact city: the centre sits within its ring-road like a fortified town protected by a moat, and key facilities like the football ground and the railway station abut the north and northeast sectors of the four-lane earthworks.

I walked into the centre and it was immediately apparent that the Road to Wembley was generating additional traffic. There were bouncers outside the city centre bars and thronging hordes within. Elsewhere, the January sales were drawing crowds of their own. Those would have been the last January sales before what became known as the Credit Crunch and subsequently the Financial Crisis of 2007-08. They must have been relatively carefree times, but the faces of the shoppers had that tinge of anxiety that comes from worrying that a bargain is getting away somewhere.

A quiet drink at street level was out of the question. I found a café on the top floor of a department store and, reasoning that this could be the last meal of the day, ordered a simple lunch. Are department store cafés always on the top floor so that you have to pass through the entire store to get to them? If so, why do they allow you to sidestep the goods by taking a lift?

For cultural sustenance I relied entirely on the Collegiate Church of St Peter – since its position on a grassy knoll lies between the centre and the football ground I could hardly miss it. Even so, I should have gone to the Wolverhampton Art Gallery, which has a café on top of its other attractions, which in most respects would exceed those of Bonmarché, at least from my point of view. I also missed the UK's first set of traffic lights, still controlling the flow at Princess Square and still bearing the original black and white banding.

St Peter's is a thoroughly agreeable surprise. A statue of Lady Wulfrun, for whom the city is named, stands proudly in front. Noble of brow, she gazes unblinkingly into the future of her town. But the oddest features of the statue by Sir Charles Wheeler are, regrettably, her breasts.

They are strangely independent. Neither unusually large nor misshapen, they protrude symmetrically from the panels of her cape as though lifted and separated to the point of no recall. They make Wulfrun look like an early experiment in genetic engineering, after the idea of a woman with a single central breast had been discarded. They look less like a bosom than a model of a minor volcano field. Women concerned to find a well-fitting bra will measure the distance between their breasts in fingers; in Wulfrun's case hands would be more likely, as if measuring a horse. Her son Wulfric means 'Spot', a dog's name, and both of them sound like 'wolf' – it looks as though there's a variant of the Romulus and Remus story being presented here.

These are not ideas to entertain on entering a church. Their first effect is to drive from your mind the actual dedication of the building. The dark, sturdy and somewhat masculine structure will stay in your mind as the Church of St Wulfrun, or some similar expression of Wulfrulatry. Then there's the danger, ever-present in a church at the best of times, of yielding to an unseemly fit of giggles.

Better, perhaps, to approach the church from the south, where the stem of an Anglo-Saxon cross (supposedly from a Mercian monastery, although traces of no such building have been found) should put you into a more suitably sombre frame of mind.

By the time I got to Molineux I was in a more respectful mood and took as much pleasure from the ground as I had expected to. That's a lower division reflex – anticipating a beating, the humble fan looks for compensations. In the event Oldham were good value for the draw, but order was restored in the replay, which they lost 0-2.

Wolverhampton Wanderers 2 Oldham 2

Molineux, 6 January 2007

Wycombe Wanderers

High Wycombe lies in a deep valley, which makes it a dramatic town to approach by road from north or south. The A404 drops into the town by a long and impressive slope, from which the sweep of the road climbing out of the valley on the opposite side is an almost Alpine prospect.

I specify 'by road' rather than 'by car' because I arrived for this fixture on a bicycle. Unlike the Aston Villa game almost 20 years earlier, there was real cycling involved. I was living about 20 miles away across the ridges of the Chilterns. 'About 20 miles' is another case of imprecision on which I need to enlarge: when I set out, I estimated the distance at no more than 18 miles; this turned out to be a crucial miscalculation.

Why was a man in his 59th year cycling at all? Since moving house in 2007 it had become my preferred, indeed my only, form of exercise. The beauty of my new home, for a cyclist whose best years were behind him, was that the routes out of the town in half the available directions were soon if not immediately flat, into Aylesbury Vale. Several others could be made flat by using the towpaths of various canals. The remainder, up steep hills into the Chiltern hinterland, could be stored away as challenges to be tackled when I felt up to them.

April was early in the season – I was and am a fair-weather cyclist – and the obvious route to High Wycombe promised hills. The path alongside the Wendover Arm of the Grand Union Canal sidestepped some of the early slopes but it added to the distance. There was, furthermore, no avoiding the climb into the Chilterns at some point. Because I planned to go via Hughenden, the former home of Benjamin Disraeli, I committed myself to the Missenden road out of Butlers Cross. From the top of that hill, it was miraculously downhill most of the rest of the way.

Hughenden itself muttered a low warning to me for later in the day. The lane at that point is called Valley Road, and the house sits on the brow of a hill at the end of a short drive to the west. I dismounted and pushed as soon as the gradient set in. Thus I arrived at the home of Victoria's favourite Prime Minister fresh and in good shape, but it was early to be out of the saddle. The thought of the return journey began to prey on my mind.

Hughenden is good value, inside and out. The house is not so large that fatigue ever threatens to set in, and it somehow retains a lived-in feel. The dining chair with the legs cut back, so that the petite Victoria could sit with the soles of her feet on the floor, was a highlight.

It was a pleasant, sunny day and I admired the formal gardens around the house as much as the interiors. In the courtyard café, I chose Lancashire hotpot from the menu by way of superstition. Chatting to fellow diners, I found myself to be the only Lancastrian but relatively local: there was a couple from Northumberland at my table and, adjacent, a family from Canada.

Rested and refuelled I coasted the rest of the way into Wycombe. The football ground, Adams Park, is on the western margins of the town where an industrial estate merges into farmland. One of the club's main car-parks is on a hillside above the stadium and I'm told that games have been postponed on particularly wet days because of the difficulty of getting cars up there.

No such problems on a dry April Saturday. As for cyclists, I anchored my bike to a low fence outside a light-industrial unit. I removed anything detachable – pump, lamps (in case I had miscalculated lighting-up time) and the handlebar computer which, I couldn't help noticing, recorded a mileage slightly in excess of 22 for the journey to the ground.

Of the match itself, two memories stand out. One was the relentless tension that arose from the perilous league positions of both clubs. The other was the temperature, which dipped as the afternoon wore on.

Oldham took the lead with a fine goal from Portuguese attacking midfielder Filipe Morais. They then lost it and, with barely 10 minutes remaining, spinelessly conceded a second. The conviction began to grow in me that I would be warmer on the bike; and as I sidled towards the exit, in the 90th minute, Oldham won a penalty. Standing close to the corner flag, I watched Robbie Simpson take it. Square on, it was difficult to tell where the ball had gone except that it hit the net. I left the ground in a much better frame of mind.

My route home was carefully planned to avoid the steady uphill slog back the way I'd come, through Wycombe, past Hughenden and eventually to Butlers Cross. I took a more westerly tack, to West Wycombe and then north to Princes Risborough. Turning east from there through the Kimbles, I reasoned, I could skirt the Chilterns escarpment and return to Wendover and the sanctuary of its towpath without too much difficulty. The price, as at the beginning of the day's journey, was a few extra miles.

By the time I reached a village called Ellesborough the flaws in my plan were fully exposed. The skirting tactic was not working; I was ascending and descending spurs thrown out from the Chiltern escarpment like a rucked-up carpet. The milometer was already reading plenty more than the 36 miles I had reckoned on. My hamstrings began to complain. Worse, I discovered that resting them on the downhill sections did not help – they simply stiffened and threatened to give up more quickly at the next call on their services.

There were good country pubs along the route and I wondered whether serious rest and a morale-boosting drink would help. But that might take the ride into the twilight zone, and I didn't want to be picking my way along the towpath of the Wendover Arm in the dark. I had lights, but my bicycle lights were intended more to allow the bike to be seen than to illuminate its course with water alongside. I pressed on.

The road from Ellesborough to Wendover is not flat, but the promise of the towpath was enough of a psychological boost to get my hamstrings through the immediate ordeal.

When I reached the A41, however, faced either by the long climb up Aston Hill or the longer, flatter circuit to the Grand Union, I got off and hobbled up the hill. Slightly refreshed, I was in the saddle when I reached home. I vowed never to try to cycle more than 35 miles in a day ever again. So far the need has not arisen.

The 2011-12 season finished three weeks later. Oldham stayed up, with an 11pt cushion... over Wycombe Wanderers, who were relegated by finishing in 21st place.

Wycombe Wanderers 2 Oldham 2
Adams Park, 14 April 2012

Yeovil Town

I'd passed up several opportunities to go to Yeovil with a friend who was born there. I'm sure he would have been pleased to show me round, although I never heard him speak well of the place.

In fact I'm still not sure what there is in Yeovil to admire – a helicopter museum, perhaps? That would be appropriate, since one of my memories of Yeovil is of going round in circles.

Eventually I made the journey on my own, and by car. Yeovil looked quite attractive as I drove around it on a bright and unseasonally warm March day. It looked much the same on my second circuit, but the shortage of recognisable names on the road signs was making orientation difficult. I began to wonder whether I would have done better to stop en route, where there were certainly interesting places – Sherbourne, with not one but two castles, for example.

But to build myself up for the match in Yeovil I went instead to the nearby village of East Coker to visit the church where the ashes of TS Eliot lie. Can there be a more appropriately named place for ashes?

However, visiting it was easier said than done. East Coker is an elusive little village and the church of St Michael and All Angels stands in an unnamed satellite that might be thought of as South Coker. The absence from the map of anywhere called Coker doesn't help. On the road signs, there is nothing to tell you that anything out of the ordinary might be found in the vicinity.

Eventually I found the church through no more sophisticated a piece of navigation than that its tower was visible from the road. I parked on a lane that appeared to serve a country seat and walked up to the church.

Eliot's ashes happen to be here because the poet apparently felt drawn to his ancestral hearth. His forebears had lived in the area for 200 years before Andrew Eliot and his son, also called Andrew, emigrated to Massachusetts around 1670. TS Eliot returned simply to see where the family came from; he was sufficiently impressed to draw from East Coker the title and symbolism of a poem and now remains there for eternity.

It doesn't really matter how you feel about *The Waste Land*. If you don't know what to make of it, join the club. And you may as well take at face value the assertion (by people who are paid to know these things) that it is possibly the most important poem of the 20th century. That alone would make East Coker a significant literary landmark. But when you consider that *The Waste Land* was published in 1922, the same year as *Ulysses* – arguably the greatest novel ever – you may feel you're close to the heart of some extraordinary artistic nexus.

Not that St Michael and All Angels itself will inspire such thoughts. It's an attractive, tidy but unassuming country church and the memorial to TS Eliot has a provisional air. A simple plaque on the west wall, below a plain but intricately leaded window, asks for your prayers for the repose of the souls of Thomas Stearns Eliot and Esmé Valerie Eliot.

To the right, perched on a miniature column of the kind inexplicably popular in garden centres all over the country, is a photograph of a bust of the poet. This proxy portrait makes him look like Alec Guinness; the besuited bank clerk who occasionally essays a smile in his photographs is absent.

Behind this display, some sort of drainage pipe rises up the wall. To the left, lingering alongside a handsome compound column, stands a statue whose face has been hacked off by crazed religious reformers. A curiously modern crucifix presides over the memorial and opportunities to buy leaflets are many. In all other respects the distinction Eliot has conferred on East Coker remains an unsweated asset.

This search for and appreciation of roots seems to be a particularly American characteristic – certainly I've never known an Australian to waste much time over visiting the mother country and searching through churchyards. But it isn't universal. By coincidence I am typing this in a building not a quarter of a mile from where the great-grandfather of the first President of the United States was born. But John Washington was born on the wrong side of the sheets. Although the first-born of Lawrence Washington and his wife Amphyllis Twigden, he was relegated to the chorus of minor bequests when his father died – the bulk of the inheritance went to his legitimate younger brother. John emigrated to seek his fortune, married well and founded a dynasty. There is no record locally of any of the American Washingtons returning to Tring to provide it with a tourist attraction. Amphyllis Twigden, though... what a name.

And the football? The curse of Oldham Athletic struck again. Yeovil won and, shortly afterwards, were relegated. If their decline follows the trajectories of such previous Pyrrhic victors as Hereford United, Torquay United and Tranmere Rovers, they will shortly drop out of the football league altogether.

TS Eliot was certainly aware of football. In a book called *Notes Towards the Definition of Culture* in 1948, he included the FA Cup Final in a list of things that defined English cultural life.

"The term culture... includes all the characteristic activities and interests of a people; Derby Day, Henley Regatta, Cowes, the 12th of August, a cup final, the dog races, the pin table, the dart board, Wensleydale cheese, boiled cabbage cut into sections, beetroot in vinegar, 19th-century Gothic churches and the music of Elgar. The reader can make his own list..."

Does that mean old Tom liked football? The reader can make up his own mind as well as his own list. For myself, I'd say that the absence of capitals on "a cup final" and other proletarian pursuits contrasts tellingly with their proliferation on 'society' events.

Yeovil Town 2 Oldham 1
Huish Park, 7 March 2015

Index

About the author

David Guest has been a journalist for over 35 years, working for most of that time as a freelance writer and editor in diverse areas of the media. He has also been a computer programmer, an ice-cream man and a board-game designer.

He was born in Lancashire and finished his formal education in Yorkshire. Apart from a period in Australia he has spent most of his working life in the south of England.

- www.facebook.com/david.guest.9674
- @DavidAlanGuest
- d.guest@btinternet.com

www.townsof2halves.co.uk

A Pressure of the Hand

"It would be an insecure storyteller who began his tale with a story borrowed from someone else. Over to Antoine de Saint-Exupéry, then..."

So begins David Guest's debut novel, *A Pressure of the Hand*. It's a tale of first love recalled largely through letters exchanged forty-odd years earlier.

The letters were written by Grace, a 17-year-old placed in an impossible position by the demands on her from family, school and her beloved. The lovesick recipient of her letters puts her on the highest of pedestals, proposing Grace as the high-point of human evolution. "Fossil remains found in East Africa in 1974 are known for the sake of simplicity as Lucy, now commonly regarded as the Mother of the Human Race. Lucy is the first of a pair of bookends, and eventually another individual will match her at the other end of the shelf."

A Pressure of the Hand
Rosewood Publishing
ISBN 978-0-9956787-0-5

Also available in e-book form, ISBN 978-0-9956787-1-2